JUMP
AT HOME
GRADE
4

NEW EDITION

JUMP AT HOME GRADE 4

NEW EDITION

Worksheets for the JUMP Math Program

JOHN MIGHTON

ANANSI

First published in 2004 by House of Anansi Press Inc.

Revised edition published in 2010 by House of Anansi Press Inc.
www.houseofanansi.com

Some of the material in this book has previously been published by JUMP Math.

Every reasonable effort has been made to contact the holders of copyright for materials reproduced in this work. The publishers will gladly receive information that will enable them to rectify any inadvertent errors or omissions in subsequent editions.

23 22 21 20 19   6 7 8 9 10

Library and Archives Canada Cataloguing in Publication

Cataloguing data available from Library and Archives Canada

Library of Congress Control Number: 2010924085

Acknowledgements
In writing the worksheets for this volume, I received an enormous amount of help from JUMP staff and volunteers.
Contributing Authors – Katie Baldwin, James Bambury, Dana Born, Kate Green, Allison Hall, Margaret McClintock, Laura Miggiani, Raegan Mighton, Ravi Negi, and Sudha Shrestha.
Layout Team – Katie Baldwin, James Bambury, Dana Born, Kate Green, Mahbuba Haq, Laura Miggiani, Ravi Negi, Sudha Shrestha, Linda Thai, and Laura Visentin.
Proofing and Editing Team – Katie Baldwin, James Bambury, Nandita Biswas-Mellamphy, the team at Capital One (particularly Andrew Cowan, Geoff Thiessen Sebastian Grobys, and Yuanhui Lang), Stephen Hong, Imogen Jenkins, Paul Mates, Margaret McClintock, Laura Miggiani, Chloe Mighton, Alex Oehlert, Sindi Sabourin, Jeremy Sills, Oliver Stock, Sayaka Yajima, and Hyun Youk.
Answer Key Team – Katie Baldwin, James Bambury, Dana Born, the team at Capital One (particularly Andrew Cowan, Geoff Thiessen, Sebastian Grobys, and Yuanhui Lang), Stephen Hong, John Lim, Laura Miggiani, Alex Oehlert, Sindi Sabourin, and Hyun Youk.
Support Team – Jon Alexander, Krisztina Benczik, the Fields Institute, Laura Gass, Midori Hyndman, the JUMP Board, Jonathan Kassian, Richard Michael, Lynne Patterson, Philip Spencer, and the teachers, administrators, and support staff at our partner schools.
The following people gave us helpful suggestions and advice – Nicki Boycott, Liam Carmichael, Helen Garland, Ken Scott, and Isaac Stein.

This book, like the JUMP program itself, is made possible by the efforts of the volunteers and staff of JUMP Math.

 Canada Council for the Arts **Conseil des Arts du Canada**

We acknowledge for their financial support of our publishing program the Canada Council for the Arts, the Ontario Arts Council, and the Government of Canada.

Printed and bound in Canada

Contents

Unit 3: Measurement 1

Unit 4: Logic and Systematic Search 1

Unit 5: Patterns & Algebra 2

Unit 6: Number Sense 2

Unit 7: Measurement 2

Introduction: About JUMP Math

There is a prevalent myth in our society that people are born with mathematical talent, and others simply do not have the ability to succeed. Recent discoveries in cognitive science are challenging this myth of ability. The brain is not hard-wired, but continues to change and develop throughout life. Steady, incremental learning can result in the emergence of new abilities.

The carefully designed mathematics in the JUMP Math program provide the necessary skills and knowledge to give your child the joy of success in mathematics. Through step-by-step learning, students celebrate success with every question, thereby increasing achievement and reducing math anxiety.

John Mighton: Founder of JUMP Math

"Nine years ago I was looking for a way to give something back to my local community. It occurred to me that I should try to help kids who needed help with math. Mathematicians don't always make the best teachers because mathematics has become obvious to them; they can have trouble seeing why their students are having trouble. But because I had struggled with math myself, I wasn't inclined to blame my students if they couldn't move forward."

— John Mighton, *The End of Ignorance*

JUMP Math, a national charity dedicated to improving mathematical literacy, was founded by John Mighton, a mathematician, bestselling author, and award-winning playwright. The organization grew out of John's work with a core group of volunteers in a "tutoring club"; their goal was to meet the needs of the most challenged students from local schools. Over the next three years John developed the early material — simple handouts for the tutors to use during their one-on-one teaching sessions with individual students. This period was one of experimentation in developing the JUMP Math method. Eventually, John began to work in local inner-city schools, by placing tutors in the classrooms. This led to the next period of innovation: using the JUMP Math method on small groups of students.

Teachers responded enthusiastically to the success they saw in their students and wanted to adapt the method for classroom use. In response, the needs of the teachers for curriculum-based resources were met by the development of workbooks. These started out as a series of three remedial books with limited accompanying teacher materials, released in fall 2003. The effectiveness of these workbooks led quickly to the development of grade-specific, curriculum-based workbooks. The grade-specific books were first released in 2004. Around that time, the power of teacher networks in creating learning communities was beginning to take shape.

Inspired by the work he has done with thousands of students over the past twenty years, John has systematically developed an approach to teaching mathematics that is based on fostering brain plasticity and emergent intelligence, and on the idea that children have more potential in mathematics than is generally believed. Linking new research in cognitive science to his extensive observations of students, John calls for a re-examination of the assumptions that underlie current methods of teaching mathematics.

JUMP Math, as a program and as an organization, developed in response to the needs of the students, teachers, schools, and communities where John and the volunteers were working. Recognizing the potential of all students to succeed in mathematics, and to succeed in school, was the motivation that John needed to dedicate more than ten years of his life developing a mathematics program that achieved his vision.

JUMP Math: An Innovative Approach

In only ten years, JUMP Math has gone from John's kitchen table to a thriving organization reaching more than 50,000 students with high-quality learning resources and training for 2,000 teachers. It continues to work with community organizations to reach struggling students through homework clubs and after-school programs. Through the generous support of our sponsors, JUMP Math donates resources to classrooms and homework clubs across Canada. The organization has also inspired thousands of community volunteers and teachers to donate their time as tutors, mentors, and trainers.

JUMP Math is unique; it builds on the belief that every child can be successful at mathematics by
- Promoting positive learning environments and building confidence through praise and encouragement;
- Maintaining a balanced approach to mathematics by concurrently addressing conceptual and procedural learning;
- Achieving understanding and mastery by breaking mathematics down into small sequential steps;
- Keeping all students engaged and attentive by "raising the bar" incrementally; and,
- Guiding students strategically to explore and discover the beauty of mathematics.

JUMP Math recognizes the importance of reducing math anxiety. Research in psychology has shown that our brains are extremely fallible: Our working memories are poor, we are easily overwhelmed by too much new information, and we require a good deal of practice to consolidate skills and concepts. These mental challenges are compounded when we are anxious. The JUMP approach has been shown to reduce math anxiety significantly.

JUMP Math scaffolds mathematical concepts rigorously and completely. The materials were designed by a team of mathematicians and educators who have a deep understanding of and a love for mathematics. Concepts are introduced in rigorous steps, and prerequisite skills are included in the lesson. Breaking down concepts and skills into steps is often necessary even with the more able students. Math is a subject in which a gifted student can become a struggling student almost overnight, because mathematical knowledge is cumulative.

Consistent with emerging brain research, JUMP Math provides materials and methods that minimize differences between students, allowing teachers, tutors, and parents to more effectively improve student performance in mathematics. Today, parents have access to this unique innovation in mathematics learning with the revised JUMP at Home books.

JUMP Math at Home

JUMP at Home has been developed by mathematicians and educators to complement the mathematics curriculum that your child learns at school. Each grade covers core skills and knowledge to help your child succeed in mathematics. The program focuses on building number sense, pattern recognition, and foundations for algebra.

JUMP at Home is designed to boost every student's confidence, skills, and knowledge. Struggling students will benefit from practice in small steps, while good students will be provided with new ways to understand concepts that will help them enjoy mathematics even more and to exceed their own expectations.

JUMP Math in Schools

JUMP Math also publishes full curriculum-based resources — including student workbooks, teacher guides with daily lesson plans, and blackline masters — that cover all of the Ontario and the Western Canada mathematics curriculum. For more information, please visit the JUMP Math website, www.jumpmath.org, to find out how to order.

Evidence that JUMP Math Works

JUMP Math is a leader in promoting third-party research about its work. A recent study by researchers at the Ontario Institute for Studies in Education (OISE), the University of Toronto, and Simon Fraser University found that in JUMP Math classrooms conceptual understanding improved significantly for weaker students. In Lambeth, England, researchers reported that after using JUMP Math for one year, 69 percent of students who were two years behind were assessed at grade level.

Cognitive scientists from The Hospital for Sick Children in Toronto recently conducted a randomized-controlled study of the effectiveness of the JUMP math program. Studies of such scientific rigour remain relatively rare in mathematics education research in North America. The results showed that students who received JUMP instruction outperformed students who received the methods of instruction their teachers would normally use, on well-established measures of math achievement.

Using JUMP at Home

Helping your child discover the joy of mathematics can be fun and productive. You are not the teacher but the tutor. When having fun with mathematics, remember the JUMP Math T.U.T.O.R. principles:

Take responsibility for learning:
> If your child doesn't understand a concept, it can always be clarified further or explained differently. As the adult, you are responsible for helping your child understand. If they don't get it, don't get frustrated — get creative!

Use positive reinforcement:
> Children like to be rewarded when they succeed. Praise and encouragement build excitement and foster an appetite for learning. The more confidence a student has, the more likely they are to be engaged.

Take small steps:
> In mathematics, it is always possible to make something easier. Always use the JUMP Math worksheets to break down the question into a series of small steps. Practice, practice, practice!

Only indicate correct answers:
> Your child's confidence can be shaken by a lack of success. Place checkmarks for correct answers, then revisit questions that your child is having difficulty with. Never use Xs!

Raise the bar:
> When your child has mastered a particular concept, challenge them by posing a question that is slightly more difficult. As your child meets these small challenges, you will see their focus and excitement increase.

And remember: if your child is falling behind, teach the number facts! It is a serious mistake to think that students who don't know their number facts can always get by in mathematics using a calculator or other aids. Students can certainly perform operations on a calculator, but they cannot begin to solve problems if they lack a sense of numbers: students need to be able to see patterns in numbers, and to make estimates and predictions about numbers, in order to have any success in mathematics. We have put together some fun activities to help you and your child get ready for mathematics!

Introductory Unit on Fractions

"In the twenty years that I have been teaching mathematics to children, I have never met an educator who would say that students who lack confidence in their intellectual or academic abilities are likely to do well in school. Our introductory unit has been carefully designed and tested with thousands of students to boost confidence. It has proven to be an extremely effective tool for convincing even the most challenged student that they can do well in mathematics."

— John Mighton

Cognitive scientists have discovered that in order for the brain to be "ready to learn" it cannot be distracted by anxiety. If your child struggles with mathematics or has "math anxiety," be sure to start JUMP Math with the introductory unit on Fractions found at www.jumpmath.org.

In recent years, research has shown that students are more apt to do well in subjects when they believe they are capable of doing well. It seems obvious, then, that any math program that aims to harness the potential of every student must start with an exercise that builds the confidence of every student. The introductory unit on Fractions was designed for this purpose. It has proven to be an extremely effective tool for convincing even the most challenged students that they can do well in mathematics.

The method used in the Introductory Unit can be described as guided discovery. The individual steps that you will follow in teaching the unit are extremely small, so even the weakest student needn't be left behind. Throughout the unit, students are expected to:

- Discover or extend patterns or rules on their own;
- See what changes and what stays the same in sequences of mathematical expressions; and
- Apply what they have learned to new situations.

Students become very excited at making these discoveries and meeting these challenges as they learn the material. For many, it is the first time they have ever been motivated to pay attention to mathematical rules and patterns or to try to extend their knowledge in new cases.

How Does the Introductory Unit Build Confidence?

The introductory unit on Fractions has been specifically designed to build confidence by:

- Requiring that students possess only a few very simple skills. To achieve a perfect score on the final test in the unit, students need only possess three skills. These skills can be taught to the most challenged students in a very short amount of time. Students must be able to do these three things:
  1) Skip count on their fingers.
  2) Add one-digit numbers.
  3) Subtract one-digit numbers.
- Eliminating heavy use of language. Mathematics functions as its own symbolic language. Since the vast majority of children are able to perform the most basic operations (counting and grouping objects into sets) long before they become expert readers, mathematics is the lone subject in which the vast majority of kids are naturally equipped to excel at an early age. By removing language as a barrier, students can realize their full potential in mathematics.
- Allowing you to continually provide feedback. Moving on too quickly is both a hindrance to a student's confidence and an impediment to their eventual success. In the introductory unit, the mathematics are broken down into small steps so that you can quickly identify difficulties and help as soon as they arise.
- Keeping the student engaged through the excitement of small victories. Children respond more quickly to praise and success than to criticism and threats. If students are encouraged, they feel an incentive to learn. Students enjoy exercising their minds and showing off to a caring adult.

Since the introductory unit is about building confidence, work with your child to ensure that they are successful. Celebrate every correct answer. Take your time. Encourage your child. And, most importantly, have fun!

Work on Mental Math

Included in *JUMP at Home Grade 4* is a Mental Math unit, which will provide you with strategies and techniques for sharpening your child's math brain. Mental math is the foundation for all further study in mathematics. Students who cannot see number patterns often become frustrated and disillusioned with their work. Consistent practice in mental math allows students to become familiar with the way numbers interact, enabling them to make simple calculations quickly and effectively without always having to recall their number facts.

Mental math confronts people at every turn, making the ability to quickly calculate numbers an invaluable asset. Calculating how much change you are owed at a grocery store or deciding how much of a tip to leave at a restaurant are both real-world examples of mental math in action. For this reason, it may be the single most relevant strand of mathematics to everyday life.

How Can a Parent Best Use Math Time?

To keep your child engaged and attentive, consider breaking up your half-hour math time together into thirds:

- **First 10 Minutes:** Use this time to focus on Mental Math. This will sharpen your child's mental number skills, and they will find the remainder of the session much more enjoyable if they are not constantly struggling to remember their number facts.
- **Second 10 Minutes:** Use this time to work on grade-specific material. These worksheets have been designed by mathematicians and educators to fill gaps in learning, strengthen basic skills, and reinforce fundamental concepts.
- **Final 10 Minutes:** Save this portion of the session for math games, cards, or board games.

It is important to remember that mathematics can be fun! Liven up things by playing games and being as active as possible. If the opportunity to visually demonstrate a concept arises, JUMP at it! Have your child sort out change, look around them for geometric objects, or pace out a perimeter.

"Children will never fulfill their extraordinary potential until we remember how it felt to have so much potential ourselves. There was nothing we weren't inspired to look at or hold, or that we weren't determined to find out how to do. Open the door to the world of mathematics so your child can pass through."
— John Mighton

Mental Math Skills: Addition and Subtraction

PARENT:

If your child doesn't know their addition and subtraction facts, teach them to add and subtract using their fingers by the methods taught below. You should also reinforce basic facts using drills, games and flash cards. There are mental math strategies that make addition and subtraction easier: Some effective strategies are taught in the next section. (Until your child knows all their facts, allow them to add and subtract on their fingers when necessary.)

To **add** $4 + 8$, Grace says the greater number (8) with her fist closed. She counts up from 8, raising one finger at a time. She stops when she has raised the number of fingers equal to the lesser number (4):

8   9   10   11   12

She said "12" when she raised her 4th finger, so: $4 + 8 = 12$

1. Add:
   a) $5 + 2 =$ _____
   b) $3 + 2 =$ _____
   c) $6 + 2 =$ _____
   d) $9 + 2 =$ _____

   e) $2 + 4 =$ _____
   f) $2 + 7 =$ _____
   g) $5 + 3 =$ _____
   h) $6 + 3 =$ _____

   i) $11 + 4 =$ _____
   j) $3 + 9 =$ _____
   k) $7 + 3 =$ _____
   l) $14 + 4 =$ _____

   m) $21 + 5 =$ _____
   n) $32 + 3 =$ _____
   o) $4 + 56 =$ _____
   p) $39 + 4 =$ _____

To **subtract** $9 - 5$, Grace says the lesser number (5) with her fist closed. She counts up from 5 raising one finger at a time. She stops when she says the greater number (9):

5   6   7   8   9

She has raised 4 fingers when she stops, so: $9 - 5 = 4$

2. Subtract:
   a) $7 - 5 =$ _____
   b) $8 - 6 =$ _____
   c) $5 - 3 =$ _____
   d) $5 - 2 =$ _____

   e) $9 - 6 =$ _____
   f) $10 - 5 =$ _____
   g) $11 - 7 =$ _____
   h) $17 - 14 =$ _____

   i) $33 - 31 =$ _____
   j) $27 - 24 =$ _____
   k) $43 - 39 =$ _____
   l) $62 - 58 =$ _____

PARENT:

To prepare for the next section (Mental Math), teach your child to add 1 to any number mentally (by counting forward by 1 in their head) and to subtract 1 from any number (by counting backward by 1).

Mental Math Skills: Addition and Subtraction *(continued)*

PARENT: Children who don't know how to add, subtract, or estimate readily are at a great disadvantage in mathematics. Children who have trouble memorizing addition and subtraction facts can still learn to mentally add and subtract numbers in a short time if they are given daily practice in a few basic skills.

SKILL 1 – Adding 2 to an Even Number

This skill has been broken down into a number of sub-skills. After teaching each sub-skill, you should give your child a short diagnostic quiz to verify that they have learned the skill. I have included sample quizzes for Skills 1 to 4.

i) *Naming the next one-digit even number:*

Numbers that have ones digit 0, 2, 4, 6, or 8 are called the *even numbers*. Using drills or games, teach your child to say the sequence of one-digit even numbers without hesitation. Ask them to imagine the sequence going on in a circle so that the next number after 8 is 0 (0, 2, 4, 6, 8, 0, 2, 4, 6, 8, . . .). Then play the following game: name a number in the sequence and ask your child to give the next number in the sequence. Don't move on until they have mastered the game.

ii) *Naming the next greatest two-digit even number:*

Case 1 – Numbers that end in 0, 2, 4, or 6
Write an even two-digit number that ends in 0, 2, 4 or 6 on a piece of paper. Ask your child to name the next greatest even number. They should recognize that if a number ends in 0, then the next even number ends in 2; if it ends in 2 then the next even number ends in 4, etc. For instance, the number 54 has ones digit 4, so the next greatest even number will have ones digit 6.

> **QUIZ**
>
> Name the next greatest even number:
>
> a) 52 : _____   b) 64 : _____   c) 36 : _____   d) 22 : _____   e) 80 : _____

Case 2 – Numbers that end in 8
Write the number 58 on a piece of paper. Ask your child to name the next greatest even number. Remind them that even numbers must end in 0, 2, 4, 6, or 8. But 50, 52, 54, and 56 are all less than 58, so the next greatest even number is 60. Your child should see that an even number ending in 8 is always followed by an even number ending in 0 (with a tens digit that is one higher).

> **QUIZ**
>
> Name the next greatest even number:
>
> a) 58 : _____   b) 68 : _____   c) 38 : _____   d) 48 : _____   e) 78 : _____

iii) *Adding 2 to an even number:*

Point out to your child that adding 2 to any even number is equivalent to finding the next even number: e.g., $46 + 2 = 48$, $48 + 2 = 50$, etc. Knowing this, your child can easily add 2 to any even number.

Mental Math Skills: **Addition and Subtraction** *(continued)*

> **QUIZ**
>
> Add:
>
> a) $26 + 2 =$ ___   b) $82 + 2 =$ ___   c) $40 + 2 =$ ___   d) $58 + 2 =$ ___   e) $34 + 2 =$ ___

SKILL 2 – Subtracting 2 from an Even Number

i) *Finding the preceding one-digit even number:*

Name a one-digit even number and ask your child to give the preceding number in the sequence. For instance, the number that comes before 4 is 2, and the number that comes before 0 is 8. (Remember: the sequence is circular.)

ii) *Finding the preceding two-digit even number:*

Case 1 – Numbers that end in 2, 4, 6, or 8
Write a two-digit number that ends in 2, 4, 6, or 8 on a piece of paper. Ask your child to name the preceding even number. They should recognize that if a number ends in 2, then the preceding even number ends in 0; if it ends in 4, then the preceding even number ends in 2, etc. For instance, the number 78 has ones digit 8, so the preceding even number has ones digit 6.

> **QUIZ**
>
> Name the preceding even number:
>
> a) 48 : _____   b) 26 : _____   c) 34 : _____   d) 62 : _____   e) 78 : _____

Case 2 – Numbers that end in 0
Write the number 80 on a piece of paper and ask your child to name the preceding even number. They should recognize that if an even number ends in 0, then the preceding even number ends in 8 (but the ones digit is one less). So the even number that comes before 80 is 78.

> **QUIZ**
>
> Name the preceding even number:
>
> a) 40 : _____   b) 60 : _____   c) 80 : _____   d) 50 : _____   e) 30 : _____

ii) *Subtracting 2 from an even number:*

Point out to your child that subtracting 2 from any even number is equivalent to finding the preceding even number: e.g., $48 - 2 = 46$, $46 - 2 = 44$, etc.

> **QUIZ**
>
> Subtract:
>
> a) $58 - 2 =$ ___   b) $24 - 2 =$ ___   c) $36 - 2 =$ ___   d) $42 - 2 =$ ___   e) $60 - 2 =$ ___

Mental Math Skills: Addition and Subtraction *(continued)*

SKILL 3 – Adding 2 to an Odd Number

i) *Naming the next one-digit odd number:*

Numbers that have ones digit 1, 3, 5, 7, or 9 are called *odd numbers*. Using drills or games, teach your child to say the sequence of one-digit odd numbers without hesitation. Ask them to imagine the sequence going on in a circle so that the next number after 9 is 1 (1, 3, 5, 7, 9, 1, 3, 5, 7, 9, . . .). Then play the following game: name a number in the sequence and ask your child to give the next number in the sequence. Don't move on until they have mastered the game.

ii) *Naming the next greatest two-digit odd number:*

<u>Case 1 – Numbers that end in 1, 3, 5, or 7</u>
Write an odd two-digit number that ends in 1, 3, 5, or 7 on a piece of paper. Ask your child to name the next greatest odd number. They should recognize that if a number ends in 1, then the next odd number ends in 3; if it ends in 3, then the next odd number ends in 5, etc. For instance, the number 35 has ones digit 5, so the next greatest odd number will have ones digit 7.

> QUIZ
>
> Name the next greatest odd number:
>
> a) 51 : _____   b) 65 : _____   c) 37 : _____   d) 23 : _____   e) 87 : _____

<u>Case 2 – Numbers that end in 9</u>
Write the number 59 on a piece of paper. Ask your child to name the next greatest odd number. Remind them that odd numbers must end in 1, 3, 5, 7, or 9. But 51, 53, 55, and 57 are all less than 59. The next greatest odd number is 61. Your child should see that an odd number ending in 9 is always followed by an odd number ending in 1 (with a tens digit that is one higher).

> QUIZ
>
> Name the next greatest odd number:
>
> a) 59 : _____   b) 69 : _____   c) 39 : _____   d) 49 : _____   e) 79 : _____

iii) *Adding 2 to an odd number:*

Point out to your child that adding 2 to any odd number is equivalent to finding the next odd number: e.g., 47 + 2 = 49, 49 + 2 = 51, etc. Knowing this, your child can easily add 2 to any odd number.

> QUIZ
>
> Add:
>
> a) 27 + 2 = ___   b) 83 + 2 = ___   c) 41 + 2 = ___   d) 59 + 2 = ___   e) 35 + 2 = ___

Mental Math Skills: Addition and Subtraction (continued)

SKILL 4 – Subtracting 2 from an Odd Number

i) *Finding the preceding one-digit odd number:*

Name a one-digit odd number and ask your child to give the preceding number in the sequence. For instance, the number that comes before 3 is 1, and the number that comes before 1 is 9. (Remember: the sequence is circular.)

ii) *Finding the preceding two-digit odd number:*

Case 1 – Numbers that end in 3, 5, 7, or 9
Write a two-digit number that ends in 3, 5, 7, or 9 on a piece of paper. Ask your child to name the preceding odd number. They should recognize that if a number ends in 3, then the preceding odd number ends in 1; if it ends in 5, then the preceding odd number ends in 3, etc. For instance, the number 79 has ones digit 9, so the preceding odd number has ones digit 7.

QUIZ

Name the preceding odd number:

a) 49 : _____   b) 27 : _____   c) 35 : _____   d) 63 : _____   e) 79 : _____

Case 2 – Numbers that end in 1
Write the number 81 on a piece of paper and ask your child to name the preceding odd number. They should recognize that if an odd number ends in 1, then the preceding odd number ends in 9 (but the ones digit is one less). So the odd number that comes before 81 is 79.

QUIZ

Name the preceding odd number:

a) 41 : _____   b) 61 : _____   c) 81 : _____   d) 51 : _____   e) 31 : _____

iii) *Subtracting 2 from an odd number:*

Point out to your child that subtracting 2 from any odd number is equivalent to finding the preceding odd number: e.g., $49 - 2 = 47$, $47 - 2 = 45$, etc.

QUIZ

Subtract:

a) $59 - 2 =$____   b) $25 - 2 =$____   c) $37 - 2 =$____   d) $43 - 2 =$____   e) $61 - 2 =$____

SKILLS 5 and 6

Once your child can add and subtract the numbers 1 and 2, then they can easily add and subtract the number 3: Add 3 to a number by first adding 2, then adding 1 (e.g., $35 + 3 = 35 + 2 + 1$). Subtract 3 from a number by subtracting 2, then subtracting 1 (e.g., $35 - 3 = 35 - 2 - 1$).

Mental Math Skills: **Addition and Subtraction** *(continued)*

PARENT: All of the addition and subtraction tricks you teach your child should be reinforced with drills, flashcards, and tests. Eventually they should memorize their addition and subtraction facts and shouldn't have to rely on the mental math tricks. One of the greatest gifts you can give your child is to teach them their number facts.

SKILLS 7 and 8

Add 4 to a number by adding 2 twice (e.g., $51 + 4 = 51 + 2 + 2$). Subtract 4 from a number by subtracting 2 twice (e.g., $51 - 4 = 51 - 2 - 2$).

SKILLS 9 and 10

Add 5 to a number by adding 4 then 1. Subtract 5 by subtracting 4 then 1.

SKILL 11

Your child can add pairs of identical numbers by doubling (e.g., $6 + 6 = 2 \times 6$). They should either memorize the 2 times table or they should double numbers by counting on their fingers by 2s.

Add a pair of numbers that differ by 1 by rewriting the larger number as 1 plus the smaller number (then use doubling to find the sum): e.g., $6 + 7 = 6 + 6 + 1 = 12 + 1 = 13$; $7 + 8 = 7 + 7 + 1 = 14 + 1 = 15$.

SKILLS 12, 13, and 14

Add a one-digit number to 10 by simply replacing the zero in 10 with the one-digit number: e.g., $10 + 7 = 17$.

Add 10 to any two-digit number by simply increasing the tens digit of the two-digit number by 1: e.g., $53 + 10 = 63$.

Add a pair of two-digit numbers (with no carrying) by adding the ones digits of the numbers and then adding the tens digits: e.g., $23 + 64 = 87$.

SKILLS 15 and 16

To add 9 to a one-digit number, subtract 1 from the number and then add 10: e.g., $9 + 6 = 10 + 5 = 15$; $9 + 7 = 10 + 6 = 16$. (Essentially, your child simply has to subtract 1 from the number and then stick a 1 in front of the result.)

To add 8 to a one-digit number, subtract 2 from the number and add 10: e.g., $8 + 6 = 10 + 4 = 14$; $8 + 7 = 10 + 5 = 15$.

SKILLS 17 and 18

To subtract a pair of multiples of ten, simply subtract the tens digits and add a zero for the ones digit: e.g., $70 - 50 = 20$.

To subtract a pair of two-digit numbers (without carrying or regrouping), subtract the ones digit from the ones digit and the tens digit from the tens digit: e.g., $57 - 34 = 23$.

Mental Math — Further Strategies *(continued)*

Further Mental Math Strategies

1. Your child should be able to explain how to use the strategies of "rounding the subtrahend (i.e., the number you are subtracting) up to the nearest multiple of ten."

   Examples:

   Subtrahend

   Subtrahend rounded to the nearest tens

   a) $37 - 19 = 37 - 20 + 1$ ← You must add 1 because 20 is 1 greater than 19.

   b) $64 - 28 = 64 - 30 + 2$ ← You must add 2 because 30 is 2 greater than 28.

   c) $65 - 46 = 65 - 50 + 4$

   Practice Questions:

   a) $27 - 17 = 27 - \underline{\quad} + \underline{\quad}$

   b) $52 - 36 = 52 - \underline{\quad} + \underline{\quad}$

   c) $76 - 49 = 76 - \underline{\quad} + \underline{\quad}$

   d) $84 - 57 = 84 - \underline{\quad} + \underline{\quad}$

   e) $61 - 29 = 61 - \underline{\quad} + \underline{\quad}$

   f) $42 - 18 = 42 - \underline{\quad} + \underline{\quad}$

   PARENT: This strategy works well with numbers that end in 6, 7, 8, or 9.

2. Your child should be able to explain how to subtract by thinking of adding.

   Examples:

   Count by ones from 45 to the nearest tens (50)

   Count from 50 until you reach the first number (62)

   a) $62 - 45 = 5 + 12 = 17$ ← The sum of counting up to the nearest ten and the original number is the difference.

   b) $46 - 23 = 3 + 20 = 23$

   c) $73 - 17 = 6 + 50 = 56$ ← What method did we use here?

   Practice Questions:

   a) $88 - 36 = \underline{\quad} + \underline{\quad} = \underline{\quad}$

   b) $58 - 21 = \underline{\quad} + \underline{\quad} = \underline{\quad}$

   c) $43 - 17 = \underline{\quad} + \underline{\quad} = \underline{\quad}$

   d) $74 - 28 = \underline{\quad} + \underline{\quad} = \underline{\quad}$

   e) $93 - 64 = \underline{\quad} + \underline{\quad} = \underline{\quad}$

   f) $82 - 71 = \underline{\quad} + \underline{\quad} = \underline{\quad}$

3. Your child should be able to explain how to "use doubles."

   Examples:

   Minuend

   If you add the subtrahend to itself, and the sum is equal to the minuend, then the subtrahend is the same as the difference.

   a) $12 - 6 = 6$ $6 + 6 = 12$ ← Same value as minuend

   b) $8 - 4 = 4$

   Subtrahend plus itself

   Practice Questions:

   a) $6 - 3 = \underline{\quad}$

   b) $10 - 5 = \underline{\quad}$

   c) $14 - 7 = \underline{\quad}$

   d) $18 - 9 = \underline{\quad}$

   e) $16 - 8 = \underline{\quad}$

   f) $20 - 10 = \underline{\quad}$

Mental Math Exercises

PARENT: Teaching the material on these Mental Math worksheets may take several lessons. Your child will need more practice than is provided on these pages. These pages are intended as a test to be given when you are certain your child has learned the materials fully.

PARENT: Teach skills 1, 2, 3 and 4 as outlined on pages xvii–xx before you allow your child to answer Questions 1 through 12:

1. Name the <u>even</u> number that comes <u>after</u> the number. Answer in the blank provided:

   a) 32 _____   b) 46 _____   c) 14 _____   d) 92 _____   e) 56 _____

   f) 30 _____   g) 84 _____   h) 60 _____   i) 72 _____   j) 24 _____

2. Name the <u>even</u> number that comes <u>after</u> the number:

   a) 28 _____   b) 18 _____   c) 78 _____   d) 38 _____   e) 68 _____

3. Add:
   REMEMBER: Adding 2 to an even number is the same as finding the next even number.

   a) $42 + 2 =$ _____   b) $76 + 2 =$ _____   c) $28 + 2 =$ _____   d) $16 + 2 =$ _____

   e) $68 + 2 =$ _____   f) $12 + 2 =$ _____   g) $36 + 2 =$ _____   h) $90 + 2 =$ _____

   i) $70 + 2 =$ _____   j) $24 + 2 =$ _____   k) $66 + 2 =$ _____   l) $52 + 2 =$ _____

4. Name the <u>even</u> number that comes <u>before</u> the number:

   a) **38** _____   b) **42** _____   c) **56** _____   d) **72** _____   e) **98** _____

   f) **48** _____   g) **16** _____   h) **22** _____   i) **66** _____   j) **14** _____

5. Name the <u>even</u> number that comes <u>before</u> the number:

   a) **30** _____   b) **70** _____   c) **60** _____   d) **10** _____   e) **80** _____

6. Subtract:
   REMEMBER: Subtracting 2 from an even number is the same as finding the preceding even number.

   a) $46 - 2 =$ _____   b) $86 - 2 =$ _____   c) $90 - 2 =$ _____   d) $14 - 2 =$ _____

   e) $54 - 2 =$ _____   f) $72 - 2 =$ _____   g) $12 - 2 =$ _____   h) $56 - 2 =$ _____

   i) $32 - 2 =$ _____   j) $40 - 2 =$ _____   k) $60 - 2 =$ _____   l) $26 - 2 =$ _____

7. Name the <u>odd</u> number that comes <u>after</u> the number:

   a) 37 _____   b) 51 _____   c) 63 _____   d) 75 _____   e) 17 _____

   f) 61 _____   g) 43 _____   h) 81 _____   i) 23 _____   j) 95 _____

8. Name the <u>odd</u> number that comes <u>after</u> the number:

   a) 69 _____   b) 29 _____   c) 9 _____   d) 79 _____   e) 59 _____

Mental Math Exercises *(continued)*

9. Add:
    REMEMBER: Adding 2 to an odd number is the same as finding the next odd number.

    a) $25 + 2 =$ _____   b) $31 + 2 =$ _____   c) $47 + 2 =$ _____   d) $33 + 2 =$ _____

    e) $39 + 2 =$ _____   f) $91 + 2 =$ _____   g) $5 + 2 =$ _____   h) $89 + 2 =$ _____

    i) $11 + 2 =$ _____   j) $65 + 2 =$ _____   k) $29 + 2 =$ _____   l) $17 + 2 =$ _____

10. Name the <u>odd</u> number that comes <u>before</u> the number:
    a) **39** _____   b) **43** _____   c) **57** _____   d) **17** _____   e) **99** _____

    f) **13** _____   g) **85** _____   h) **79** _____   i) **65** _____   j) **77** _____

11. Name the <u>odd</u> number that comes <u>before</u> the number:
    a) **21** _____   b) **41** _____   c) **11** _____   d) **91** _____   e) **51** _____

12. Subtract:
    REMEMBER: Subtracting 2 from an odd number is the same as finding the preceding odd number.

    a) $47 - 2 =$ _____   b) $85 - 2 =$ _____   c) $91 - 2 =$ _____   d) $15 - 2 =$ _____

    e) $51 - 2 =$ _____   f) $73 - 2 =$ _____   g) $11 - 2 =$ _____   h) $59 - 2 =$ _____

    i) $31 - 2 =$ _____   j) $43 - 2 =$ _____   k) $7 - 2 =$ _____   l) $25 - 2 =$ _____

PARENT: Teach skills 5 and 6 as outlined on page xx before you allow your child to answer Questions 13 and 14.

13. Add 3 to the number by adding 2, then adding 1 (e.g., $35 + 3 = 35 + 2 + 1$):

    a) $23 + 3 =$ _____   b) $36 + 3 =$ _____   c) $29 + 3 =$ _____   d) $16 + 3 =$ _____

    e) $67 + 3 =$ _____   f) $12 + 3 =$ _____   g) $35 + 3 =$ _____   h) $90 + 3 =$ _____

    i) $78 + 3 =$ _____   j) $24 + 3 =$ _____   k) $6 + 3 =$ _____   l) $59 + 3 =$ _____

14. Subtract 3 from the number by subtracting 2, then subtracting 1 (e.g., $35 - 3 = 35 - 2 - 1$):
    a) $46 - 3 =$ _____   b) $87 - 3 =$ _____   c) $99 - 3 =$ _____   d) $14 - 3 =$ _____

    e) $8 - 3 =$ _____   f) $72 - 3 =$ _____   g) $12 - 3 =$ _____   h) $57 - 3 =$ _____

    i) $32 - 3 =$ _____   j) $40 - 3 =$ _____   k) $60 - 3 =$ _____   l) $28 - 3 =$ _____

15. Fred has 49 stamps. He gives 2 stamps away. How many stamps does he have left?

16. There are 25 minnows in a tank. Alice adds 3 more to the tank. How many minnows are now in the tank?

Mental Math Exercises *(continued)*

PARENT: Teach skills 7 and 8 as outlined on page xxi.

17. Add 4 to the number by adding 2 twice (e.g., $51 + 4 = 51 + 2 + 2$):

   a) $42 + 4 =$ _____   b) $76 + 4 =$ _____   c) $27 + 4 =$ _____   d) $17 + 4 =$ _____

   e) $68 + 4 =$ _____   f) $11 + 4 =$ _____   g) $35 + 4 =$ _____   h) $8 + 4 =$ _____

   i) $72 + 4 =$ _____   j) $23 + 4 =$ _____   k) $60 + 4 =$ _____   l) $59 + 4 =$ _____

18. Subtract 4 from the number by subtracting 2 twice (e.g., $26 - 4 = 26 - 2 - 2$):

   a) $46 - 4 =$ _____   b) $86 - 4 =$ _____   c) $91 - 4 =$ _____   d) $15 - 4 =$ _____

   e) $53 - 4 =$ _____   f) $9 - 4 =$ _____   g) $13 - 4 =$ _____   h) $57 - 4 =$ _____

   i) $40 - 4 =$ _____   j) $88 - 4 =$ _____   k) $69 - 4 =$ _____   l) $31 - 4 =$ _____

PARENT: Teach skills 9 and 10 as outlined on page xxi.

19. Add 5 to the number by adding 4, then adding 1 (or add 2 twice, then add 1):

   a) $84 + 5 =$ _____   b) $27 + 5 =$ _____   c) $31 + 5 =$ _____   d) $44 + 5 =$ _____

   e) $63 + 5 =$ _____   f) $92 + 5 =$ _____   g) $14 + 5 =$ _____   h) $16 + 5 =$ _____

   i) $9 + 5 =$ _____   j) $81 + 5 =$ _____   k) $51 + 5 =$ _____   l) $28 + 5 =$ _____

20. Subtract 5 from the number by subtracting 4, then subtracting 1 (or subtract 2 twice, then subtract 1):

   a) $48 - 5 =$ _____   b) $86 - 5 =$ _____   c) $55 - 5 =$ _____   d) $69 - 5 =$ _____

   e) $30 - 5 =$ _____   f) $13 - 5 =$ _____   g) $92 - 5 =$ _____   h) $77 - 5 =$ _____

   i) $45 - 5 =$ _____   j) $24 - 5 =$ _____   k) $91 - 5 =$ _____   l) $8 - 5 =$ _____

PARENT: Teach skill 11 as outlined on page xxi.

21. Add:

   a) $6 + 6 =$ _____   b) $7 + 7 =$ _____   c) $8 + 8 =$ _____

   d) $5 + 5 =$ _____   e) $4 + 4 =$ _____   f) $9 + 9 =$ _____

22. Add by thinking of the larger number as a sum of two smaller numbers. The first one is done for you:

   a) $6 + 7 = 6 + 6 + 1$ b) $7 + 8 =$ _____   c) $6 + 8 =$ _____

   d) $4 + 5 =$ _____   e) $5 + 7 =$ _____   f) $8 + 9 =$ _____

Mental Math Exercises *(continued)*

PARENT: Teach skills 12, 13, and 14 as outlined on page xxi.

23. a) $10 + 3 =$ _____   b) $10 + 7 =$ _____   c) $5 + 10 =$ _____   d) $10 + 1 =$ _____

    e) $9 + 10 =$ _____   f) $10 + 4 =$ _____   g) $10 + 8 =$ _____   h) $10 + 2 =$ _____

24. a) $10 + 20 =$ _____   b) $40 + 10 =$ _____   c) $10 + 80 =$ _____   d) $10 + 50 =$ _____

    e) $30 + 10 =$ _____   f) $10 + 60 =$ _____   g) $10 + 10 =$ _____   h) $70 + 10 =$ _____

25. a) $10 + 25 =$ _____   b) $10 + 67 =$ _____   c) $10 + 31 =$ _____   d) $10 + 82 =$ _____

    e) $10 + 43 =$ _____   f) $10 + 51 =$ _____   g) $10 + 68 =$ _____   h) $10 + 21 =$ _____

    i) $10 + 11 =$ _____   j) $10 + 19 =$ _____   k) $10 + 44 =$ _____   l) $10 + 88 =$ _____

26. a) $20 + 30 =$ _____   b) $40 + 20 =$ _____   c) $30 + 30 =$ _____   d) $50 + 30 =$ _____

    e) $20 + 50 =$ _____   f) $40 + 40 =$ _____   g) $50 + 40 =$ _____   h) $40 + 30 =$ _____

    i) $60 + 30 =$ _____   j) $20 + 60 =$ _____   k) $20 + 70 =$ _____   l) $60 + 40 =$ _____

27. a) $20 + 23 =$ _____   b) $32 + 24 =$ _____   c) $51 + 12 =$ _____   d) $12 + 67 =$ _____

    e) $83 + 14 =$ _____   f) $65 + 24 =$ _____   g) $41 + 43 =$ _____   h) $70 + 27 =$ _____

    i) $31 + 61 =$ _____   j) $54 + 33 =$ _____   k) $28 + 31 =$ _____   l) $42 + 55 =$ _____

PARENT: Teach skills 15 and 16 as outlined on page xxi.

28. a) $9 + 3 =$ _____   b) $9 + 7 =$ _____   c) $6 + 9 =$ _____   d) $4 + 9 =$ _____

    e) $9 + 9 =$ _____   f) $5 + 9 =$ _____   g) $9 + 2 =$ _____   h) $9 + 8 =$ _____

29. a) $8 + 2 =$ _____   b) $8 + 6 =$ _____   c) $8 + 7 =$ _____   d) $4 + 8 =$ _____

    e) $5 + 8 =$ _____   f) $8 + 3 =$ _____   g) $9 + 8 =$ _____   h) $8 + 8 =$ _____

PARENT: Teach skills 17 and 18 as outlined on page xxi.

30. a) $40 - 10 =$ _____   b) $50 - 10 =$ _____   c) $70 - 10 =$ _____   d) $20 - 10 =$ _____

    e) $40 - 20 =$ _____   f) $60 - 30 =$ _____   g) $40 - 30 =$ _____   h) $60 - 50 =$ _____

31. a) $57 - 34 =$ _____   b) $43 - 12 =$ _____   c) $62 - 21 =$ _____   d) $59 - 36 =$ _____

    e) $87 - 63 =$ _____   f) $95 - 62 =$ _____   g) $35 - 10 =$ _____   h) $17 - 8 =$ _____

Mental Math (Advanced)

<u>Multiples of Ten</u>

NOTE: In the exercises below, you will learn several ways to use multiples of ten in mental addition or subtraction.

I $542 + 214 = 542 + 200 + 10 + 4 = 742 + 10 + 4 = 752 + 4 = 756$

   $827 - 314 = 827 - 300 - 10 - 4 = 527 - 10 - 4 = 517 - 4 = 513$

   Sometimes you will need to carry:

   $545 + 172 = 545 + 100 + 70 + 2 = 645 + 70 + 2 = 715 + 2 = 717$

---

1. Warm up:

    a) $536 + 100 =$ _____   b) $816 + 10 =$ _____   c) $124 + 5 =$ _____   d) $540 + 200 =$ _____

    e) $234 + 30 =$ _____   f) $345 + 300 =$ _____   g) $236 - 30 =$ _____   h) $442 - 20 =$ _____

    i) $970 - 70 =$ _____   j) $542 - 400 =$ _____   k) $160 + 50 =$ _____   l) $756 + 40 =$ _____

2. Write the second number in expanded form and add or subtract one digit at a time. The first one is done for you:

    a) $564 + 215 =$ _____ *564 + 200 + 10 + 5* _____ $=$ _____ 779 _____

    b) $445 + 343 =$ _____ $=$ _____

    c) $234 + 214 =$ _____ $=$ _____

3. Add or subtract mentally (one digit at a time):

    a) $547 + 312 =$ _____   b) $578 - 314 =$ _____   c) $845 - 454 =$ _____

II   If one of the numbers you are adding or subtracting is close to a number that is a multiple of ten, add the multiple of ten and then add or subtract an adjustment factor:

   $645 + 99 = 645 + 100 - 1 = 745 - 1 = 744$

   $856 + 42 = 856 + 40 + 2 = 896 + 2 = 898$

III   Sometimes in subtraction it helps to think of a multiple of ten as a sum of 1 and a number consisting entirely of 9s (e.g., $100 = 1 + 99$; $1000 = 1 + 999$). You never have to borrow or exchange when you are subtracting from a number consisting entirely of 9s.

   $100 - 43 = 1 + 99 - 43 = 1 + 56 = 57$ ◄———— *Do the subtraction, using 99 instead of 100, and then add 1 to your answer.*

   $1000 - 543 = 1 + 999 - 543 = 1 + 456 = 457$

---

4. Use the tricks you've just learned:

    a) $845 + 91 =$ _____   b) $456 + 298 =$ _____   c) $100 - 84 =$ _____   d) $1000 - 846 =$ _____

Mental Math Game: Modified Go Fish

PURPOSE:

If children know the pairs of one-digit numbers that add up to particular **target numbers**, they will be able to mentally break sums into easier sums.

EXAMPLE:

As it is easy to add any one-digit number to 10, you can add a sum more readily if you can decompose numbers in the sum into pairs that add to ten. For example:

$$7 + 5 = 7 + 3 + 2 = 10 + 2 = 12$$

These numbers add to 10.

To help children remember pairs of numbers that add up to a given target number, I developed a variation of "Go Fish" that I have found very effective.

THE GAME:

Pick any target number and remove all the cards with value greater than or equal to the target number out of the deck. In what follows, I will assume that the target number is 10, so you would take all the tens and face cards out of the deck (aces count as one).

The dealer gives each player six cards. If a player has any pairs of cards that add to 10, they are allowed to place these pairs on the table before play begins.

Player 1 selects one of the cards in their hand and asks Player 2 for a card that adds to 10 with the chosen card. For instance, if Player 1's chosen card is a 3, they may ask Player 2 for a 7.

If Player 2 has the requested card, Player 1 takes it and lays it down along with the card from their hand. Player 1 may then ask for another card. If Player 2 does not have the requested card, they say, "Go fish," and Player 1 must pick up a card from the top of the deck. (If this card adds to 10 with a card in Player 1's hand, they may lay down the pair right away.) It is then Player 2's turn to ask for a card.

Play ends when one player lays down all of their cards. Players receive 4 points for laying down all of their cards first and 1 point for each pair they have laid down.

PARENT: If your child is having difficulty, I would recommend that you start with pairs of numbers that add to 5. Take all cards with value greater than 4 out of the deck. Each player should be dealt only four cards to start with.

I have worked with several children who have had a great deal of trouble sorting their cards and finding pairs that add to a target number. I have found that the following exercise helps:

Give your child only three cards, two of which add to the target number. Ask them to find the pair that adds to the target number. After your child has mastered this step with three cards, repeat the exercise with four cards, then five cards, and so on.

PARENT: You can also give your child a list of the pairs that add to the target number. As your child gets used to the game, gradually remove pairs from the list so that they learn the pairs by memory.

Hundreds Charts

1	2	3	4	5	6	7	8	9	10
11	12	13	14	15	16	17	18	19	20
21	22	23	24	25	26	27	28	29	30
31	32	33	34	35	36	37	38	39	40
41	42	43	44	45	46	47	48	49	50
51	52	53	54	55	56	57	58	59	60
61	62	63	64	65	66	67	68	69	70
71	72	73	74	75	76	77	78	79	80
81	82	83	84	85	86	87	88	89	90
91	92	93	94	95	96	97	98	99	100

1	2	3	4	5	6	7	8	9	10
11	12	13	14	15	16	17	18	19	20
21	22	23	24	25	26	27	28	29	30
31	32	33	34	35	36	37	38	39	40
41	42	43	44	45	46	47	48	49	50
51	52	53	54	55	56	57	58	59	60
61	62	63	64	65	66	67	68	69	70
71	72	73	74	75	76	77	78	79	80
81	82	83	84	85	86	87	88	89	90
91	92	93	94	95	96	97	98	99	100

1	2	3	4	5	6	7	8	9	10
11	12	13	14	15	16	17	18	19	20
21	22	23	24	25	26	27	28	29	30
31	32	33	34	35	36	37	38	39	40
41	42	43	44	45	46	47	48	49	50
51	52	53	54	55	56	57	58	59	60
61	62	63	64	65	66	67	68	69	70
71	72	73	74	75	76	77	78	79	80
81	82	83	84	85	86	87	88	89	90
91	92	93	94	95	96	97	98	99	100

1	2	3	4	5	6	7	8	9	10
11	12	13	14	15	16	17	18	19	20
21	22	23	24	25	26	27	28	29	30
31	32	33	34	35	36	37	38	39	40
41	42	43	44	45	46	47	48	49	50
51	52	53	54	55	56	57	58	59	60
61	62	63	64	65	66	67	68	69	70
71	72	73	74	75	76	77	78	79	80
81	82	83	84	85	86	87	88	89	90
91	92	93	94	95	96	97	98	99	100

Introduction

How to Learn Your Times Tables in 5 Days

PARENT:

Trying to do math without knowing your times tables is like trying to play the piano without knowing the location of the notes on the keyboard. Your child will have difficulty seeing patterns in sequences and charts, solving proportions, finding equivalent fractions, decimals and percents, solving problems etc. if they don't know their tables.

Using the method below, you can teach your child their tables in a week or so. (If you set aside five or ten minutes a day to work with them, the pay-off will be enormous.) There is really no reason for your child not to know their tables!

DAY 1: Counting by 2s, 3s, 4s, and 5s

If you have completed the JUMP Fractions unit, you should already know how to count and multiply by 2s, 3s, 4s, and 5s. If you do not know how to count by these numbers you should memorize the hands:

If you know how to count by 2s, 3s, 4s, and 5s, then you can multiply by any combination of these numbers. For instance, to find the product of 3×2, count by 2s until you have raised 3 fingers:

  2   4   6 $3 \times 2 =$

DAY 2: The 9 Times Table

The numbers you say when you count by 9s are called the **multiples** of 9 (0 is also a multiple of 9). The first ten multiples of 9 (after 0) are 9, 18, 27, 36, 45, 54, 63, 72, 81, and 90. What happens when you add the digits of any of these multiples of 9 (such as $1 + 8$ or $6 + 3$)? The sum is always 9!

Here is another useful fact about the 9 times table: Multiply 9 by any number between 1 and 10 and look at the tens digit of the product. The tens digit is always one less than the number you multiplied by:

$9 \times 4 = 36$ $9 \times 8 = 72$ $9 \times 2 = 18$

3 is one less than 4   7 is one less than 8   1 is one less than 2

You can find the product of 9 and any number by using the two facts given above. For example, to find 9×7, follow these steps:

Step 1: $9 \times 7 = $ __ __ $9 \times 7 = $ __ __

Subtract 1 from the number   Now you know the tens digit
you are multiplying by 9: $7 - 1 = 6$ of the product.

How to Learn Your Times Tables in 5 Days *(continued)*

Step 2: $9 \times 7 = \underline{6}\ \underline{\ \ }$ $9 \times 7 = \underline{6}\ \underline{3}$

These two digits add to 9.   So the missing digit is $9 - 6 = 3$
                                                          (You can do the subtraction on your fingers if necesary.)

Practise these two steps for all of the products of 9: 9×2, 9×3, 9×4, and so on.

DAY 3: The 8 Times Table

There are two patterns in the digits of the 8 times table. Knowing these patterns will help you remember how to count by 8s.

Step 1: You can find the ones digit of the first five multiples of 8, by starting at 8 and counting backwards by 2s.

8
6
4
2
0

Step 2: You can find the tens digit of the first five multiples of 8, by starting at 0 and counting up by 1s.

08
16
24
32
40

Step 3: You can find the ones digit of the next five multiples of 8 by repeating step 1.

8
6
4
2
0

Step 4: You can find the remaining tens digits by starting at 4 and counting by 1s.

48
56
64
72
80

(Of course you do not need to write the 0 in front of the 8 for the product 1×8.)

Practise writing the multiples of 8 (up to 80) until you have memorized the complete list. Knowing the patterns in the digits of the multiples of 8 will help you memorize the list very quickly. Then you will know how to multiply by 8.

$8 \times 6 = 48$

Count by 8 until you have 6 fingers up: 8, 16, 24, 32, 40, 48.

How to Learn Your Times Tables in 5 Days *(continued)*

DAY 4: The 6 Times Table

If you have learned the 8 and 9 times tables, then you already know 6×9 and 6×8.

And if you know how to multiply by 5 up to 5×5, then you also know how to multiply by 6 up to 6×5! That is because you can always calculate 6 times a number by calculating 5 times the number and then adding the number itself to the result. The pictures below show how this works for 6×4:

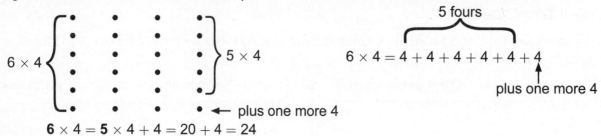

$$6 \times 4 = 5 \times 4 + 4 = 20 + 4 = 24$$

Similarly: $6 \times 2 = 5 \times 2 + 2;$ $6 \times 3 = 5 \times 3 + 3;$ $6 \times 5 = 5 \times 5 + 5.$

Knowing this, you only need to memorize 2 facts:

$$6 \times 6 = 36 \qquad 6 \times 7 = 42$$

Or, if you know 6×5, you can find 6×6 by calculating $6 \times 5 + 5$.

DAY 5: The 7 Times Table

If you have learned the 6, 8, and 9 times tables, then you already know 6×7, 8×7, and 9×7.

And since you also already know $1 \times 7 = 7$, you only need to memorize 5 facts:

$$2 \times 7 = 14 \qquad 3 \times 7 = 21 \qquad 4 \times 7 = 28 \qquad 5 \times 7 = 35 \qquad 7 \times 7 = 49$$

If you are able to memorize your own phone number, then you can easily memorize these 5 facts!

NOTE: You can use doubling to help you learn the facts above: 4 is double 2, so 4×7 (28) is double 2×7 (14); 6 is double 3, so 6×7 (42) is double 3×7 (21).

Try this test every day until you have learned your times tables.

1. $3 \times 5 =$ _____	2. $8 \times 4 =$ _____	3. $9 \times 3 =$ _____	4. $4 \times 5 =$ _____
5. $2 \times 3 =$ _____	6. $4 \times 2 =$ _____	7. $8 \times 1 =$ _____	8. $6 \times 6 =$ _____
9. $9 \times 7 =$ _____	10. $7 \times 7 =$ _____	11. $5 \times 8 =$ _____	12. $2 \times 6 =$ _____
13. $6 \times 4 =$ _____	14. $7 \times 3 =$ _____	15. $4 \times 9 =$ _____	16. $2 \times 9 =$ _____
17. $9 \times 9 =$ _____	18. $3 \times 4 =$ _____	19. $6 \times 8 =$ _____	20. $7 \times 5 =$ _____
21. $9 \times 5 =$ _____	22. $5 \times 6 =$ _____	23. $6 \times 3 =$ _____	24. $7 \times 1 =$ _____
25. $8 \times 3 =$ _____	26. $9 \times 6 =$ _____	27. $4 \times 7 =$ _____	28. $3 \times 3 =$ _____
29. $8 \times 7 =$ _____	30. $1 \times 5 =$ _____	31. $7 \times 6 =$ _____	32. $2 \times 8 =$ _____

Base Ten Blocks

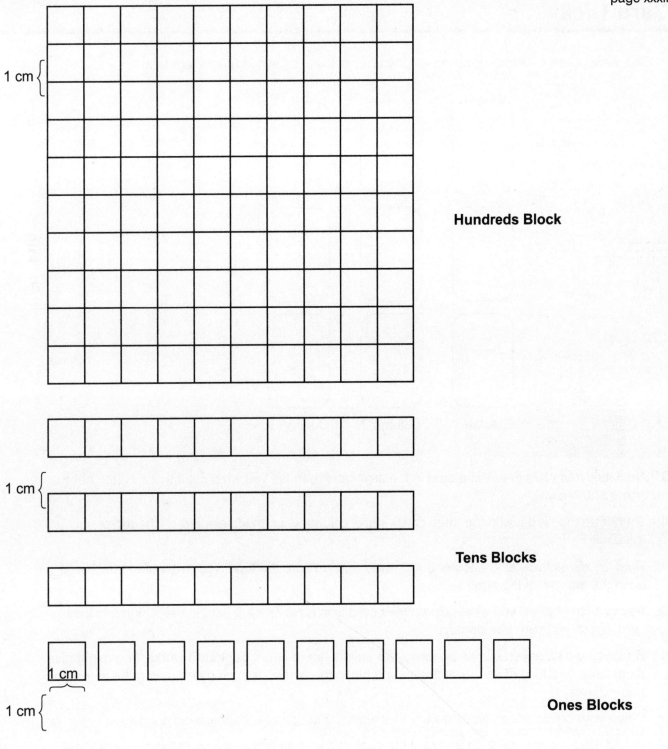

1 cm

Hundreds Block

1 cm

Tens Blocks

1 cm

1 cm

Ones Blocks

Introduction

Card Trick

1. First, deal out nine cards – face up – in the arrangement shown in the picture below:

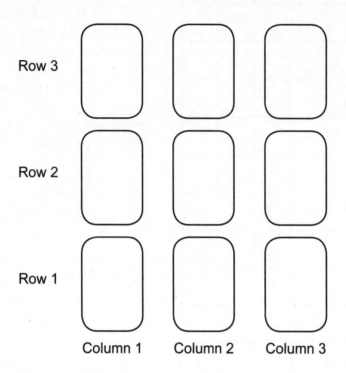

Row 3

Row 2

Row 1

Column 1 Column 2 Column 3

2. Next ask your child to select a card in the array and then tell you what column it's in (but not the name of the card).

3. Gather up the cards, with the three cards in the column your child selected on the top of the deck.

4. Deal the cards face up in another 3 × 3 array making sure the top three cards of the deck end up in the top row of the array.

5. Ask your child to tell you what column their card is in now. The top card in that column is their card, which you can now identify!

6. Repeat the trick several times and ask your child to try to figure out how it works. You might give them hints by telling them to watch how you place the cards, or even by repeating the trick with a 2 × 2 array.

When your child understands how the trick works, you can ask the following questions:

✓ Would there be any point to the trick if the subject told the person performing the trick both the row and the column number of the card they had selected? Clearly there would be no trick if the performer knew both numbers. Two pieces of information are enough to unambiguously identify a position in an array or graph. This is why graphs are such an efficient means of representation: two numbers can identify any location in two-dimensional space (in other words, on a flat sheet of paper). This discovery, made over 300 years ago by the French mathematician René Descartes, was one of the simplest and most revolutionary steps in the history of mathematics and science: his idea of representing position using numbers underlies virtually all modern mathematics, science, and technology.

Elimination Game

Find the special number in each square by reading the clues and eliminating.
REMEMBER: Zero is an even number.

1. Cross out numbers that are…

a)

4	3	9
7	9	8
1	6	5

Odd
Less than 4
Greater than 5
What number is left?

b)

4	2	3
5	1	7
0	9	8

Even
Less than 4
Greater than 6
What number is left?

c)

4	20	9
11	6	16
5	3	18

Even
Multiples of 3
Greater than 10
What number is left?

d)

4	20	9
15	6	16
5	3	18

Multiples of 2
Multiples of 3
Multiples of 4
What number is left?

BONUS: Cross out numbers **with**…

a)

42	31	92
27	99	88
21	66	52

Ones digit 2
Tens digit 2
Both digits are the same
What number is left?

b)

24	3	9
7	89	83
1	6	52

One digit
Tens digit 8
Ones digit 2
What number is left?

No unauthorized copying   **Games, Activities, and Puzzles**

Match the Numbers

1. a) Draw a line between all the pairs of numbers that add to 10:

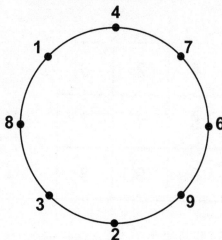

b) Draw a line between all the pairs of numbers that add to 10:

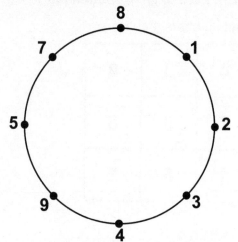

c) Draw a line between all the pairs of numbers that add to 10:

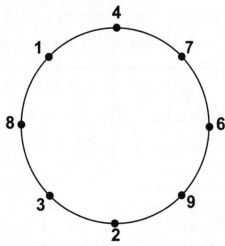

d) Draw a line between all the pairs of numbers that add to 10:

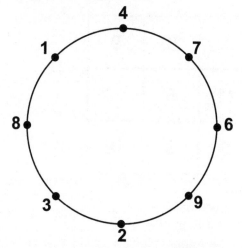

e) Draw a line between all the pairs of numbers that add to 100:

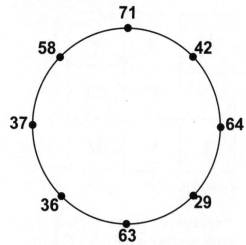

f) Draw a line between all the pairs of numbers that add to 100:

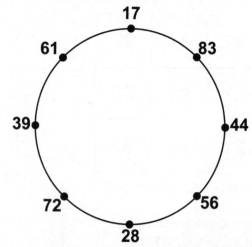

No unauthorized copying **Games, Activities, and Puzzles**

Define a Number

Each statement describes at least one whole number between 1 and 100.

A The number is even.	B The number is odd.	C You can count to the number by 4s.
D You can count to the number by 3s.	E You can count to the number by 25s.	F You can count to the number by 100s.
G If you multiplied the number by 5, the product would be larger than 100.	H The number has 3 digits.	I The ones digit is one less than the tens digit. The ones digit is 5.
J The number has 3 or more digits.	K The sum of its digits is greater than 9.	L The number has 2 digits and the ones digit is greater than the tens digit.
M The number is less than 40.	N If you rolled two dice and added the numbers together, you could get the number.	O The number is less than 25.
P The ones digit of this number is divisible by 3.	Q You can get this number by multiplying another number by itself (**EXAMPLE:** 9 = 3 × 3).	R The ones digit of this number is more than the tens digit.

1. Name a number that statement **D** applies to: _____

2. Name a number that statement **C** and **O** apply to: _____

3. Name three numbers that statements **N** and **A** apply to: _____, _____, _____

4. a) Name a number that statements **B**, **D**, **G** and **O** apply to: _____

   b) Name a number that statements **D**, **L** and **O** apply to: _____

5. a) Which statements apply to both the number 22 and the number 30? _____

   b) Which statements apply to both the number 12 and the number 32? _____

6. Can you find four numbers that statement **Q** applies to? _____, _____, _____, _____

Guess and Check Game

1. Solve each puzzle below by placing 3 pennies in the shapes below.
   Draw your solution (using dots for pennies):

   Example: Gloria places 3 pennies in the following figure so that there is:

   - an even number in the circle (**REMEMBER: Zero is an even number**),
   - an odd number in the square, and an odd number in the pentagon.

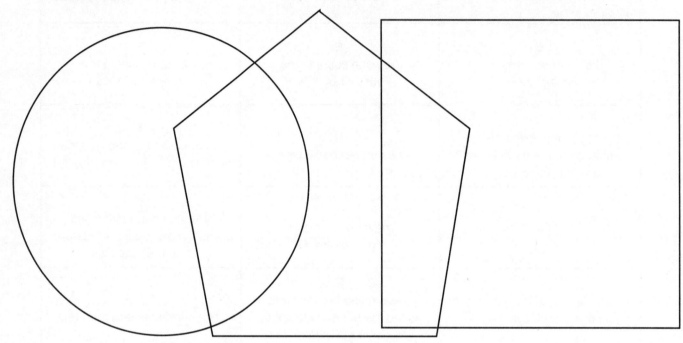

Can you place 3 pennies so you have...

Answer:

Remember:
'0' is an
<u>even number</u>

a) an <u>even</u> number in the circle,
an <u>even</u> number in the pentagon, and
an <u>even</u> number in the square?

b) an <u>odd</u> number in the circle,
an <u>even</u> number in the pentagon, and
an <u>even</u> number in the square?

c) an <u>even</u> number in the circle,
an <u>odd</u> number in the pentagon, and
an <u>even</u> number in the square?

d) an <u>odd</u> number in the circle,
an <u>odd</u> number in the pentagon, and
an <u>odd</u> number in the square?

Hidden Letters

Can you find the hidden letter in each grid of numbers by shading the correct boxes?
The first one is started for you.

1. Shade all the numbers exactly divisible by 5:

a)
60	50	95
25	6	32
85	5	65
200	48	54
40	11	19

b)
10	30	25
35	26	58
15	33	28
55	53	42
45	20	50

c)
45	50	65
25	11	27
40	15	43
75	57	63
70	35	20

a)
85	90	20
60	88	11
5	95	50
53	48	65
45	155	25

b)
30	70	55
50	47	35
75	15	80
90	26	10
10	17	40

2. Shade all the numbers exactly divisible by 2:

a)
8	3	9
26	7	13
4	22	16
18	11	10
20	12	6

b)
14	17	2
8	19	6
20	10	18
16	21	12
4	3	22

c)
20	28	4
29	8	15
23	30	9
17	16	1
31	24	5

a)
38	23	4
34	25	40
6	45	32
28	17	8
16	48	28

b)
9	13	8
29	33	12
22	50	32
18	55	44
42	36	28

3. Shade all the numbers exactly divisible by 3:

a)
24	15	12
36	5	16
18	21	9
27	11	22
3	18	30

b)
6	9	21
4	30	25
16	33	31
20	24	28
31	15	19

c)
9	27	21
36	2	15
12	6	18
24	19	13
30	22	7

Egyptian Writing

NS4-1: Place Value – Ones, Tens, Hundreds, and Thousands

1. Teach your child Egyptian writing to show place value.

   Example: Write 234 in Egyptian writing:

   Ask your child what is different about Egyptian writing? Answer: You have to show the number of ones, tens, etc. individually: i.e. If you have 7 ones you have to draw seven strokes (|||||||). In the Arabic system we use, a single digit (7) tells you how many ones there are. Your child might want to try to invent their own number systems:

   a) 1 =   (stroke)

   b) 10 = ∩ (arch)

   c) 100 = ♀ (coiled rope)

   d) 1000 = ⚲ (lotus flower)

   e) 10 000 = ⋀ (finger)

NS4-12: Regrouping

1. Ask your child to show the regrouping in question 1 with base ten blocks.

2. If you taught your child Egyptian writing (see Extension for NS4-1: Place Value – Ones, Tens, Hundreds, and Thousands) you could ask them to show regrouping using Egyptian writing.

   EXAMPLE:

Sums and Differences

Give your child a set of cards with the numbers 1 to 8 on them.

a) Ask your child to arrange the cards in two rows as shown so that the difference between the number is as small as possible.

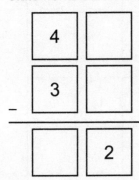

Solution:

5	1	2	3
4	8	7	6

b) Ask your child to place the eight cards so that the three subtraction statements below are correct.

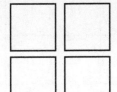

PARENT: As a warm up for exercise 3 a) above, ask your child to place the cards from 1 to 4 in the array to make the smallest difference.

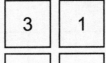

Solution:

3	1
2	4

More Challenging: Place the cards 1 to 6 in the array to make the smallest difference.

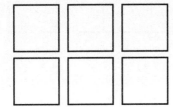

Solution:

4	1	2
3	6	5

No unauthorized copying   **Games, Activities, and Puzzles**

Money

NOTE: Here is another exercise that will help your child visualize regrouping two digit numbers. (For this exercise you will need real or play money dimes, pennies, and cards that have been divided into ten squares.)

Add: 38 + 25

Step 1:   Make a model of the two numbers by placing dimes on the tens cards and pennies on the ones cards.

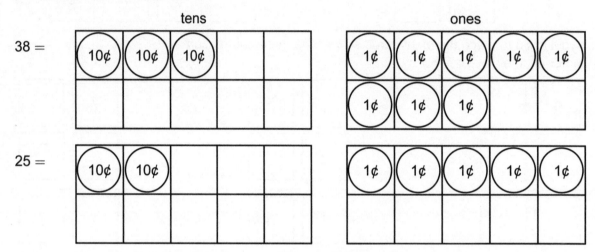

Step 2:   Move as many pennies from the lower ones-card as you need to fill the upper ones-card.

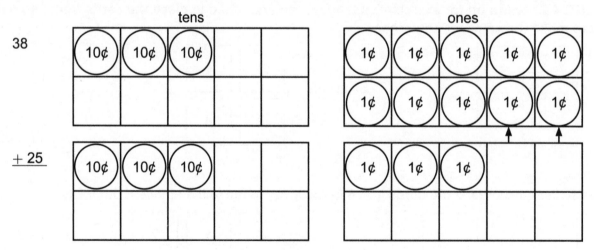

Money *(continued)*

Step 3: Exchange the ten pennies on the upper ones card for a dime and place the dime in the upper tens card. (This is the equivalent to the carrying step.) Notice that there are only 3 pennies left on the lower ones car:

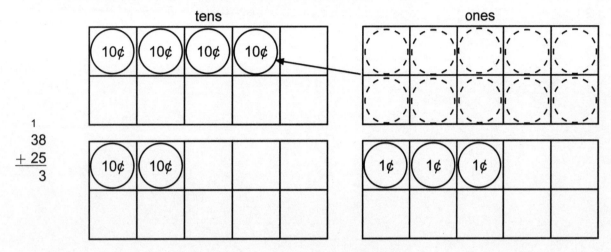

$$\begin{array}{r} \overset{1}{38} \\ +\ 25 \\ \hline 3 \end{array}$$

Step 4: Move all the coins to the upper cards and count the total (63).

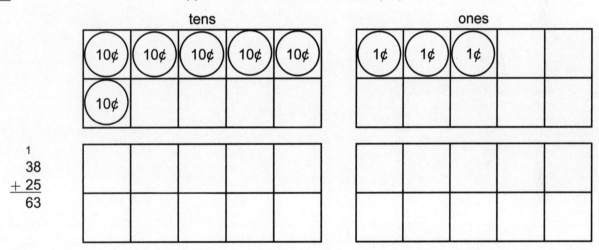

$$\begin{array}{r} \overset{1}{38} \\ +\ 25 \\ \hline 63 \end{array}$$

PA4-1: Counting

Helen finds the **difference** between 15 and 12 by counting on her fingers. She says "12" with her fist closed, then counts to 15, raising one finger at a time:

    12   13   14   15

When she says "15," she has raised 3 fingers. So the difference or "gap" between 12 and 15 is 3.

----

1. Find the difference between the numbers by counting up. Write your answer in the circle:
   (If you know your subtraction facts, you may find the answer without counting.)

   a) 2 ◯ 5   b) 3 ◯ 8   c) 6 ◯ 8   d) 4 ◯ 9

   e) 12 ◯ 16   f) 13 ◯ 17   g) 21 ◯ 26   h) 37 ◯ 39

   i) 26 ◯ 29   j) 32 ◯ 37   k) 24 ◯ 29   l) 44 ◯ 47

   m) 51 ◯ 55   n) 46 ◯ 49   o) 28 ◯ 32   p) 34 ◯ 39

   q) 89 ◯ 91   r) 62 ◯ 71   s) 87 ◯ 89   t) 59 ◯ 63

   BONUS:

   u) 96 ◯ 101   v) 79 ◯ 83   w) 98 ◯ 104   x) 117 ◯ 122

   y) 219 ◯ 223   z) 146 ◯ 151   aa) 99 ◯ 108   bb) 99 ◯ 107

PARENT:
To help your child recognize the gap between numbers, give your child daily practice with the mental math exercises provided on pages xxx–xxxiv.

What number added to 6 gives 9?   6 + ☐? = 9

Anne finds the answer using a **number line**.
She puts her finger on 6 and counts the
number of spaces between 6 and 9:

She counts 3 spaces, so: 6 + ☐3 = 9

and: 9 is 3 **more than** 6

and: 3 is called the **difference** between 9 and 6

----

2. Use the number line (or count up) to find the **difference** between the numbers:

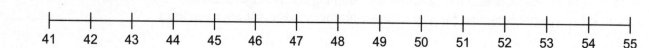

a) 42 ◯ 45   b) 43 ◯ 47   c) 51 ◯ 54   d) 44 ◯ 51

e) 42 ◯ 44   f) 49 ◯ 53   g) 47 ◯ 48   h) 45 ◯ 49

3. Use the number line (or count up) to find the **difference** between the numbers.
    Write your answer in the box:

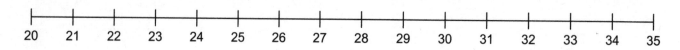

a) 23 + ☐ = 25   b) 22 + ☐ = 26   c) 24 + ☐ = 27

d) ☐ + 22 = 24   e) 23 + ☐ = 30   f) ☐ + 28 = 31

⬡   BONUS:
       4. Fill in the missing numbers:

a) 25 is _____ more than 23   b) 30 is _____ more than 27   c) 53 is _____ more than 46

d) 32 is _____ more than 29   e) 28 is _____ more than 25   f) 26 is _____ more than 25

g) 50 is _____ more than 49   h) 47 is _____ more than 43   i) 53 is _____ more than 48

Patterns & Algebra 1

What number is 4 **more** than 16? (Or: What is 16 + 4?)

Alissa finds the answer by counting on her fingers. She says 16 with her fist closed, then counts up from 16 until she has raised 4 fingers:

| 16 | 17 | 18 | 19 | 20 |

The number 20 is 4 **more** than 16.

---

1. Add the number in the circle to the number beside it. Write your answer in the blank:

a) 5 ④ _____   b) 8 ② _____   c) 7 ③ _____   d) 3 ④ _____

e) 17 ⑤ _____   f) 18 ④ _____   g) 14 ⑧ _____   h) 19 ⑥ _____

i) 30 ⑧ _____   j) 27 ⑨ _____   k) 34 ⑦ _____   l) 32 ⑤ _____

BONUS:

m) 67 ② _____   n) 85 ⑤ _____   o) 42 ③ _____   p) 68 ④ _____

q) 54 ⑥ _____   r) 63 ⑤ _____   s) 98 ④ _____   t) 93 ⑧ _____

2. Fill in the missing numbers:

a) _____ is 4 more than 6   b) _____ is 6 more than 5   c) _____ is 5 more than 7

d) _____ is 1 more than 19   e) _____ is 6 more than 34   f) _____ is 5 more than 18

g) _____ is 8 more than 29   h) _____ is 7 more than 24   i) _____ is 8 more than 37

Angel wants to continue the number pattern: 6 , 8 , 10 , 12 , _?_

Step 1:   She finds the **difference** between the first two numbers:

⌃2⌄ ⌃ ⌄ ⌃ ⌄ ⌃ ⌄
6 , 8 , 10 , 12 , _?_

Step 2:   She checks that the difference between the other numbers
           in the pattern is also 2:

⌃2⌄ ⌃2⌄ ⌃2⌄ ⌃2⌄
6 , 8 , 10 , 12 , _?_

Step 3:   To continue the pattern, Angel adds 2 to the last number
           in the sequence:

6 , 8 , 10 , 12 , _14_

PARENT:
Your child should count on their fingers if necessary to carry out the steps above.

- -

1. Extend the following patterns. Start by finding the gap between the numbers:

a) 1 , 3 , 5 , ____ , ____ , ____   b) 0 , 2 , 4 , ____ , ____ , ____

c) 3 , 7 , 11 , ____ , ____ , ____   d) 2 , 6 , 10 , ____ , ____ , ____

e) 1 , 4 , 7 , ____ , ____ , ____   f) 5 , 9 , 13 , ____ , ____ , ____

BONUS:

g) 1 , 11 , 21 , ____ , ____ , ____   h) 5 , 12 , 19 , ____ , ____ , ____

i) 21 , 24 , 27 , ____ , ____ , ____   j) 86 , 88 , 90 , ____ , ____ , ____

Use increasing sequences to solve these problems.

2. Mary reads 5 pages of her book each night. Last night she was on page 72.

    What page will she reach tonight? _____ And tomorrow night? _____

3. Jane runs 12 blocks on Monday. Each day she runs 4 blocks further than the day before.

    How far does she run on Tuesday? _____ And on Wednesday? _____

    On what day of the week will she run 28 blocks? _____

PA4-4: Counting Backwards

What number **subtracted** from 8 gives 5?

$$8 - \boxed{?} = 5$$

Mary finds the answer using a **number line**:

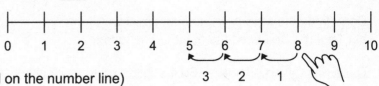

She puts her finger on 8 and counts (backward on the number line)
to find the number of spaces between 8 and 5.

She counts 3 spaces, so: $8 - \boxed{3} = 5$ and: 5 is 3 **less than** 8

----

1. Use the number line to find the difference between the two numbers. Write your answer in the box:

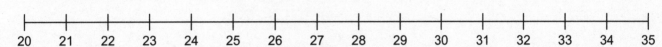

 a) $27 - \boxed{} = 24$ b) $26 - \boxed{} = 23$ c) $29 - \boxed{} = 27$

 d) $25 - \boxed{} = 21$ e) $28 - \boxed{} = 24$ f) $30 - \boxed{} = 25$

 g) $32 - \boxed{} = 29$ h) $35 - \boxed{} = 34$ i) $30 - \boxed{} = 24$

2. What number must you **subtract** from the bigger number to get the smaller number? Write your answer in the circle (with a minus sign, as shown in the first question below):

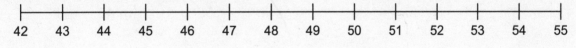

 a) 47 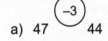 44   b) 45 ◯ 43   c) 51 ◯ 48   d) 54 ◯ 43

 e) 48 ◯ 41   f) 49 ◯ 44   g) 54 ◯ 47   h) 52 ◯ 43

BONUS:
3. Fill in the missing numbers:

 a) 47 is ____ less than 50   b) 51 is ____ less than 55   c) 46 is ____ less than 51

 d) 49 is ____ less than 51   e) 48 is ____ less than 54   f) 45 is ____ less than 52

 g) 44 is ____ less than 49   h) 43 is ____ less than 51   i) 52 is ____ less than 55

JUMP at Home Grade 4   No unauthorized copying   **Patterns & Algebra 1**

What number must you subtract from 22 to get 18?

Dana finds the answer by counting backwards on her fingers. She uses the number line to help:

22   21   20   19   18

Dana has raised 4 fingers. So 4 subtracted from 22 gives 18.

----

4. What number must you **subtract** from the greater number to get the lesser number?

    NOTE: Find the answer by counting backwards on your fingers. (If you know your subtraction facts, you can write the answer directly.) Use the number line to help you.

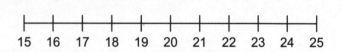

15   16   17   18   19   20   21   22   23   24   25

a) 23 (-3) 20   b) 24 ( ) 19   c) 21 ( ) 16   d) 22 ( ) 15

e) 24 ( ) 17   f) 19 ( ) 16   g) 23 ( ) 17   h) 25 ( ) 19

5. Find the gap between the numbers by counting backwards on your fingers:

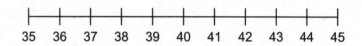

35   36   37   38   39   40   41   42   43   44   45

a) 42 (-4) 38   b) 41 ( ) 39   c) 42 ( ) 37   d) 38 ( ) 37

e) 41 ( ) 37   f) 40 ( ) 36   g) 42 ( ) 35   h) 43 ( ) 35

6. Find the gap between the numbers by counting backwards on your fingers (or by using your subtraction facts):

a) 86 ( ) 81   b) 58 ( ) 52   c) 50 ( ) 48   d) 80 ( ) 78

e) 52 ( ) 47   f) 67 ( ) 63   g) 45 ( ) 36   h) 62 ( ) 56

i) 58 ( ) 51   j) 101 ( ) 97   k) 82 ( ) 76   l) 97 ( ) 89

PARENT:
Spend extra time working with your child if they need more practice finding the gap between pairs of numbers by subtracting or counting backwards. Your child will not be able to extend or describe patterns if they cannot find the gap between pairs of numbers.

Patterns & Algebra 1

What number is 3 less than 9?   (Or: What is 9 – 3?)

Keitha finds the answer by counting on her fingers.
She says 9 with her fist closed and counts backwards
until she has raised 3 fingers:

9   8   7   6

The number 6 is 3 **less than** 9.

----

1. Subtract the number in the circle from the number beside it. Write your answer in the blank:

    a) 3 (-2) _____   b) 12 (-3) _____   c) 8 (-4) _____   d) 9 (-1) _____

    e) 8 (-5) _____   f) 10 (-4) _____   g) 5 (-1) _____   h) 9 (-2) _____

    BONUS:

    i) 28 (-4) _____   j) 35 (-6) _____   k) 57 (-8) _____   l) 62 (-4) _____

2. Fill in the missing numbers:

    a) _____ is 4 less than 7   b) _____ is 2 less than 9   c) _____ is 3 less than 8

    d) _____ is 5 less than 17   e) _____ is 4 less than 20   f) _____ is 6 less than 25

    g) _____ is 7 less than 28   h) _____ is 4 less than 32   i) _____ is 5 less than 40

3. Extend the following **decreasing** patterns:
    HINT: It is important to start by first finding the gap between the numbers.

Example:
       ◯   ◯   ◯   ◯   ◯
    11 , 9 , 7 , ____ , ____ , ____

Step 1

    11 (-2) 9 (-2) 7 (-2) ____ , ____ , ____

Step 2
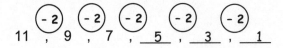
    11 (-2) 9 (-2) 7 (-2) 5 , 3 , 1

a) 10 , 9 , 8 , ____ , ____ , ____

b) 14 , 12 , 10 , ____ , ____ , ____

c) 23 , 22 , 21 , ____ , ____ , ____

d) 24 , 21 , 18 , ____ , ____ , ____

e) 90 , 80 , 70 , ____ , ____ , ____

f) 45 , 40 , 35 , ____ , ____ , ____

1. Extend the following patterns, using the "gap" provided:

Example 1:

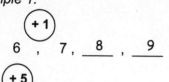

6 , 7, _8_ , _9_ ___

a) 5 , 10, ___ , ___ , ___

c) 3 , 6, ___ , ___ , ___

e) 12 , 14 , ___ , ___ , ___

g) 14 , 13, ___ , ___ , ___

Example 2:

8 , 6, _4_ , _2_ ___

b) 1 , 4 , ___ , ___ , ___

d) 6 , 8, ___ , ___ , ___

f) 10 , 15 , ___ , ___ , ___

h) 16 , 14 , ___ , ___ , ___

2. Extend the following patterns by first finding the "gap":

HINT: You should first check that the gap is the same between each pair of numbers!

Example:

3 , 5 , 7 , ___

<u>Step 1:</u>

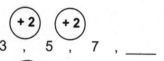

3 , 5 , 7 , ___

a) 5 , 8 , 11 , ___ , ___

c) 6 , 10 , 14 , ___ , ___

e) 21 , 24 , 27 , ___ , ___

g) 25 , 23 , 21 , ___ , ___

<u>Step 2:</u>

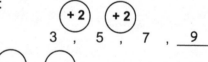

3 , 5 , 7 , _9_

b) 2 , 4 , 6 , ___ , ___

d) 1 , 3 , 5 , ___ , ___

f) 12 , 17 , 22 , ___ , ___

h) 59 , 54 , 49 , ___ , ___

BONUS:

3. Rachel has a box of 24 chocolates. She eats 3 each day.

How many are left after 5 days? _____

4. Emi has saved $17. She saves $4 each day.

How much money has she saved after 4 days? _____

PARENT:
This section provides a basic introduction to pattern rules. For more advanced work involving word problems, applications and communication, see sections PA4-11 to 17.

1. Continue the following sequences by **adding** the number given:

   a) (add 3)   31, 34, ____, ____, ____   b) (add 5)   70, 75, ____, ____, ____

   c) (add 2)   24, 26, ____, ____, ____   d) (add 10)   50, 60, ____, ____, ____

2. Continue the following sequences, **subtracting** by the number given:

   a) (subtract 2)   14, 12, ___, ___, ___   b) (subtract 3)   15, 12, ___, ___, ___

   c) (subtract 5)   75, 70, ___, ___, ___   d) (subtract 3)   66, 63, ___, ___, ___

3. Continue the following sequences by **adding** the number given:

   a) (add 4)   31, 35, ____, ____, ____   b) (add 9)   11, 20, ____, ____, ____

   c) (add 6)   10, 16, ____, ____, ____   d) (add 7)   70, 77, ____, ____, ____

4. Continue the following sequences by **subtracting** the number given:

   a) (subtract 4)   46, 42, ___, ___, ___   b) (subtract 7)   49, 42, ___, ___, ___

   c) (subtract 3)   91, 88, ___, ___, ___   d) (subtract 5)   131, 126, ____, ____, ____

BONUS:

5. Create a pattern of your own. After writing down the pattern in the blanks, give the rule you used:

   _____ , _____ , _____ , _____ , _____   My rule: _____

6. Which one of the following sequences was made by adding 3? Circle it:
   HINT: Check all the numbers in the sequence.

   a) 3, 5, 9, 12   b) 3, 6, 8, 12   c) 3, 6, 9, 12

7. 　　　　　　　　　　**72, 64, 56, 48, 40, ...**

   Zannat says this sequence was made by subtracting 7 each time. Faruq says it was made by subtracting 8. Who is right? Explain:

   _____

   _____

1. The following sequences were made by **adding** a number repeatedly. In each case, say what number was added:

   a) 2, 5, 8, 11   add ____

   b) 3, 6, 9, 12   add ____

   c) 15, 17, 19, 21   add ____

   d) 44, 46, 48, 50   add ____

   e) 41, 46, 51, 56   add ____

   f) 19, 22, 25, 28   add ____

   g) 243, 245, 247, 249   add ____

   h) 21, 27, 33, 39   add ____

   i) 15, 18, 21, 24   add ____

   j) 41, 45, 49, 53   add ____

2. The following sequences were made by **subtracting** a number repeatedly. In each case, say what number was subtracted:

   a) 18, 16, 14, 12   subtract ____

   b) 35, 30, 25, 20   subtract ____

   c) 100, 99, 98, 97   subtract ____

   d) 41, 38, 35, 32   subtract ____

   e) 17, 14, 11, 8   subtract ____

   f) 99, 97, 95, 93   subtract ____

   g) 180, 170, 160, 150   subtract ____

   h) 100, 95, 90, 85   subtract ____

   i) 27, 25, 23, 21   subtract ____

   j) 90, 84, 78, 72   subtract ____

3. State the rule for the following patterns:

   a) 119, 112, 105, 98, 91   subtract ____

   b) 1, 9, 17, 25, 33, 41   add ____

   c) 101, 105, 109, 113   _____

   d) 110, 99, 88, 77,   _____

4. For the following pattern, use the first three numbers in the pattern to find the rule. Then continue the pattern by filling in the blanks:

   12, 17, 22, _____, _____, _____   The rule is: _____

5.   **5, 8, 11, 14, 17, ...**

   Keith says the pattern rule is "Start at 5 and subtract 3 each time." Jane says the rule is "Add 4 each time." Molly says the rule is "Start at 5 and add 3 each time."

   a) Whose rule is correct? _____

   b) What mistakes did the others make?_____

   _____

Patterns & Algebra 1

PA4-9: Introduction to T-Tables

Abdul makes a **growing pattern** with blocks.

He records the number of blocks in each figure in a chart or T-table. He also records the number of blocks he adds each time he makes a new figure:

Figure 1   Figure 2   Figure 3

Figure	# of Blocks
1	3
2	5
3	7

② Number of blocks **added** each time
②

The number of blocks in the figures are 3, 5, 7, …

Abdul writes a rule for this number pattern:

RULE: Start at 3 and add 2 each time.

----

1. Abdul makes another growing pattern with blocks. How many blocks does he add to make each new figure? Write your answer in the circles provided. Then write a rule for the pattern:

a)

Figure	Number of Blocks
1	3
2	7
3	11

Rule:

b)

Figure	Number of Blocks
1	2
2	6
3	10

Rule:

c)

Figure	Number of Blocks
1	2
2	4
3	6

Rule:

d)

Figure	Number of Blocks
1	1
2	6
3	11

Rule:

e)

Figure	Number of Blocks
1	5
2	9
3	13

Rule:

f)

Figure	Number of Blocks
1	12
2	18
3	24

Rule:

Patterns & Algebra 1

g)

Figure	Number of Blocks
1	2
2	10
3	18

Rule:

h)

Figure	Number of Blocks
1	3
2	6
3	9

Rule:

i)

Figure	Number of Blocks
1	6
2	13
3	20

Rule:

BONUS:

2. Extend the number pattern. How many blocks would be used in the 6th figure?

a)

Figure	Number of Blocks
1	2
2	7
3	12

b)

Figure	Number of Blocks
1	3
2	6
3	9

c)

Figure	Number of Blocks
1	3
2	8
3	13

3. Amy makes a growing pattern with blocks. After making the 3rd figure, she only has 14 blocks left. Does she have enough blocks to complete the 4th figure?

a)

Figure	Number of Blocks
1	3
2	7
3	11

YES   NO

b)

Figure	Number of Blocks
1	7
2	10
3	13

YES   NO

c)

Figure	Number of Blocks
1	1
2	5
3	9

YES   NO

4. In a notebook, make a chart to show how many squares will be needed to make the **fifth figure** in each pattern:

a)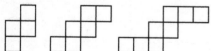

b)

Patterns & Algebra 1

PA4-10: T-Tables

1. Count the number of line segments in each set of figures by marking each line segment as you count as shown in the example:

   HINT: Count around the outside of the figure first.

   Example: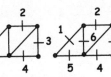

   a)  ____

   b) 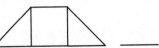 ____

   c) 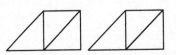 ____

   d) 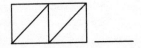 ____

   e)  ____

   f) 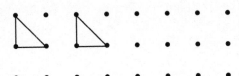 ____

2. Continue the pattern below, then complete the chart:

   Figure 1

   Figure 2

   Figure 3

   Figure 4

   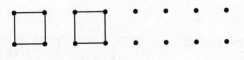

Figure	Number of Line Segments
1	4
2	8
3	
4	

   How many line segments would

   Figure 5 have? _____

3. Continue the pattern below, then complete the chart:

   Figure 1

   Figure 2

   Figure 3

   Figure 4

Figure	Number of Line Segments
1	
2	
3	
4	

   How many line segments would

   Figure 5 have? _____

     Patterns & Algebra 1

PA4-10: T-Tables *(continued)*

4. Continue the pattern below, then complete the chart:

Figure 1

Figure 2

Figure 3

Figure 4

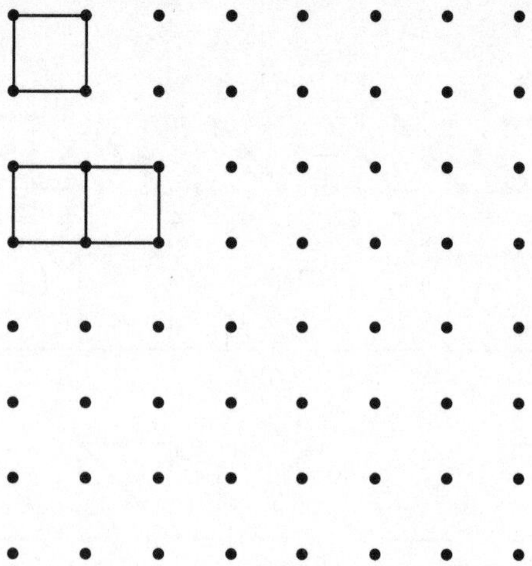

Figure	Number of Line Segments
1	
2	
3	
4	

a) How many line segments would Figure 5 have? ______________

b) How many line segments would Figure 6 have? ______________

c) How many line segments would Figure 7 have? ______________

5. Continue the pattern below, then complete the chart:

Figure 1

Figure 2

Figure 3

Figure 4

Figure 5

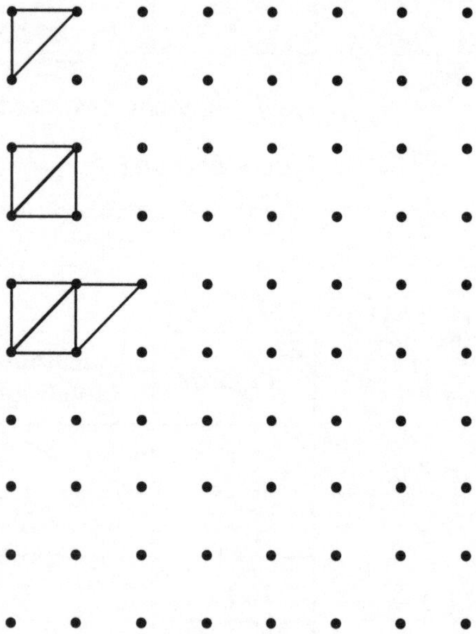

Figure	Number of Line Segments
1	
2	
3	
4	
5	

a) How many line segments would Figure 6 have? ______________

b) How many line segments would Figure 7 have? ______________

c) How many line segments would Figure 8 have? ______________

PA4-10: T-Tables *(continued)*

6. Extend the chart. How many young would five animals have?

a)
Arctic Fox	Number of Cubs
1	5
2	10

b)
Wood-chuck	Number of Pups
1	4
2	8

c)
Osprey	Number of Eggs
1	3
2	6

d)
White Tailed Deer	Number of Fawns
1	2
2	4

7. How much money would Claude earn for four hours of work?

a)
Hours Worked	Dollars Earned in an Hour
1	$14

b)
Hours Worked	Dollars Earned in an Hour
1	$12

c)
Hours Worked	Dollars Earned in an Hour
1	$15

8. Step 1

Step 2

Step 3

Hexagons	Triangles

Peter wants to make a border for a picture using triangles and hexagons. He has 6 hexagons and 9 triangles.

Does he have enough triangles to use all 6 hexagons? _____

9. Hanna wants to make Christmas ornaments like the one shown below. She has 5 trapezoids (the shaded figure).

Fill in the chart to show how many triangles she will need:

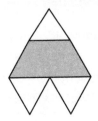

Trapezoids	Triangles

No unauthorized copying

Patterns & Algebra 1

PA4-11: Patterns Involving Time

For the exercises on this page you will need to know:

The Days of the Week: **Monday, Tuesday, Wednesday, Thursday, Friday, Saturday, Sunday.**

The Months of the Year: **January, February, March, April, May, June, July, August, September, October, November, December.**

1. Harry starts work on Tuesday morning.
   He repairs 4 bikes each day.

Day	Total Number of Bikes Repaired
Tuesday	4

   How many bikes has he repaired by Friday evening?

2. Meryl saves $20 in July.
   She saves $10 each month after that.

Month	Dollars Saved
July	$20

   How much has she saved by the end of October?

3. During a snow storm, 5 cm of snow had fallen by 6 pm.
   3 cm of snow fell every hour after that.

Hour	Depth of Snow
6 pm	5 cm

   How deep was the snow at 9 pm?

4. Adria's maple sapling grows 3 cm in May.
   It grows 6 cm each month after that.

Month	Height of Sapling
May	

   How high is the sapling by the end of August?

 In a notebook, make a chart to solve the following problems.

5. Karen writes 14 pages of her book in February.
   She writes 8 pages every month after that.
   How many pages has she written by the end of June?

6. Mario starts work on Wednesday morning.
   He plants 5 trees each day.
   How many trees has he planted by Friday evening?

Patterns & Algebra 1

7. Sandhu lights a candle at 6 pm. It is 30 cm high.

    At 7 pm, the candle is 27 cm high.

    At 8 pm, it is 24 cm high.

a) How many cm does the candle burn
    down every hour?

    Write your answers (with a minus sign)
    in the circles provided:

b) How high is the candle at 11 pm?

    _____

Hour	Height of the Candle
6 pm	30 cm
7 pm	27 cm
8 pm	24 cm
9 pm	
10 pm	

8. Abdullah has $35 in his savings account at
    the end of March.

    He spends $7 each month.

Month	Savings
March	$35

How much does he have in his account
at the end of June?

9. Allishah has $38 in her savings account at
    the end of October.

    She spends $6 each month.

Month	Savings

How much does she have at the end
of January?

10. Karen has $57 in her savings account at the
    end of June.

    She spends $6 each month.

Month	Savings

How much does she have at the end of
September?

11. A fish tank contains 20L of water at 5 pm.

    3L of water leak out each hour.

Time	Amount of Water in Tank

How much water is left at 8 pm?

1. Write the place value of the underlined digit:

    a) 35<u>6</u>4 | tens | b) 1<u>3</u>36 | |

    c) 25<u>6</u> | | d) <u>1</u>230 | |

    REMEMBER:

    4 3 7 5

    thousands   tens   ones

    hundreds

    e) <u>3</u>859 | | f) 5<u>7</u>45 | | g) 23<u>8</u> | |

    h) 6<u>2</u>14 | | i) 8<u>7</u> | | j) <u>9</u>430 | |

2. Give the place value of the number 5 in each of the numbers below:
    HINT: First underline the 5 in each question.

    a) 5640 | | b) 547 | | c) 451 | |

    d) 2415 | | e) 1257 | | f) 5643 | |

    g) 1563 | | h) 56 | | i) 205 | |

3. You can also write numbers using a place value chart:

    Example:

    In a place value chart, the number 3264 is:

thousands	hundreds	tens	ones
3	2	6	4

    Write the following numbers into the place value chart. The first one has been done for you:

	thousands	hundreds	tens	ones
a) 5231	5	2	3	1
b) 8053				
c) 489				
d) 27				
e) 9104				
f) 4687				

NS4-2: Place Value

The number 2 836 is a **4-digit number**:

- The **digit** 2 stands for 2 000 – the **value** of the digit 2 is 2 000
- The **digit** 8 stands for 800 – the **value** of the digit 8 is 800
- The **digit** 3 stands for 30 – the **value** of the digit 3 is 30
- The **digit** 6 stands for 6 – the **value** of the digit 6 is 6

----

1. Write the **value** of each digit:

a) 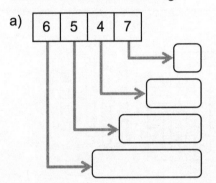   b) 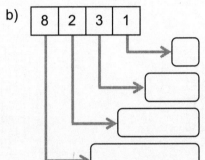   c)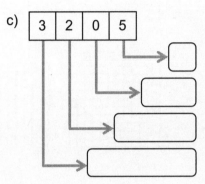

2. What does the digit 3 stand for in each number? The first one is done for you:

a) 237

  30

b) 5 235

c) 6 382

d) 3 280

e) 4 305

f) 6 732

g) 3 092

h) 5 883

i) 3 852

j) 1 003

k) 1 300

l) 231

3. Fill in the blanks:

a) In the number 6 572, the **digit** 5 stands for_____ .

b) In the number 4 236, the **digit** 3 stands for_____ .

c) In the number 2 357, the **digit** 7 stands for_____ .

d) In the number 8 021, the **value** of the digit 8 is_____ .

e) In the number 6 539, the **value** of the digit 5 is_____ .

f) In the number 3 675, the **value** of the digit 7 is_____ .

g) In the number 1 023, the digit _____ is in the **tens place**.

h) In the number 1 729, the digit _____ is in the **hundreds place**.

i) In the number 7 253, the digit _____ is in the **thousands place**.

1. For each question below, give the number represented by the picture. Write each number in expanded word form first:

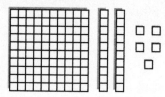

Example:

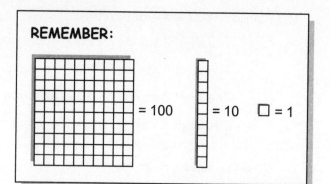

<u>1</u> hundreds + <u>2</u> tens + <u>5</u> ones = 125

a)

___ hundreds + ___ tens + ___ ones =

b)

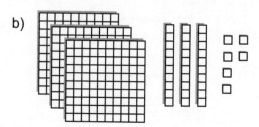

___ hundreds + ___ tens + ___ ones =

c)

___ hundreds + ___ tens + ___ ones =

d)

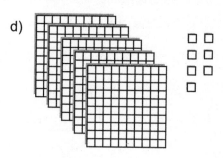

___ hundreds + ___ tens + ___ ones =

2. Using the grid paper below, draw the base-ten model for the following numbers:

a) 123

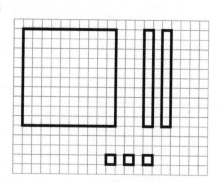

b) 132

3. In a notebook, draw base-ten models for: a) 68   b) 350   c) 249

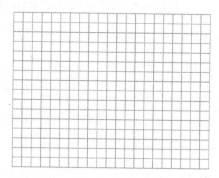

4. For each question below, give the number
   represented by the picture. Write each number
   in expanded form (numerals and words) first:

Example:

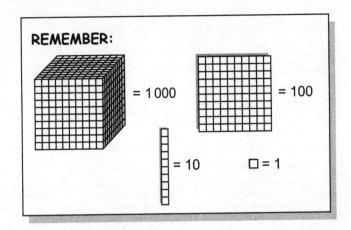

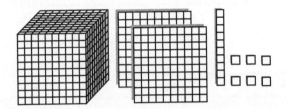

__1__ thousands + __2__ hundreds + __1__ tens + __6__ ones = | 1 216 |

a)

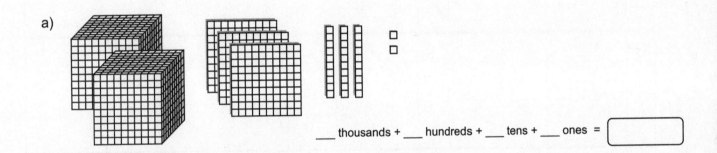

___ thousands + ___ hundreds + ___ tens + ___ ones =

b)

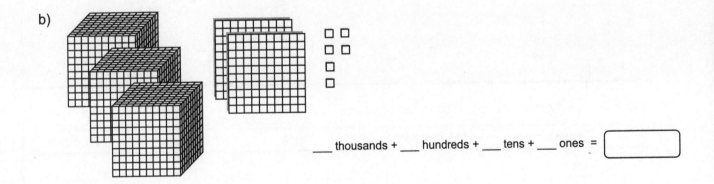

___ thousands + ___ hundreds + ___ tens + ___ ones =

c)

_____ =

Steps for drawing a thousands cube:

Step 1
Draw a square:

Step 2
Draw lines from
3 of its vertices:

Step 3
Join the lines:

5. Represent the given numbers with the base ten blocks in the place value chart. The first one has been started for you:

	Number	Thousands	Hundreds	Tens	Ones
a)	2 314				
b)	1 245				
c)	3 143				

6. Write the numbers for the given base ten blocks:

	Thousands	Hundreds	Tens	Ones	Number
a)					_____
b)					_____

NS4-4: Representation in Expanded Form

1. Expand the following numbers using **numerals** and **words**. The first one is done for you:

   a) 2427 = __2__ thousands + __4__ hundreds + __2__ tens + __7__ ones

   b) 4569 = ____ thousands + ____ hundreds + ____ tens + ____ ones

   c) 3875 = _____

   d) 7210 = _____

   e) 623 = _____

2. Write the number in expanded form (using **numerals**). The first one is done for you:

   a) 2613 = 2000 + 600 + 10 + 3   b) 27 =

   c) 48 =   d) 1232 =

   e) 6103 =   f) 3570 =

   g) 598 =   h) 2901 =

3. Write the number for each sum:

   a) 30 + 6 =   b) 50 + 2 =   c) 60 + 5 =

   d) 400 + 60 + 8 =   e) 500 + 20 + 3 =   f) 3000 + 200 + 50 + 3 =

   g) 5000 + 700 + 20 + 1 =   h) 600 + 40 + 5 =   i) 8000 + 900 + 70 + 2 =

   BONUS:

   j) 600 + 7 =   k) 900 + 6 =   l) 800 + 70 =

   m) 5000 + 100 =   n) 5000 + 20 =   o) 6000 + 2 =

   p) 8000 + 10 + 3 =   q) 9000 + 4 =   r) 4000 + 100 + 5 =

   s) 6000 + 300 + 20 =   t) 8000 + 200 =   u) 3000 + 10 =

4. Find the missing numbers:

a) 200 + 70 + _____ = 273

b) 300 + _____ + 6 = 386

c) 6 000 + 800 + _____ + 7 = 6 827

d) 1 000 + 400 + _____ + 5 = 1 475

e) 9 000 + _____ + 20 + 5 = 9 825

f) 5 000 + _____ + 60 + 3 = 5 263

BONUS:

g) 7 000 + 200 + _____ = 7 202

h) 6 000 + 300 + _____ = 6 320

i) _____ + 300 = 7 300

j) 6 000 + _____ = 6 080

k) 9 000 + _____ + _____ = 9 260

l) 1 000 + _____ + _____ = 1 703

m) 7 000 + _____ + _____ = 7 021

n) 9 000 + _____ = 9 900

5. Write each number in expanded form. Then draw a base ten model.

Example: 3 213 = ┃ 3 000 + 200 + 10 + 3 ┃

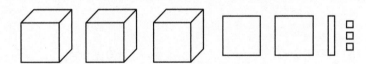

a) 2 317 = ┃ _____ + _____ + _____ + _____ ┃

b) 1 446 = ┃ _____ + _____ + _____ + _____ ┃

BONUS:
6. Feliz has:

- 1 000 stamps from Canada
- 200 stamps from Portugal
- 30 stamps from Spain
- 9 stamps from Egypt

How many stamps does he have in total? _____

Eugene makes a **model** of the number 342 using base ten materials. He writes the number in **expanded form**, using **numerals and words** and using **numerals alone**:

342 = 3 hundreds + 4 tens + 2 ones   *expanded form (using numerals and words)*

342 = 300 + 40 + 2   *expanded form (using numerals)*

---

1. Draw a model of each number using base ten materials. Then write the number in expanded form using numerals and words **and** using numerals. The first one is done for you:

a) 125

125 = ___1 hundred + 2 tens + 5 ones___

125 = ___100 + 20 + 5___

b) 234

234 = _____

234 = _____

c) 307

307 = _____

307 = _____

Answer the following questions in a notebook.

2. Write numerals for the following number words:

a) forty-one   b) twenty-nine   c) three hundred forty-six

d) one hundred ninety   e) sixty-five   f) five hundred two

g) three hundred forty-six   h) one thousand, six   i) four thousand seven
                                 hundred twelve

3. Write number words for the following numbers:

a) 952   b) 3 000   c) 4 700   d) 6 040   e) 2 981   f) 5 862

4. Represent the number 275 in four different ways: by sketching a base ten model, with number words, and in expanded form (2 ways).

1. Write the number in each box. Write the name of each number on the line below. Then, circle the larger number in each pair:

a) (i)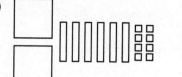

(ii)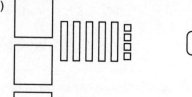

_____   _____

b) (i)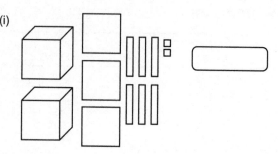

(ii)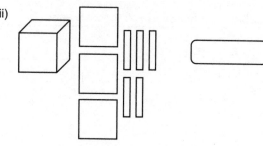

_____   _____

c) Explain how you knew which number in part b) of Question 1 was greater:

_____

_____

2. Write the number in each box. Then circle the larger number in each pair:

   HINT: If there is the same number of thousands, count the number of hundreds or tens.

a) (i)

(ii)

b) (i)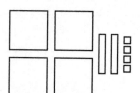

(ii)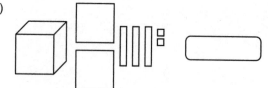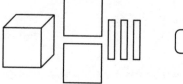

3. In a notebook, draw base-ten models for the following pairs of numbers. Circle the larger number:

   a) four hundred sixteen   460

   b) one thousand three hundred   1 007

NS4-7: Comparing and Ordering Numbers

1. Write the **value** of each digit. Then complete the sentence:

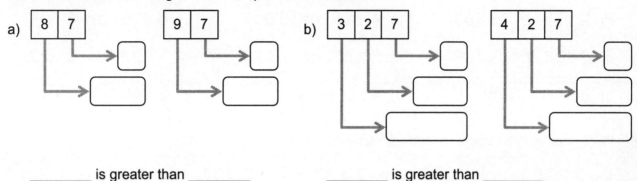

a) | 8 | 7 | | 9 | 7 |

b) | 3 | 2 | 7 | | 4 | 2 | 7 |

_____ is greater than _____   _____ is greater than _____

2. Circle the pair of digits that are different in each pair of numbers. Then write the greater number in the box:

a) 2475
   2465
   [2 475]

b) 1360
   1260
   [   ]

c) 4852
   4858
   [   ]

d) 6325
   7325
   [   ]

e) 384
   584
   [   ]

f) 2906
   2904
   [   ]

g) 875
   865
   [   ]

h) 238
   231
   [   ]

3. Read the numbers from left to right. Circle the first pair of digits you find that are different. Then write the greater number in the box:

a) 1583
   1597
   [1597]

b) 6293
   6542
   [   ]

c) 5769
   6034
   [   ]

d) 9432
   9431
   [   ]

4. Read the numbers from left to right. Underline the first pair of digits you find that are different. Then circle the greater number:

a) 2 342   (2 351)   b) 5 201   5 275   c) 6 327   6102

d) 7 851   7923   e) 5542   5540   f) 9234   8723

g) 3502   3501   h) 6728   7254   i) 2113   2145

5. Circle the greater number:

    a) 2 175 or 3 603   b) 4 221 or 5 012   c) 6 726 or 6 591

    d) 3 728 or 3 729   e) 8 175 or 8 123   f) 5 923 or 6 000

    g) 387 or 389   h) 418 or 481   i) 2 980 or 298

6. Write < or > in the box to make each statement true:

    a) 3 275 ☐ 4 325   b) 2 132 ☐ 2 131   c) 5 214 ☐ 5 216

    d) 528 ☐ 3 257   e) 7 171 ☐ 7 105   f) 287 ☐ 25

    BONUS:

    g) 12 357 ☐ 12 321   h) 75 273 ☐ 75 301

7. Circle the greater number in each pair:

    a) 62 or sixty-three

    b) one hundred eighty-eight or 191

    c) seventy-six or 71

    d) 3725 or four thousand thirty

    e) eight thousand two hundred fifty or 8 350

    f) one thousand one hundred six or 2 107

    g) 6 375 or six thousand three hundred eighty-five

8. Mark each number on the number line. Then circle the greatest number:

    A. 5 800   **B.** 5 700   **C.** 5 200

    5000   6000

9. Fill in the boxes with any number that will make the statement true:

    a) ☐ ☐ 7 < 3 ☐ 2   b) ☐ 2 ☐ > 5 ☐ 9

Answer the following questions in a notebook.

10. Which number must be greater (no matter what numbers are placed in the boxes)? Explain.

    ☐ 4 7   or   ☐ ☐ 2 3

11. How many whole numbers are greater than 5 900 and less than 6 000?

12. Montreal is 539 km away from Toronto. Ottawa is 399 km away from Toronto. Which city is further from Toronto?

1. Write "10 more" or "10 less" in the blanks:

    a) 90 is _____ than 80

    b) 30 is _____ than 40

    c) 10 is _____ than 20

    d) 100 is _____ than 90

2. Write "100 more" or "100 less" in the blanks:

    a) 600 is _____ than 500

    b) 700 is _____ than 800

    c) 700 is _____ than 600

    d) 800 is _____ than 900

3. Write "1000 more" or "1000 less" in the blanks:

    a) 7000 is _____ than 6000

    b) 1000 is _____ than 2000

4. Write the value of the digits. Then say how much more or less the first number is than the second:

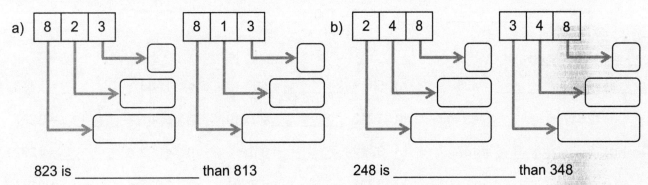

a) 823 is _____ than 813

b) 248 is _____ than 348

5. Circle the pair of digits that are different. Then fill in the blanks:

    a) 2 6 5 2
        2 7 5 2

        2652 is ____100 less____ than 2752

    b) 1382
        1482

        1382 is _____ than 1482

    c) 6830
        7830

        6830 is _____ than 7830

    d) 3621
        2621

        3621 is _____ than 2621

    e) 8405
        8415

        8405 is _____ than 8415

    f) 5871
        5872

        5871 is _____ than 5872

1. Fill in the blanks:

   a) _____ is 10 more than 287

   b) _____ is 10 less than 363

   c) _____ is 10 less than 1982

   d) _____ is 10 more than 3603

   e) _____ is 100 more than 592

   f) _____ is 100 less than 4135

   g) _____ is 100 more than 6821

   h) _____ is 100 less than 3295

   i) _____ is 1000 less than 8305

   j) _____ is 1000 more than 4253

2. Fill in the blanks:

   a) 743 + 10 = _____

   b) 2382 + 10 = _____

   c) 9035 + 10 = _____

   d) 1270 + 100 = _____

   e) 1952 + 100 = _____

   f) 8321 + 1000 = _____

   g) 357 − 10 = _____

   h) 683 − 10 = _____

   i) 932 − 100 = _____

   j) 2487 − 100 = _____

   k) 1901 − 100 = _____

   l) 5316 − 1000 = _____

3. Fill in the blanks:

   a) 485 + _____ = 495

   b) 503 + _____ = 603

   c) 1483 + _____ = 1493

   d) 2617 + _____ = 2717

   e) 3210 − _____ = 2210

   f) 6387 − _____ = 6287

   g) 287 − _____ = 187

   h) 325 − _____ = 315

   i) 4392 − _____ = 4292

   j) 7001 − _____ = 6001

   k) 2301 − _____ = 2201

   l) 8027 + _____ = 8127

4. Fill in the blanks:

   a) 93 + 10 = _____

   b) 295 + 10 = _____

   c) 394 + 10 = _____

   d) 2492 + 10 = _____

   e) 5395 + 10 = _____

   f) 8096 + 10 = _____

   g) 3972 + 100 = _____

   h) 4923 + 100 = _____

   i) 6902 + 100 = _____

   j) 892 + _____ = 902

   k) 597 + _____ = 607

   l) 8122 + _____ = 8222

   m) 301 − 10 = _____

   n) 2507 − 10 = _____

   o) 9397 + 10 = _____

BONUS:

5. Continue the patterns:

   a) 508, 518, 528, _____, _____

   b) 6532, 6542, 6552, _____, _____

   c) 1482, 1492, _____, 1512, _____

   d) 8363, _____, _____, 8393, 8403

1. Count by 10s to continue the pattern:

    a) 30, 40, 50, _____, _____, _____   b) 10, 20, 30, _____, _____, _____

    c) 50, 60, 70, _____, _____, _____   d) 23, 33, 43, _____, _____

    e) 27, 37, 47, _____, _____, _____   f) 15, 25, 35, _____, _____, _____

    g) 49, 59, 69, _____, _____, _____   h) 1, 11, 21, _____, _____

    i) 100, 110, 120, _____, _____, _____   j) 160, 170, 180, _____, _____, _____

2. Count by 100s to continue the pattern:

    a) 100, 200, 300, _____, _____, _____   b) 600, 700, 800, _____, _____, _____

    c) 300, 400, 500, _____, _____, _____   d) 1 000, 1 100, 1 200, _____, _____, _____

3. There are 100 jelly beans in a bag. How many jelly beans would there be in:

    a) 2 bags? _____   b) 4 bags? _____   c) 5 bags? _____

4. Count by 100s to complete the pattern. The first one has been done for you:

    a) 101, 201, 301, <u>401</u>, <u>501</u>   b) 110, 210, 310, _____, _____

    c) 227, 327, 427, _____, _____, _____   d) 399, 499, 599, _____, _____, _____

    e) 45, 145, 245, _____, _____, _____   f) 525, 625, 725, _____, _____, _____

5. Count by 1000s to continue the pattern:

    a) 1 000, 2 000, _____, _____, _____   b) 6 000, 7 000, _____, _____, _____

6. There are 1000 nails in a bag. How many nails would there be in:

    a) 3 bags? _____   b) 4 bags? _____   c) 5 bags? _____

7. Count down by 100s:

    a) 700, 600, 500, _____, _____, _____   b) 1 000, 900, 800, _____, _____, _____

    c) 2200, 2100, _____, _____, _____   d) 5 100, 5 000, _____, _____, _____

8. Count down by 1000s:

    a) 9 000, 8 000, 7 000, _____, _____   b) 5 000, 4 000, _____, _____, _____

1. Create the greatest possible **three-digit** number using the digits given (use each digit only once):

   a) 4, 3, 2 [   ]   b) 7, 8, 9 [   ]   c) 0, 4, 1 [   ]

   BONUS: Now make the greatest possible four-digit number:

   d) 5, 1, 2, 8 [   ]   e) 4, 9, 1, 5 [   ]   f) 6, 1, 5, 4 [   ]

2. Use the digits to create the greatest number, the least number and any number in between (use each digit exactly once):

	Digits	Greatest Number	Number in Between	Least Number
a)	5 7 2 1			
b)	4 9 8 6			
c)	2 7 7 5			

3. Arrange the numbers in order, starting with the **least** number:

   a) 175, 162, 187

   _____ , _____ , _____

   b) 7251, 7385, 7256

   _____ , _____ , _____

   c) 3950, 3850, 3270

   _____ , _____ , _____

   d) 9432, 9484, 9402

   _____ , _____ , _____

   e) 2023, 2027, 2100

   _____ , _____ , _____

   f) 4201, 4110, 4325

   _____ , _____ , _____

4. List all the three-digit numbers you can make using the digits provided. Then circle the greatest one:
   NOTE: Use each number only once.

   a) 3, 4, and 5   b) 6, 1, and 7

Carl has 5 tens blocks and 17 ones blocks. He regroups 10 ones as 1 tens block:

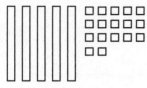 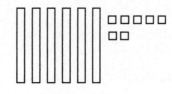

5 tens + 17 ones   =   6 tens + 7 ones

----

1. Regroup 10 ones as 1 tens block:

a)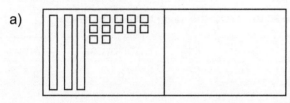

___ tens + ___ ones = ___ tens + ___ ones

b)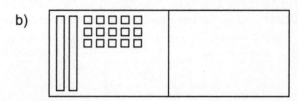

___ tens + ___ ones = ___ tens + ___ ones

c)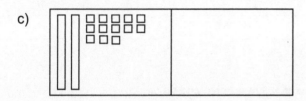

___ tens + ___ ones = ___ tens + ___ ones

d)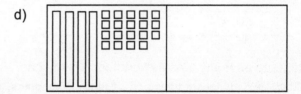

___ tens + ___ ones = ___ tens + ___ ones

2. Complete the charts by regrouping as many ones as tens as you can. The first one has been done:
   REMEMBER: 10 ones = 1 ten, 20 ones = 2 tens, 30 ones = 3 tens, and so on.

a)
tens	ones
6	②5
6 +②= 8	5
= 85

b)
tens	ones
8	32
=

c)
tens	ones
5	31
=

d)
tens	ones
7	17
=

e)
tens	ones
6	29
=

f)
tens	ones
1	52
=

3. Regroup ones as tens:

a) 23 ones = ___ tens + ___ ones   b) 56 ones = ___ tens + ___ ones   c) 86 ones = ___ tens + ___ ones

d) 58 ones = ___ tens + ___ ones   e) 18 ones = ___ tens + ___ ones   f) 72 ones = ___ tens + ___ ones

g) 80 ones = ___ tens + ___ ones   h) 7 ones = ___ tens + ___ ones   i) 98 ones = ___ tens + ___ ones

Mehmet has 2 hundreds blocks, 15 tens blocks, and 6 ones blocks. He regroups 10 tens blocks as 1 hundreds block:

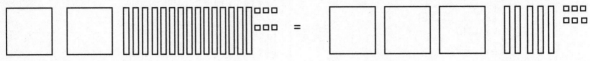

2 hundreds + 15 tens + 6 ones   3 hundreds + 5 tens + 6 ones

- -

4. Complete the charts by regrouping 10 tens as 1 hundred:

   PARENT: For at least one question below, have your child model the exchange using base 10 materials.

a)

hundreds	tens
5	11
5 + 1 = 6	1

b)

hundreds	tens
2	15

c)

hundreds	tens
6	17

d)

hundreds	tens
6	12

e)

hundreds	tens
2	17

f)

hundreds	tens
5	10

5. Regroup as many tens as hundreds as you can:

   REMEMBER: 10 tens = 1 hundred, 20 tens = 2 hundreds, 30 tens = 3 hundreds, and so on.

   a) 3 hundreds + 13 tens + 4 ones = ____ hundreds + ____ tens + ____ ones

   b) 5 hundreds + 21 tens + 1 ones = ____ hundreds + ____ tens + ____ ones

   c) 3 hundreds + 10 tens + 5 ones = _____

   d) 1 hundreds + 34 tens + 7 ones = _____

6. Regroup tens as hundreds or ones as tens. The first one has been done for you:

   a) 4 hundreds + 2 tens + 19 ones = <u>4 hundreds + 3 tens + 9 ones</u>

   b) 7 hundreds + 25 tens + 2 ones = _____

   c) 2 hundreds + 43 tens + 6 ones = _____

   d) 7 hundreds + 1 tens + 61 ones = _____

   e) 0 hundreds + 26 tens + 3 ones = _____

Maya has 1 thousands block, 11 hundreds blocks, 1 tens block and 2 ones blocks.
She regroups 10 hundreds blocks as 1 thousands block:

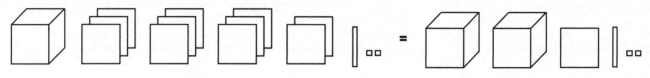

1 thousand + 11 hundreds + 1 ten + 2 ones   2 thousands + 1 hundred + 1 ten + 2 ones

----

7. Complete the charts by regrouping 10 hundreds as 1 thousand:

    PARENT: For at least one question, have your child model the exchange using base 10 materials.

a)

thousands	hundreds
3	12
3 + 1 = 4	2

b)

thousands	hundreds
4	13

c)

thousands	hundreds
7	14

8. Regroup hundreds as thousands, tens as hundreds, or ones as tens. The first one has been done:

    a) 5 thousands + 12 hundreds + 3 tens + 1 one = _6_ thousands + _2_ hundreds + _3_ tens + _1_ one

    b) 3 thousands + 15 hundreds + 1 ten + 6 ones = ____ thousands + ____ hundreds + ____ ten + ____ ones

    c) 3 thousands + 26 hundreds + 5 tens + 1 one = ____ thousands + ____ hundreds + ____ tens + ____ one

    d) 6 thousands + 14 hundreds + 6 tens + 5 ones = _____

    _____

    e) 2 thousands + 18 hundreds + 0 tens + 7 ones = _____

    _____

    f) 6 thousands + 6 hundreds + 23 tens + 5 ones = _____

    _____

    g) 4 thousands + 1 hundred + 3 tens + 19 ones = _____

    _____

9. Roger wants to build a model of three thousand, two hundred twelve.

    He has 3 thousands blocks, 1 hundreds block and 24 ones blocks.

    Can he build the model?

    In a notebook, use diagrams and numbers to explain your answer.

NS4-13: Adding Two-Digit Numbers

1. Find the **sum** of the numbers below by drawing a picture and by adding the digits.
   Don't worry about drawing the model in too much detail:

a) **15 + 43**

	with base ten materials		with numerals	
	tens	ones	tens	ones
15			1	5
43			4	3
sum			5	8

b) **25 + 22**

	with base ten materials		with numerals	
	tens	ones	tens	ones
25				
22				
sum				

c) **31 + 27**

	with base ten materials		with numerals	
	tens	ones	tens	ones
31				
27				
sum				

d) **13 + 24**

	with base ten materials		with numerals	
	tens	ones	tens	ones
13				
24				
sum				

2. Add the numbers by adding the digits:

a) $\begin{array}{r} 3\ 4 \\ +\ 4\ 3 \\ \hline \end{array}$
b) $\begin{array}{r} 7\ 7 \\ +\ 1\ 2 \\ \hline \end{array}$
c) $\begin{array}{r} 5\ 4 \\ +\ 3\ 5 \\ \hline \end{array}$
d) $\begin{array}{r} 1\ 0 \\ +\ 4\ 9 \\ \hline \end{array}$
e) $\begin{array}{r} 1\ 6 \\ +\ 2\ 3 \\ \hline \end{array}$

f) $\begin{array}{r} 1\ 6 \\ +\ 2\ 1 \\ \hline \end{array}$
g) $\begin{array}{r} 5\ 2 \\ +\ 2\ 4 \\ \hline \end{array}$
h) $\begin{array}{r} 8\ 1 \\ +\ 1\ 1 \\ \hline \end{array}$
i) $\begin{array}{r} 4\ 3 \\ +\ 3\ 1 \\ \hline \end{array}$
j) $\begin{array}{r} 7\ 5 \\ +\ 1\ 4 \\ \hline \end{array}$

1. Add the numbers below by drawing a picture and by adding the digits. Use base-ten materials to show how to combine the numbers and how to regroup. (The first one has been done for you.)

a) **16 + 25**

	with base ten materials		with numerals	
	tens	ones	tens	ones
16		☐☐☐☐☐ ☐	1	6
25		☐☐☐☐☐	2	5
sum		☐☐☐☐☐ ☐☐☐☐☐ ☐ (exchange 10 ones for a ten)	3	11
		☐ (after regrouping)	4	1

b) **25 + 37**

	with base ten materials		with numerals	
	tens	ones	tens	ones
25				
37				
sum				

c) **29 + 36**

	with base ten materials		with numerals	
	tens	ones	tens	ones
29				
36				
sum				

d) **17 + 35**

	with base ten materials		with numerals	
	tens	ones	tens	ones
17				
35				
sum				

2. Add the numbers by regrouping:

    <u>Step 1</u>:   Regroup 10 ones as 1 ten.

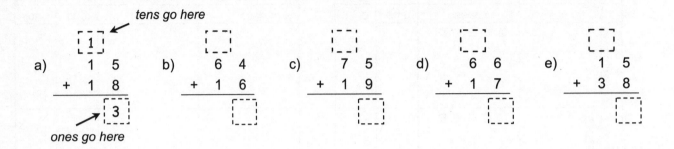

tens go here

a)   [1]   b)   [   ]   c)   [   ]   d)   [   ]   e)   [   ]

a) 1 5   b) 6 4   c) 7 5   d) 6 6   e) 1 5

  + 1 8   + 1 6   + 1 9   + 1 7   + 3 8

    [3]   [   ]   [   ]   [   ]   [   ]

ones go here

f)   [1]   g)   [   ]   h)   [   ]   i)   [   ]   j)   [   ]

f) 1 3   g) 2 4   h) 5 4   i) 2 7   j) 4 6

  + 1 9   + 3 8   + 1 8   + 6 9   + 4 8

    [   ]   [   ]   [   ]   [   ]   [   ]

    <u>Step 2</u>:   Add the numbers in the tens column.

k)   [1]   l)   [1]   m)   [1]   n)   [1]   o)   [1]

k) 1 2   l) 1 3   m) 1 5   n) 2 6   o) 3 8

  + 1 8   + 1 7   + 2 8   + 2 6   + 2 7

  [3][0]   [   ][0]   [   ][3]   [   ][2]   [   ][5]

3. Add the numbers by regrouping. The first one has been done for you:

     1

a) 3 6   b) 3 7   c) 5 9   d) 3 7   e) 5 7

  + 1 8   + 1 8   + 1 8   + 4 3   + 2 6

   5 4

f) 6 3   g) 5 8   h) 1 8   i) 5 9   j) 7 5

  + 2 9   + 4 7   + 7 7   + 1 3   + 1 6

1. Rewrite each money amount in dimes and pennies:

   a) 51¢ = __5__ dimes + __1__ penny   b) 23¢ =____ dimes +____ pennies

   c) 67¢ =____ dimes +____ pennies   d) 92¢ =____ dimes +____ pennies

   e) 84¢ =____ dimes +____ pennies   f) 70¢ =____ dimes +____ pennies

   g) 2¢ =____ dimes +____ pennies   h) 5¢ =____ dimes +____ pennies

2. Show how to regroup 10 pennies as 1 dime:

   a)
dimes	pennies
2	12
3	2

   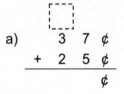
   After regrouping

   b)
dimes	pennies
5	13

   c)
dimes	pennies
7	17

   d)
dimes	pennies
4	18

3. Find the total number of dimes and pennies. Then regroup:

   a)
dimes	pennies
3	5
2	6
5	11
6	1

   Total after regrouping { 6 | 1

   b)
dimes	pennies
2	6
3	6

   c)
dimes	pennies
5	2
2	9

   d)
dimes	pennies
3	3
4	9

4. Add by regrouping 10 pennies as 1 dime:

   a) 3 7 ¢   b) 2 3 ¢   c) 2 6 ¢   d) 4 7 ¢   e) 2 8 ¢
     + 2 5 ¢   + 4 9 ¢   + 3 7 ¢   + 6 7 ¢   + 4 8 ¢
   ─────────   ─────────   ─────────   ─────────   ─────────
         ¢   ¢   ¢   ¢   ¢

5. Add by lining up the dimes and pennies in the grid. The first one is started for you:

   a) 15¢ + 17¢   b) 23¢ + 27¢   c) 48¢ + 59¢   d) 26¢ + 34¢   e) 27¢ + 85¢

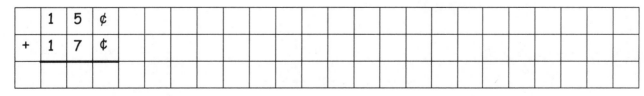

Dalha adds 152 + 273 using base 10 materials:

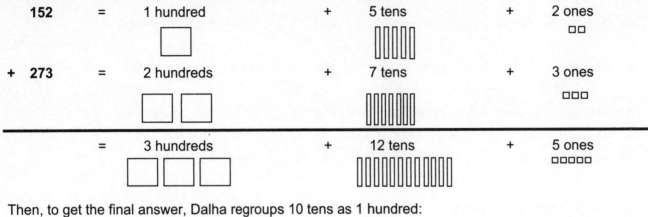

| **152** | = | 1 hundred | + | 5 tens | + | 2 ones |
| **+ 273** | = | 2 hundreds | + | 7 tens | + | 3 ones |

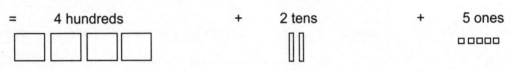

| | = | 3 hundreds | + | 12 tens | + | 5 ones |

Then, to get the final answer, Dalha regroups 10 tens as 1 hundred:

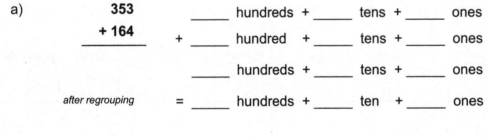

| | = | 4 hundreds | + | 2 tens | + | 5 ones |

- -

1. Add the numbers using base 10 materials or a picture (and record your work below):

a)
$$\begin{array}{r} 353 \\ + 164 \\ \hline \end{array}$$

_____ hundreds + _____ tens + _____ ones

+ _____ hundred + _____ tens + _____ ones

_____ hundreds + _____ tens + _____ ones

after regrouping = _____ hundreds + _____ ten + _____ ones

b)
$$\begin{array}{r} 462 \\ + 375 \\ \hline \end{array}$$

_____ hundreds + _____ tens + _____ ones

+ _____ hundreds + _____ tens + _____ ones

_____ hundreds + _____ tens + _____ ones

after regrouping = _____ hundreds + _____ tens + _____ ones

2. Add. You will need to regroup. The first one is started for you:

a)
```
  1
  5 2 6
+ 2 9 3
───────
    1 9
```

b)
```
  □
  6 4 5
+ 1 8 3
───────
```

c)
```
  □
  3 7 4
+ 4 6 2
───────
```

d)
```
  4 8 2
+ 4 7 7
───────
```

e)
```
  2 8 4
+ 5 9 5
───────
```

3. Add. You will need to regroup ones as tens:

a)
```
  □
  3 2 8
+   1 4
───────
```

b)
```
  □
  2 4 7
+ 5 1 6
───────
```

c)
```
  □
  9 1 5
+   4 5
───────
```

d)
```
  3 4 6
+ 2 0 5
───────
```

e)
```
  2 1 8
+ 3 4 8
───────
```

4. Add, regrouping where necessary:

a)   5 6 4   b)   2 4 8   c)   5 2 6   d)   1 6 4   e)   4 4 4   f)   8 5 6
   + 1 5 3   + 4 2 4   + 3 4 8   + 6 7 2   + 2 0 9   + 1 3 4

5. Add by lining up the numbers correctly in the grid. The first one has been started for you:

a) 218 + 265   b) 272 + 213   c) 643 + 718   d) 937 + 25

| | 2 | 1 | 8 |
| + | 2 | 6 | 5 |

e) 146 + 273   f) 816 + 925   g) 369 + 119   h) 847 + 910

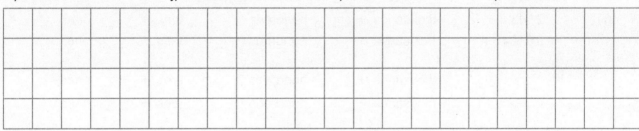

i) 387 + 203   j) 822 + 978   k) 27 + 132   l) 586 + 9

BONUS:

6. Use the pattern in your answers to a), b) and c) to find the sums in d) and e) without adding:

a)   9   b)   9 9   c)   9 9 9   d)   9 9 9 9   e)   9 9 9 9 9
     + 9   + 9 9   + 9 9 9   + 9 9 9 9   + 9 9 9 9 9

7. How do you think you would add the numbers below? Show your work in a notebook:

a) 22 + 36 + 21   b) 324 + 112 + 422   c) 131 + 204 + 351

Amber adds 1 852 + 2 321 using base 10 materials:

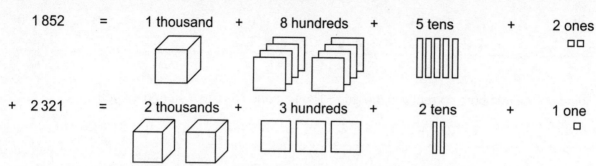

| 1 852 | = | 1 thousand | + | 8 hundreds | + | 5 tens | + | 2 ones |

| + 2 321 | = | 2 thousands | + | 3 hundreds | + | 2 tens | + | 1 one |

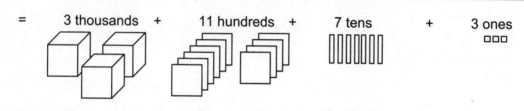

| = | 3 thousands | + | 11 hundreds | + | 7 tens | + | 3 ones |

Then, to get the final answer, Amber regroups 10 hundreds as 1 thousand:

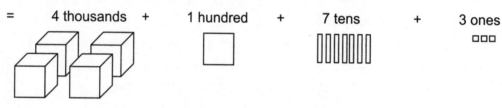

| = | 4 thousands | + | 1 hundred | + | 7 tens | + | 3 ones |

- -

1. Add the numbers using base ten materials or a picture. Record your work below:

a)
    2 543   _____ thousands + _____ hundreds + _____ tens + _____ ones

    + 3 621 + _____ thousands + _____ hundreds + _____ tens + _____ ones

                    _____ thousands + _____ hundreds + _____ tens + _____ ones

after regrouping   _____ thousands + _____ hundreds + _____ tens + _____ ones

b)
    3 824   _____ thousands + _____ hundreds + _____ tens + _____ ones

    + 1 654 + _____ thousands + _____ hundreds + _____ tens + _____ ones

                    _____ thousands + _____ hundreds + _____ tens + _____ ones

after regrouping   _____ thousands + _____ hundreds + _____ tens + _____ ones

2. Add. (You will need to regroup.) The first one is started for you:

a)
```
   1
  5 2 6 5
+ 2 9 1 2
---------
    1 7 7
```

b)
```
  6 4 5 4
+ 1 8 3 3
---------
```

c)
```
  3 7 4 7
+ 2 6 2 1
---------
```

d)
```
  1 8 2 1
+ 2 7 7 2
---------
```

e)
```
  1 8 2 4
+ 5 7 7 3
---------
```

3. Add. You will need to carry into the hundreds:

a)   3 4 8 3   b)   2 5 6 9   c)   5 4 8 6   d)   8 3 6 4   e)   1 2 9 4
    + 1 3 3 4   + 1 2 6 0   + 1 1 3 1   + 1 4 7 2   + 5 0 9 3

4. Add. You will need to carry into the tens:

a)   2 4 3 6   b)   8 1 2 7   c)   7 5 8 8   d)   5 4 2 5   e)   6 2 5 4
    + 1 1 2 5   + 1 7 4 3   + 2 1 0 8   + 2 3 4 7   + 2 6 3 9

5. Add (carrying where necessary):

a)   2 3 5 4   b)   4 6 8 3   c)   3 8 3 1   d)   6 5 2 5   e)   3 8 4 4
    + 2 8 3 1   + 1 7 4 2   + 4 8 3 3   + 1 5 3 3   + 2 7 2 3

f)   3 5 4 6   g)   7 6 2 4   h)   5 6 4 0   i)   2 9 2 5   j)   3 2 4 5
    + 4 8 2 2   + 1 6 0 1   + 3 7 1 2   + 1 7 5 1   + 3 4 3 1

6. Add by lining up the numbers correctly in the grid. In some questions you may have to carry twice:

a) 4 534 + 2 542   b) 6 754 + 1 360   c) 3 214 + 4 852   d) 2 509 + 621

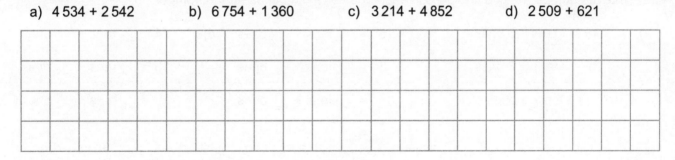

7. How do you think you might add the following numbers?

a)   2 5 3 7 2   b)   5 3 8 2 7   c)   3 8 7 6 9 1
    + 6 0 5 2 1   + 2 4 1 1 3   + 1 3 4 1 2 0

Bradley subtracts 48 – 32 by making a model of 48. He takes away 3 tens and 2 ones
(because 32 = 3 tens + 2 ones):

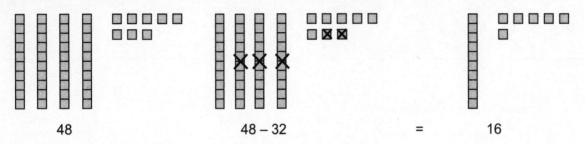

48   48 – 32   =   16

---

1. Subtract by crossing out tens and ones blocks. Draw your final answer in the right hand box:

a)

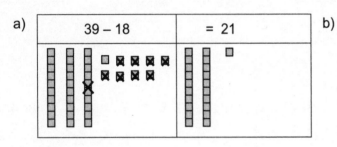

b)

| 25 – 11 | = |

c)

| 43 – 21 | = |

d)

| 45 – 32 | = |

2. Write the number of tens and ones in each number. Then subtract the number:

a)
$$45 = 4 \text{ tens} + 5 \text{ ones}$$
$$-\ 32 = 3 \text{ tens} + 2 \text{ ones}$$
$$= 1 \text{ ten} + 3 \text{ ones}$$
$$= 13$$

b)
$$57 = \_\_ \text{ tens} + \_\_ \text{ ones}$$
$$-\ 34 = \_\_ \text{ tens} + \_\_ \text{ ones}$$
$$= \_\_ \text{ tens} + \_\_ \text{ ones}$$
$$= \_\_\_\_$$

c)
$$84 = \_\_ \text{ tens} + \_\_ \text{ ones}$$
$$-\ 63 = \_\_ \text{ tens} + \_\_ \text{ ones}$$
$$= \_\_ \text{ tens} + \_\_ \text{ one}$$
$$= \_\_\_\_$$

d)
$$89 = \_\_ \text{ tens} + \_\_ \text{ ones}$$
$$-\ 56 = \_\_ \text{ tens} + \_\_ \text{ ones}$$
$$= \_\_ \text{ tens} + \_\_ \text{ ones}$$
$$= \_\_\_\_$$

e)
$$77 = \_\_ \text{ tens} + \_\_ \text{ ones}$$
$$-\ 44 = \_\_ \text{ tens} + \_\_ \text{ ones}$$
$$= \_\_ \text{ tens} + \_\_ \text{ ones}$$
$$= \_\_\_\_$$

f)
$$67 = \_\_ \text{ tens} + \_\_ \text{ ones}$$
$$-\ 45 = \_\_ \text{ tens} + \_\_ \text{ ones}$$
$$= \_\_ \text{ tens} + \_\_ \text{ ones}$$
$$= \_\_\_\_$$

3. Subtract by writing the number of tens and ones in each number:

a)
$$36 = 30 + 6$$
$$-\ \ 24 = 20 + 4$$
$$= 10 + 2$$
$$= 12$$

b)
$$84 =$$
$$-\ \ 52 =$$
$$=$$
$$=$$

c)
$$98 =$$
$$-\ \ 37 =$$
$$=$$
$$=$$

d)
$$73 =$$
$$-\ \ 12 =$$

e)
$$26 =$$
$$-\ \ 24 =$$

f)
$$88 =$$
$$-\ \ 33 =$$

4. Subtract the numbers by subtracting the digits:

a)
$$\begin{array}{r} 5\ \ 4 \\ -\ 2\ \ 3 \\ \hline \end{array}$$

b)
$$\begin{array}{r} 8\ \ 6 \\ -\ 7\ \ 3 \\ \hline \end{array}$$

c)
$$\begin{array}{r} 3\ \ 6 \\ -\ 1\ \ 5 \\ \hline \end{array}$$

d)
$$\begin{array}{r} 6\ \ 4 \\ -\ 3\ \ 2 \\ \hline \end{array}$$

e)
$$\begin{array}{r} 9\ \ 5 \\ -\ 4\ \ 2 \\ \hline \end{array}$$

f)
$$\begin{array}{r} 8\ \ 9 \\ -\ 4\ \ 0 \\ \hline \end{array}$$

5. a) Draw a picture of 543 using hundreds, tens and ones blocks. Show how you would subtract 543 − 421:

b) Now subtract the numbers by lining up the digits and subtracting. Do you get the same answer?

6. How do you think you would subtract the following numbers? Show what you think the answer would be:

a)
$$\begin{array}{r} 7\ \ 5\ \ 3\ \ 2 \\ -\ 4\ \ 1\ \ 2\ \ 1 \\ \hline \end{array}$$

b)
$$\begin{array}{r} 6\ \ 5\ \ 3\ \ 5\ \ 6 \\ -\ 4\ \ 4\ \ 2\ \ 4\ \ 5 \\ \hline \end{array}$$

c)
$$\begin{array}{r} 9\ \ 5\ \ 5\ \ 7\ \ 6\ \ 3 \\ -\ 5\ \ 2\ \ 3\ \ 0\ \ 1\ \ 1 \\ \hline \end{array}$$

NS4-19: Subtracting by Regrouping

Farkan subtracts 46 − 18 using base 10 materials:

Step 1:
Farkan represents 46 with base 10 materials.

Step 2:
8 (the ones digit of 18) is greater than 6 (the ones digit of 46) so Farkan regroups 1 tens block as 10 ones blocks.

Step 3:
Farkan subtracts 18 (he takes away 1 tens block and 8 ones blocks).

tens	ones
4	6

tens	ones
3	16

tens	ones
2	8

Here is how Farkan uses numerals to show his work:

46
− 18

Here is how Farkan shows the regrouping:

3 16
4̶6̶
− 1 8

And now Farkan can subtract 16 − 8 ones and 3 − 1 tens:

3 16
4̶6̶
− 1 8
2 8

---

1. In these questions, Farkan doesn't have enough ones to subtract. Help him by regrouping 1 tens block as 10 ones. Show how he would rewrite his subtraction statement:

a) **63 − 26**

tens	ones
6	3

tens	ones
5	13

	6	3
−	2	6

	5	13
	6̶	3̶
−	2	6

b) **64 − 39**

tens	ones
6	4

tens	ones

	6	4
−	3	9

	6	4
−	3	9

c) **42 − 19**

tens	ones
4	2

tens	ones

	4	2
−	1	9

	4	2
−	1	9

d) **35 − 27**

tens	ones
3	5

tens	ones

	3	5
−	2	7

	3	5
−	2	7

Number Sense 1

2. Subtract by regrouping. The first one is done for you:

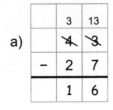

	3	13
a)	~~4~~	~~3~~
−	2	7
	1	6

b)

	5	6
−	1	8

c)

	6	4
−	3	9

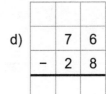

d)

	7	6
−	2	8

e)

	5	5
−	3	7

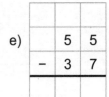

f)

	8	2
−	5	7

g)

	3	8
−	1	9

h)

	2	2
−		6

i)

	4	4
−		9

j)

	9	3
−	7	5

3. For the questions where you need to regroup, write "Help!" in the space provided. If you don't need to regroup, write "OK." Then find the answer:

a)
```
   5̸4      Help!
 − 19    4 is less than 9
 ─────
   35
```

b)
```
   77      OK
 − 56   _____
 ─────
   21
```

c)
```
   85   _____
 − 53
 ─────
```

d)
```
   95   _____
 − 18
 ─────
```

e)
```
   66   _____
 − 54
 ─────
```

f)
```
   84   _____
 − 17
 ─────
```

g)
```
   82   _____
 − 29
 ─────
```

h)
```
   26   _____
 − 15
 ─────
```

i)
```
   15   _____
 −  9
 ─────
```

j)
```
   12   _____
 −  8
 ─────
```

k)
```
   36   _____
 − 19
 ─────
```

l)
```
   52   _____
 −  9
 ─────
```

m)
```
   47   _____
 − 19
 ─────
```

n)
```
   23   _____
 −  8
 ─────
```

o)
```
   60   _____
 − 49
 ─────
```

p)
```
   82   _____
 − 41
 ─────
```

q)
```
   57   _____
 − 32
 ─────
```

r)
```
   34   _____
 − 29
 ─────
```

s)
```
   93   _____
 − 24
 ─────
```

t)
```
   82   _____
 − 24
 ─────
```

u)
```
   79   _____
 − 42
 ─────
```

4. Subtract by regrouping the hundreds as tens. The first one has been started for you:

a)
```
      2  11
      3̷  4̷  5
  -   1  6  2
  _____
```

b)
```
      5  3  8
  -   2  9  5
  _____
```

c)
```
      3  1  7
  -   1  8  6
  _____
```

d)
```
      9  4  2
  -   5  7  0
  _____
```

6. For the questions below, you will have to regroup **twice**:

Example:

Step 1
```
        4  14
     8  5̷  4̷
  -  3  6  7
  _____
```

Step 2
```
        4  14
     8  5̷  4̷
  -  3  6  7
  _____
```

Step 3
```
        14
     7  5̷  14
     8̷  5̷  4̷
  -  3  6  7
  _____
           7
```

Step 4
```
        14
     7  5̷  14
     8̷  5̷  4̷
  -  3  6  7
  _____
        8  7
```

Step 5
```
        14
     7  5̷  14
     8̷  5̷  4̷
  -  3  6  7
  _____
     4  8  7
```

a)
```
      6  3  4
  -   1  5  6
  _____
```

b)
```
      5  8  5
  -      9  6
  _____
```

c)
```
      5  0  2
  -   2  3  5
  _____
```

d)
```
      8  5  4
  -   3  7  7
  _____
```

6. To subtract 3 245 – 1 923, Sara regroups 1 thousands block as 10 hundreds blocks:

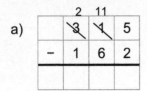  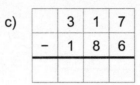

thousands	hundreds	tens	ones
3	2	4	5

thousands	hundreds	tens	ones
2	12	4	5

thousands	hundreds	tens	ones
1	3	2	2

Subtract by regrouping 1 thousand as 10 hundreds. The first one has been done for you:

a)
```
      7  13
      8̷  3̷  6  4
  -   4  8  3  1
  _____
      3  5  3  3
```

b)
```
      5  6  9  3
  -   2  7  1  1
  _____
```

c)
```
      5  7  5  8
  -   2  9  4  2
  _____
```

7. Regroup where necessary:

a)
	3	3	1	7
−	1	4	0	5

b)
	6	4	6	8
−	2	1	7	2

c)
	7	2	6	5
−	3	0	4	2

8. In the questions below, you will have to regroup **two or three times**:

a)
	8	5	3	2
−	2	7	5	4

b)
	7	6	4	1
−	4	7	5	3

c)
	6	1	3	0
−	2	2	8	3

d)
	4	3	0	2
−	1	7	2	3

e)
	3	8	5	1
−	1	9	0	9

f)
	2	8	2	3
−	1	3	2	9

g)
	5	2	8	6
−	1	7	9	8

h)
	9	2	5	7
−	4	5	2	8

9. In the questions below, you will have to regroup two or three times:

Example:

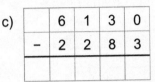
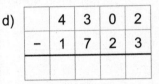

Step 1 Step 2 Step 3 Step 4

```
    0 10              9                 9  9               9  9
    1̷ 0̸ 0 0       C 1̷9̸ 10         0 1̷9̸ 1̷9̸ 10       0 1̷9̸ 1̷9̸ 10
    1̷ 0̸ 0 0       1̷ 0̸ 0 0          1̷ 0̸ 0̸ 0̸         1̷ 0̸ 0̸ 0̸
  −     3 4 1     −     3 4 1      −     3 4 1       −     3 4 1
                                                          6 5 9
```

a)
	1	0	0	0
−		4	5	7

b)
	1	0	0	
−			7	5

c)
	1	0	0	0
−		6	3	3

d)
	1	0	0	0
−		8	8	9

10. Subtract in a notebook, regrouping where necessary:

a) 8 504 − 1 230   b) 4 484 − 2 511   c) 4 302 − 1 723   d) 1 000 − 889

1. The bars in each picture represent a quantity of red and green apples. Fill in the blanks:

   a) 5 red apples
       3 green apples

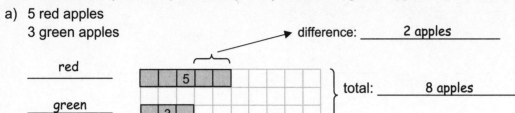

   difference: _____2 apples_____

   ___red___

   ___green___

   total: _____8 apples_____

   b) 4 green apples
       2 more red apples than green apples

   difference: _____

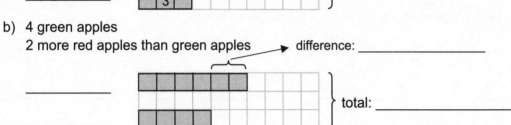

   _____

   _____

   total: _____

   c) 7 green apples
       3 more green apples than red apples

   difference: _____

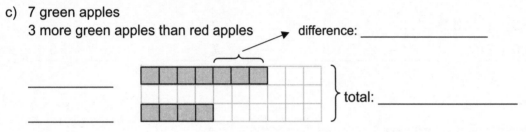

   _____

   _____

   total: _____

   d) 10 apples in total
       3 green apples

   difference: _____

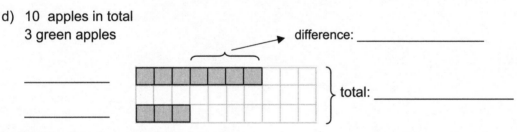

   _____

   _____

   total: _____

2. Write the missing numbers:

Red Apples	Green Apples	Total Number of Apples	How many more of one colour of apple?
2	5	7	3 more green apples than red
3		8	
	2	9	
4			1 more red apple than green

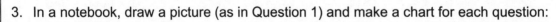

3. In a notebook, draw a picture (as in Question 1) and make a chart for each question:

   a) 4 red apples
       4 more green apples
       than red apples

   b) 12 apples in total
       7 green apples

   BONUS:

   c) 10 apples in total
       2 more red apples than
       green apples

NS4-21: Parts and Totals (Advanced)

1. The fact family for the addition statement **2 + 4 = 6** is: **4 + 2 = 6**; **6 – 4 = 2** and **6 – 2 = 4**.
   Write the fact family of equations for the following statements:

   a) 3 + 4 = 7 _____

   b) 5 + 4 = 9 _____

2. Fill in the chart:

	Green Grapes	Purple Grapes	Total Number of Grapes	How many more of one type of grape?	Fact Family	
a)	7	2	9	5 more green than purple	9 – 2 = 7 9 – 7 = 2	7 + 2 = 9 2 + 7 = 9
b)	6		10			
c)	2	9				
d)		5		4 more green than purple		

3. Use the correct symbol (+ or –):

   a) number of red apples ☐ number of green apples = total number of apples

   b) number of red apples ☐ number of green apples = how many more red than green?

   c) number of green grapes ☐ number of purple grapes = how many more green than purple?

   d) number of purple grapes ☐ number of green grapes = total number of grapes

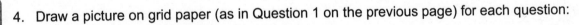

4. Draw a picture on grid paper (as in Question 1 on the previous page) for each question:

   a) Ron has 13 red stickers and 6 blue stickers.
      How many stickers does he have?

   b) Claire has 6 pets, 2 are dogs.
      The rest are cats. How many cats does she have?

   c) Peter walked 7 km. Lagi walked 3 km.
      How much further did Peter walk?

Answer the following questions in a notebook.

1. A glass can hold 255 mL of water.
   How much water can 2 glasses hold?

2. Alice's class raised $312 for charity. Sophie's class raised $287.

   a) Whose class raised more money? How do you know?

   b) How much money did the two classes raise altogether?

3. At a summer camp, 324 children are enrolled in baseball. There are 128 **more** children enrolled in swimming than in baseball.

   a) How many children are enrolled in swimming?

   b) How much children are enrolled in lessons altogether?

4. What is the greatest number you can add to 275 without having to regroup any place value?

   # 275

5. Emma flies 2 457 km on one day and 1 357 km the next day.
   How many kilometres did she fly in the two days?

6. The world's tallest tree is 110 m tall. The Skylon Tower in Niagara Falls is 156 m tall.
   How much taller is the Skylon Tower than the tallest tree?

7. 2 375 people attended a science fair one day, and 3 528 people attended the next day.
   How many people attended the fair on both days?

8. The length of Whistling Cave on Vancouver Island is 782 m. The length of Grueling Cave is 697 m.
   How much longer is Whistling Cave than Grueling Cave?

9. The border between the United States and Canada is 8 963 km long.
   The total length of the Great Wall of China, including its branches, is 6 324 km.
   How much longer than the Great Wall of China is the Canadian / US border?

Answer the following questions in a notebook.

1. In a class of 62 children, 17 are boys. How many girls are in the class? Show your work. How can you check your answer using addition?

2.

Lake Ontario	193 km
Lake Superior	350 km
Lake Michigan	307 km
Lake Huron	206 km
Lake Erie	241 km

This chart shows the lengths of the Great Lakes:

a) Write the lengths in order from shortest to longest.

b) How much longer than Lake Huron is Lake Michigan?

c) How much longer than the shortest lake is the longest lake?

3. The equation **5 + 7 = 12** is part of a fact family of equations.

The other equations in the family are: **7 + 5 = 12, 12 − 5 = 7** and **12 − 7 = 5**.

Write all the equations in the fact family for:

a) 3 + 8 = 11

b) 7 − 3 = 4

c) 19 + 5 = 24

4. Use the numbers 1, 2, 3, 4, 5, 6 to make the greatest sum possible and the greatest difference:

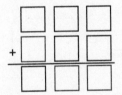 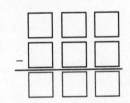

5. Find the error in Ezra's sum:

```
   2
  4 5
+ 2 7
-----
  8 1
```

6. Leonardo da Vinci, the great Italian inventor and artist, lived from 1452 to 1519.

a) How old was he when he died?

b) Leonardo painted his masterpiece the Mona Lisa in 1503. How old was he then?

7. Write the number that is:

a) ten less than 1000

b) ten more than 1000

c) 100 less than 1000

d) 100 more than 1000

8. Pens cost 49¢. Erasers cost 45¢. Ben has 95¢. Does he have enough money to buy a pen and an eraser? (Explain your answer.)

9. Josh wants to add the numbers below. He starts by adding the ones digits:

```
   1
  3 5
+ 4 7
-----
    2
```
Explain why Josh wrote the number 1 here.

     Number Sense 1

When you multiply a pair of numbers, the result is called the **product** of the numbers.

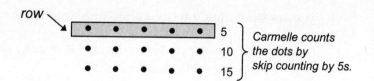

row

5
10
15

Carmelle counts the dots by skip counting by 5s.

In the **array** shown, there are 3 **rows** of dots.
There are 5 dots **in each row**.

Carmelle writes a multiplication statement for the array: **3 × 5 = 15**   (3 rows of 5 dots is 15 dots)

----

1. How many rows? How many dots in each row? Write a multiplication statement for each array:

a)

<u>__3__</u> rows

<u>__4__</u> dots in each row

<u>3 × 4 = 12</u>

b)

_____ rows

_____ dots in each row

_____

c)

_____

_____

_____

2. Write a product for each array:

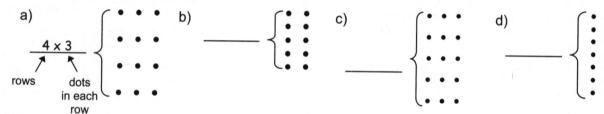

a)   <u>4 × 3</u>

rows   dots in each row

b) _____

c) _____

d) _____

 Answer the questions in a notebook.

3. Draw arrays for these products:

   a) 5 × 5

   b) 3 × 5

   c) 2 × 4

   d) 4 × 3

   e) 1 × 6

   f) 0 × 5

4. Draw an array and write a multiplication statement to find each answer:

   a) In a garden, there are 3 rows of plants. There are 5 plants in each row. How many plants are there altogether?

   b) On a bus, 4 people can sit in a row. There are 6 rows of seats on the bus. How many people can ride on the bus?

   c) Jenny planted 8 seeds in each row. There are 4 rows of seeds. How many seeds did Jenny plant?

5. Draw arrays for the products 4 × 3 and 3 × 4.

   a) Are the products the same or different?

   b) Is 6 × 4 equal to 4 × 6? Explain.

NS4-25: Multiplication and Addition

Multiplication is a short way of writing addition: $4 \times 5 = \underbrace{5 + 5 + 5 + 5}$

add 5 four times

----

1. Write a sum for each product. The first one has been done for you:

   a) $3 \times 4 = 4 + 4 + 4$ b) $2 \times 8 =$ c) $5 \times 6 =$

   d) $4 \times 2 =$ e) $3 \times 5 =$ f) $6 \times 3 =$

   g) $5 \times 7 =$ h) $2 \times 1 =$ i) $1 \times 8 =$

2. Write a product for each sum. The first one is done for you:

   a) $4 + 4 + 4 = 3 \times 4$ b) $5 + 5 + 5 =$ c) $4 + 4 =$

   d) $7 + 7 + 7 + 7 =$ e) $9 + 9 =$ f) $8 + 8 + 8 =$

   g) $2 + 2 + 2 =$ h) $9 + 9 + 9 + 9 =$ i) $1 + 1 + 1 =$

   j) $6 + 6 + 6 + 6 + 6 =$ k) $8 + 8 + 8 + 8 + 8 + 8 =$ l) $3 + 3 + 3 + 3 =$

3. Write a sum and a product for each picture. The first one has been done for you:

   a) 3 boxes; 2 pencils in each box   b) 3 boxes; 4 pencils in each box

   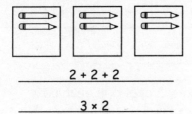   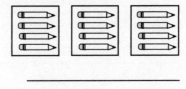

   $2 + 2 + 2$

   3×2
   _____

   c) 4 boxes; 3 pencils in each box   d) 2 boxes; 5 pencils in each box

   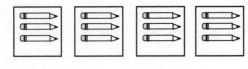   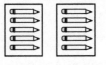

   _____   _____

   _____   _____

   e) 5 boxes; 3 pencils in each box   f) 4 boxes; 2 pencils in each box

   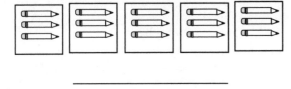   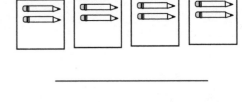

   _____   _____

   _____   _____

4. Add the numbers. Write your subtotals in the boxes provided:

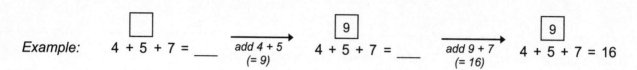

Example:　4 + 5 + 7 = ___　add 4 + 5 (= 9)　4 + 5 + 7 = ___　add 9 + 7 (= 16)　4 + 5 + 7 = 16

a) 2 + 3 + 5 = ___

b) 3 + 3 + 7 = ___

c) 5 + 4 + 3 = ___

d) 6 + 4 + 2 = ___

e) 8 + 3 + 4 = ___

f) 9 + 1 + 6 = ___

g) 4 + 3 + 3 + 2 = ___

h) 4 + 5 + 5 + 3 = ___

i) 6 + 7 + 3 + 5 = ___

5. Write a sum for each picture. Add to find out how many apples there are altogether. Check your answer by counting the apples:

a) 3 boxes; 3 apples in each box

_____

b) 4 boxes; 2 apple in each box

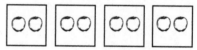

_____

c) 4 boxes; 4 apples in each box

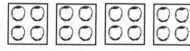

_____

d) 3 boxes; 5 apples in each box

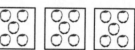

_____

 Answer the questions below in a notebook.

6. Draw a picture and write an addition statement and a multiplication statement for your picture:

　a) 3 vans
　　 7 people in each van

　b) 4 bags
　　 5 books in each bag

　c) 6 boxes
　　 4 pens in each box

　d) 5 boats
　　 4 kids in each boat

7. Write an addition statement and a multiplication statement for each question:

　a) 6 plates
　　 8 cookies in each plate

　b) 7 packets
　　 3 gifts in each packet

　c) 4 baskets
　　 7 bananas in each basket

Zainab finds the product of **3** and **5** by skip counting on a number line.

She counts off three 5s:

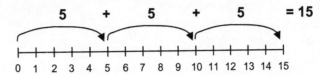

$3 \times 5 =$ 5   +   5   +   5   = 15

0 1 2 3 4 5 6 7 8 9 10 11 12 13 14 15

From the picture, Zainab can see that the product of 3 and 5 is 15.

- -

1. Show how to find the products by skip counting. Use arrows like the ones in Zainab's picture:

   a) **4 x 3 =**

   b) **7 x 2 =**

0 1 2 3 4 5 6 7 8 9 10 11 12 13 14 15   0 1 2 3 4 5 6 7 8 9 10 11 12 13 14 15

2. Use the number line to skip count by 4s, 6s and 7s. Fill in the boxes as you count:

0 1 2 3 4 5 6 7 8 9 **10** 11 12 13 14 15 16 17 18 19 **20** 21 22 23 24 25 26 27 28 29 **30** 31 32 33 34 35 36 37 38 39 **40** 41 42

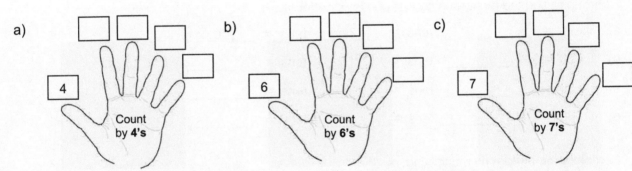

a)   4   Count by 4's   b)   6   Count by 6's   c)   7   Count by 7's

3. Find the products by skip counting on your fingers. Use the hands from Question 2 to help:

7   14   21   28   count by 7s

until you raise 4 fingers $4 \times 7 = 28$

a) $4 \times 5 =$ b) $5 \times 2 =$ c) $4 \times 4 =$ d) $2 \times 6 =$ e) $7 \times 1 =$

f) $3 \times 7 =$ g) $3 \times 3 =$ h) $6 \times 1 =$ i) $2 \times 7 =$ j) $5 \times 5 =$

k) $2 \times 2 =$ l) $7 \times 6 =$ m) $2 \times 1 =$ n) $4 \times 6 =$ o) $3 \times 6 =$

4. Find the number of items by skip counting. Write a multiplication statement for each picture:

   a) 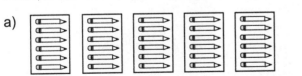   b)

   _____   _____

To multiply 3 × 20, Christie makes 3 groups containing 2 tens blocks (20 = 2 tens):

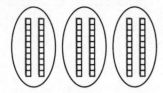

$3 \times 20 = 3 \times 2$ tens = 6 tens = 60

To multiply 3 × 200, Christie makes 3 groups containing 2 hundreds blocks (200 = 2 hundreds):

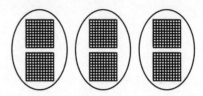

$3 \times 200 = 3 \times 2$ hundreds = 6 hundreds = 600

Christie notices a pattern: **$3 \times 2 = 6$**   **$3 \times 20 = 60$**   **$3 \times 200 = 600$**

- -

1. Draw a model for each multiplication statement, then calculate the answer. The first one is started:

   a) 4×20

   b) 2×30

   $4 \times 20 = 4 \times \underline{\ \ 2\ \ }$ tens = _____ tens = _____ $2 \times 30 = 2 \times$ _____ tens = _____ tens = _____

2. Regroup to find the answer. The first one is done for you:

   a) $3 \times 70 = 3 \times \underline{\ \ \ 7\ \ \ }$ tens = $\underline{\ \ \ 21\ \ \ }$ tens = $\underline{\ \ \ 210\ \ \ }$

   b) $3 \times 50 = 3 \times$ _____ tens = _____ tens = _____

   c) $5 \times 50 = 5 \times$ _____ tens = _____ tens = _____

   d) $4 \times 60 = 4 \times$ _____ tens = _____ tens = _____

3. Complete the pattern by multiplying:

   a) $2 \times 2 =$ _____   b) $5 \times 1 =$ _____   c) $2 \times 4 =$ _____   d) $3 \times 3 =$ _____

      $2 \times 20 =$ _____ $5 \times 10 =$ _____ $2 \times 40 =$ _____ $3 \times 30 =$ _____

      $2 \times 200 =$ _____ $5 \times 100 =$ _____ $2 \times 400 =$ _____ $3 \times 300 =$ _____

4. Multiply:

   a) $4 \times 30 =$ _____   b) $5 \times 30 =$ _____   c) $4 \times 40 =$ _____   d) $2 \times 50 =$ _____

   e) $3 \times 500 =$ _____   f) $4 \times 500 =$ _____   g) $3 \times 60 =$ _____   h) $6 \times 400 =$ _____

   i) $2 \times 700 =$ _____   j) $6 \times 70 =$ _____   k) $8 \times 40 =$ _____   l) $2 \times 900 =$ _____

Answer the following questions in a notebook.

5. Draw a base ten model (using cubes to represent thousands) to show: $4 \times 1000 = 4000$.

6. Knowing that $3 \times 2 = 6$, how can you use this fact to multiply 3×2000?

NS4-28: Mental Math

To multiply 3×23, Rosa rewrites 23 as a sum:

$$23 = 20 + 3$$

She multiplies 20 by 3: $3 \times 20 = 60$

Then she multiplies 3×3: $3 \times 3 = 9$

Finally she adds the result: $60 + 9 = 69$

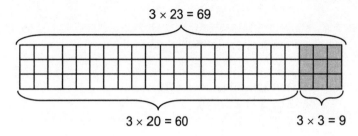

$3 \times 23 = 69$

$3 \times 20 = 60$ $3 \times 3 = 9$

The picture shows why Rosa's method works: $3 \times 23 = 3 \times 20 + 3 \times 3 = 60 + 9 = 69$

- -

1. Rewrite each multiplication statement as a sum. The first one has been done for you:

    a) $2 \times 24 = \underline{2 \times 20} + \underline{2 \times 4}$ b) $2 \times 23 = \underline{} + \underline{}$ c) $3 \times 21 = \underline{} + \underline{}$

    d) $3 \times 32 = \underline{} + \underline{}$ e) $4 \times 12 = \underline{} + \underline{}$ f) $5 \times 32 = \underline{} + \underline{}$

2. Multiply using Rosa's method. The first one has been done for you:

    a) $2 \times 13 = \underline{3 \times 10 + 3 \times 3 = 30 + 9 = 39}$

    b) $3 \times 21 = \underline{}$

    c) $2 \times 14 = \underline{}$

3. Multiply in your head by multiplying the digits separately:

    a) $3 \times 12 = \underline{}$ b) $2 \times 31 = \underline{}$ c) $4 \times 12 = \underline{}$ d) $5 \times 11 = \underline{}$

    e) $4 \times 21 = \underline{}$ f) $2 \times 43 = \underline{}$ g) $2 \times 32 = \underline{}$ h) $3 \times 33 = \underline{}$

4. Use Rosa's method to write each multiplication statement as a sum:

    a) $3 \times 213 = \underline{3 \times 200} + \underline{3 \times 10} + \underline{3 \times 3} = \underline{600 + 30 + 9} = \underline{639}$

    b) $2 \times 231 = \underline{} + \underline{} + \underline{} = \underline{} = \underline{}$

    c) $2 \times 342 = \underline{} + \underline{} + \underline{} = \underline{} = \underline{}$

5. Multiply in your head:

    a) $4 \times 112 = \underline{}$ b) $2 \times 234 = \underline{}$ c) $3 \times 233 = \underline{}$ d) $5 \times 111 = \underline{}$

    e) $3 \times 132 = \underline{}$ f) $2 \times 422 = \underline{}$ g) $4 \times 212 = \underline{}$ h) $3 \times 333 = \underline{}$

6. Yen planted 223 trees in each of 3 rows.
   How many trees did she plant altogether?

7. Paul put 240 marbles in each of 2 bags.
   How many marbles did he put in the bags?

Number Sense 1

Clara uses a chart to multiply 3 × 42:

<u>Step 1</u>
She multiplies the ones digit
of 42 by 3 (3 × 2 = 6).

<u>Step 2</u>
She multiplies the tens digit
of 42 by 3 (3 × 4 tens = 12 tens).

*She regroups 10 tens
as 1 hundred.*

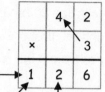

hundreds   tens

1. Use Clara's method to find the products:

a)
	3	1
×		4

b)
	5	3
×		2

c)
	4	1
×		4

d)
	2	1
×		6

e)
	3	1
×		3

f)
	7	1
×		2

g)
	6	2
×		3

h)
	8	4
×		2

i)
	5	2
×		4

j)
	2	2
×		2

k)
	2	1
×		5

l)
	5	3
×		2

m)
	4	2
×		3

n)
	4	3
×		3

o)
	6	4
×		2

p)
	7	3
×		3

q)
	5	4
×		2

r)
	6	2
×		4

s)
	7	2
×		3

t)
	9	1
×		2

u)
	6	3
×		3

v)
	8	1
×		2

w)
	5	1
×		5

x)
	7	2
×		4

y)
	6	1
×		5

z)
	7	2
×		4

aa)
	8	3
×		3

bb)
	9	1
×		9

cc)
	4	1
×		6

dd)
	6	1
×		8

ee)
	9	2
×		4

ff)
	8	5
×		1

gg)
	4	3
×		3

hh)
	6	1
×		7

ii)
	7	1
×		8

2. Find the following products. Show your work in a notebook.

a) 3 × 62   b) 2 × 74   c) 5 × 21   d) 4 × 62   e) 6 × 45   f) 7 × 23

Jane uses a chart to multiply 3 × 24:

Step 1

She multiples 4 ones by 3 (4 × 3 = 12).

She regroups 10 ones as 1 ten.

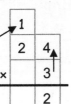

Step 2

She multiples 2 tens by 3 (3 × 2 tens = 6 tens).

She adds 1 ten to the result (6 + 1 = 7 tens):

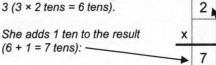

1. Using Jane's method, complete the first step of the multiplication. The first one has been done:

a)
```
 2
 1  4 ↑
 ×  5
 ─────
    0
```

b)
```
 1  4
 ×  3
 ─────
```

c)
```
 1  5
 ×  3
 ─────
```

d)
```
 3  6
 ×  2
 ─────
```

e)
```
 2  5
 ×  4
 ─────
```

2. Using Jane's method, complete the second step of the multiplication:

a)
```
 1
 2  4
 ×  4
 ─────
    6
```

b)
```
 1
 1  2
 ×  5
 ─────
    0
```

c)
```
 2
 1  4
 ×  5
 ─────
    0
```

d)
```
 2
 1  4
 ×  6
 ─────
    4
```

e)
```
 1
 2  5
 ×  3
 ─────
    5
```

f)
```
 1
 3  5
 ×  2
 ─────
    0
```

g)
```
 1
 4  7
 ×  2
 ─────
    4
```

h)
```
 1
 2  4
 ×  3
 ─────
    2
```

i)
```
 2
 2  7
 ×  3
 ─────
    1
```

j)
```
 3
 1  6
 ×  5
 ─────
    0
```

3. Using Jane's method, complete the first and second step of the multiplication:

a)
```
 2  5
 ×  2
 ─────
```

b)
```
 1  6
 ×  6
 ─────
```

c)
```
 3  5
 ×  4
 ─────
```

d)
```
 3  5
 ×  3
 ─────
```

e)
```
 3  4
 ×  3
 ─────
```

f)
```
 3  2
 ×  5
 ─────
```

g)
```
 3  7
 ×  6
 ─────
```

h)
```
 8  2
 ×  5
 ─────
```

i)
```
 2  3
 ×  7
 ─────
```

Number Sense 1

Kim multiplies 2 × 213 in 3 different ways:

1. With a chart:

	hundreds	tens	ones
	2	1	3
×			2
	4	2	6

2. In expanded form:

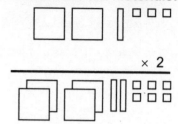

200 + 10 + 3
× 2

= 400 + 20 + 6
= 426

3. With base ten materials:

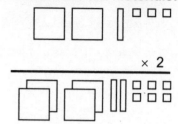

----

1. Rewrite the multiplication statement in expanded notation. Then perform the multiplication:

   a)   321   _____ + _____ + _____
        × 3   _____ × 3

              = _____ + _____ + _____

              = _____

   b)   432   _____ + _____ + _____
        × 2   _____ × 2

              = _____ + _____ + _____

              = _____

2. Multiply:

   a)   b) 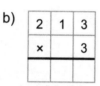   c)   d) 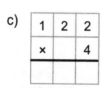   e)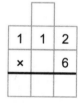

1	2	4
×		2

2	1	3
×		3

1	2	2
×		4

3	2	3
×		3

4	1	3
×		2

3. Multiply by regrouping ones as tens:

   a) 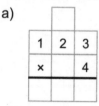   b) 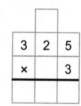   c) 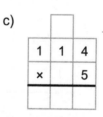   d) 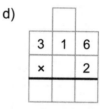   e)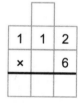

1	2	3
×		4

3	2	5
×		3

1	1	4
×		5

3	1	6
×		2

1	1	2
×		6

4. Multiply by regrouping tens as hundreds. In the last question, you will also regroup ones as tens:

   a) 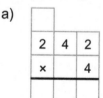   b) 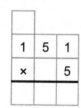   c) 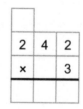   d) 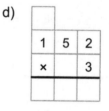   e)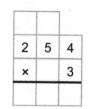

2	4	2
×		4

1	5	1
×		5

2	4	2
×		3

1	5	2
×		3

2	5	4
×		3

5. In a notebook, multiply:

   a) 4 × 242   b) 5 × 312   c) 7 × 123   d) 8 × 314   e) 9 × 253   f) 6 × 241

6. In a notebook, draw a picture to show the result of the multiplication:

   a) 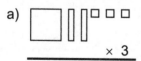   b)    c)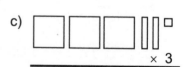

   × 3   × 3   × 3

Show your work for these questions in a notebook.

1. An octopus has 240 suckers on each arm. How many suckers does an octopus have?

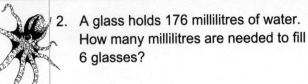

2. A glass holds 176 millilitres of water. How many millilitres are needed to fill 6 glasses?

3. On average, every North American uses 240 litres of water each day.
   a) How much does each North American use in a week?
   b) How much water would a family of 4 use in a day?

4. The **product** of 3 and 2 is 6 (3 × 2 = 6).

   The **sum** of 3 and 2 is 5 (3 + 2 = 5).

   Which is greater: the **sum** or the **product**?

5. Try finding the **sum** and the **product** of different pairs of numbers.
   (For instance, try 3 and 4, 2 and 5, 5 and 6, 1 and 7.)

   What do you notice? Is the product always greater than the sum?

6. Kyle multiplied two numbers. The product was one of the numbers, and was not zero. What was the other number?

7. Write all the pairs of numbers you can think of that multiply to give 20.
   (For an extra challenge, find all pairs of numbers that multiply to give 40.)

8. An insect called a cicada can burrow into the ground and stay there for 10 years.
   a) How many months can a cicada stay in the ground?
   b) Cicadas have been known to stay in the ground for 20 years. How can you use your answer in a) to find out how many months this is?

9. There are 3 ways to put 4 dots into rows so that each row contains the same number of dots:

   1 x 4   2 x 2   4 x 1

   How many ways can you put the following number of dots into equal rows?
   Use counters or pictures to help you find all the possibilities. Write a multiplication statement for each array.

   a) 6 dots?
   b) 8 dots?
   c) 12 dots?
   d) 16 dots?

10. Roger rode a horse around a hexagonal field with each side 325 m long.

    How far did he ride?

1. Draw an arrow to the 0 or 10 to show whether the circled number is closer to **0 or 10**:

a)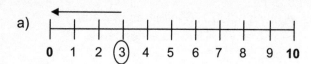

b)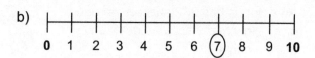

c)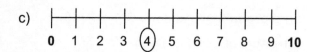

d)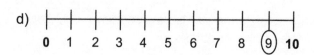

2. a) Which one digit numbers are closer to 0?_____

   b) Which are closer to 10?_____

   c) Why is 5 a special case?_____

3. Draw an arrow to show if you would round to **10 or 20 or 30**:

a)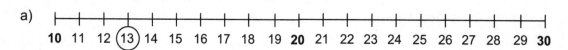

b)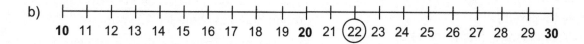

c)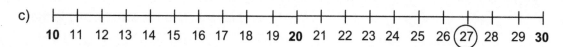

4. Draw an arrow to show which multiple of ten the number in the circle is closest to:

a)

b)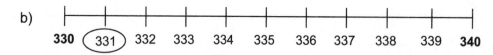

5. Circle the correct answer. Use the number lines in Questions 3 and 4 to help:

   a) The number 28 is closer to: 20   or   30   b) The number 24 is closer to: 20   or   30

   c) The number 16 is closer to: 10   or   20   d) The number 19 is closer to: 10   or   20

   e) The number 27 is closer to: 20 or 30   f) The number 12 is closer to: 10 or 20

   g) The number 251 is closer to: 250   or   260   h) The number 258 is closer to: 250   or   260

   i) The number 333 is closer to: 330 or 340   j) The number 339 is closer to: 330 or 340

6. Draw an arrow to show which multiple of ten you would round to. Then round each number to the nearest ten:

a)

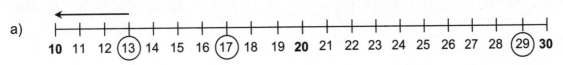

Round to   10   _____   _____

b)

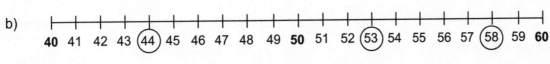

Round to   _____   _____   _____

c)

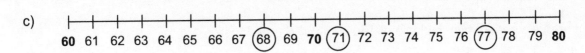

Round to   _____   _____   _____

d)

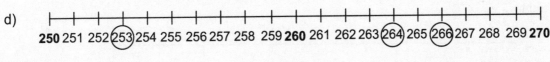

Round to   _____   _____   _____

e)

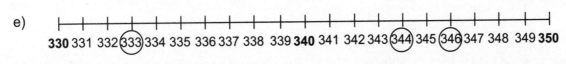

Round to   _____   _____   _____

7. Circle the correct answer:

a) 28 is closer to 20 or 30

b) 16 is closer to 10 or 20

c) 39 is closer to 30 or 40

d) 31 is closer to 30 or 40

e) 62 is closer to 60 or 70

f) 251 is closer to 250 or 260

g) 348 is closer to 340 or 350

h) 258 is closer to 250 or 260

i) 341 is closer to 340 or 35

j) 256 is closer to 250 or 260

1. Draw an arrow to show whether the circled number is closer to 0 or 100:

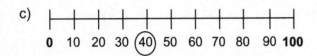

a)

b)

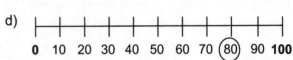

c)

d)

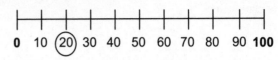

2. Is 50 closer to 0 or to 100? Why is 50 a special case?

_____

3. Circle the correct answer:

a) 80 is closer to: 0 or 100

b) 20 is closer to: 0 or 100

c) 40 is closer to: 0 or 100

d) 10 is closer to: 0 or 100

e) 60 is closer to: 0 or 100

f) 90 is closer to: 0 or 100

4. Draw an arrow to show which multiple of 100 you would round to:

a)

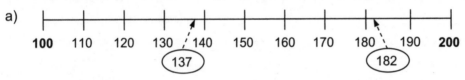

Round to _____   _____

b)

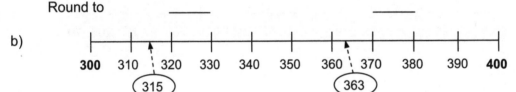

Round to _____   _____

5. Circle the correct answer:

a) The number 153 is closer to: 100 or 200

b) The number 189 is closer to: 100 or 200

c) The number 117 is closer to: 100 or 200

d) The number 135 is closer to: 100 or 200

e) The number 370 is closer to: 300 or 400

f) The number 332 is closer to: 300 or 400

BONUS:

6. Show the approximate position of each number on the line. What multiple of 100 would you round to?

a) 518   b) 576   c) 687   d) 629

Round to _____

1. Draw an arrow to show whether the circled number is closer to 0 or 1000:

a)

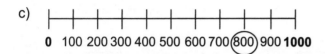

b)

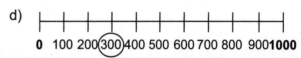

c)

d)

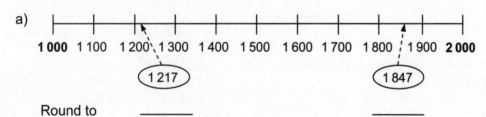

2. Is 500 closer to 0 or 1000? Why is 500 a special case?

_____

3. Circle the correct answer:

    a) 100 is closer to 0 or 1000

    b) 900 is closer to 0 or 1000

    c) 600 is closer to 0 or 1000

    d) 400 is closer to 0 or 1000

4. Draw an arrow to show which multiple of 1000 you would round to:

    a)

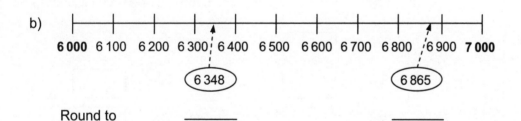

    Round to _____   _____

    b)

    Round to _____   _____

5. Circle the correct answer:

    a) The number 2953 is closer to: 2000 or 3000   b) The number 7293 is closer to: 7000 or 8000

    c) The number 5521 is closer to: 5000 or 6000   d) The number 3190 is closer to: 3000 or 4000

    6. In a notebook, write a rule for rounding a four-digit number to the nearest thousands.

NS4-36: Rounding

1. Round to the nearest **tens** place:

a) 16 [ ]

b) 23 [ ]

c) 72 [ ]

d) 66 [ ]

e) 81 [ ]

f) 93 [ ]

g) 11 [ ]

h) 52 [ ]

i) 68 [ ]

j) 37 [ ]

k) 43 [ ]

> **REMEMBER:**
>
> If the number in the ones digit is:
>
> 0, 1, 2, 3 or 4 – you round **down**
>
> 5, 6, 7, 8 or 9 – you round **up**

2. Round to the nearest **tens** place. Underline the tens digit first. Then put your pencil on the digit to the right (the ones digit). This digit tells you whether to round up or down:

a) 14̲5 [150]

b) 172 [ ]

c) 321 [ ]

d) 255 [ ]

e) 784 [ ]

f) 667 [ ]

g) 441 [ ]

h) 939 [ ]

i) 318 [ ]

j) 527 [ ]

k) 985 [ ]

l) 534 [ ]

m) 758 [ ]

n) 845 [ ]

o) 293 [ ]

3. Round the following numbers to the nearest **hundreds** place. Underline the hundreds digit first. Then put your pencil on the digit to the right (the tens digit):

> **REMEMBER:**   3̲45
>
> To round to the nearest hundreds, look at the tens digit.
>
> 0, 1, 2, 3 or 4 – you round **down**
>
> 5, 6, 7, 8 or 9 – you round **up**

a) 3̲40 [300]

b) 870 [ ]

c) 650 [ ]

d) 170 [ ]

e) 240 [ ]

f) 620 [ ]

g) 710 [ ]

h) 870 [ ]

i) 580 [ ]

j) 930 [ ]

k) 650 [ ]

l) 930 [ ]

m) 290 [ ]

n) 158 [ ]

o) 338 [ ]

p) 421 [ ]

q) 658 [ ]

r) 143 [ ]

s) 291 [ ]

t) 372 [ ]

u) 868 [ ]

v) 247 [ ]

w) 525 [ ]

x) 459 [ ]

y) 839 [ ]

NS4-36: Rounding *(continued)*

4. Round the following numbers to the nearest **hundreds** place. As in the last question, underline the hundreds digit first. Then put your pencil on the digit to the right (the tens digit):

a) 2 1̲56 → 2 200

b) 4 389 → [ ]

c) 3 229 → [ ]

d) 1 905 → [ ]

e) 5 251 → [ ]

f) 9 127 → [ ]

g) 6 472 → [ ]

h) 8 783 → [ ]

i) 7 255 → [ ]

j) 1 098 → [ ]

k) 3 886 → [ ]

l) 4 624 → [ ]

m) 8 077 → [ ]

n) 6 382 → [ ]

o) 9 561 → [ ]

p) 2 612 → [ ]

q) 5 924 → [ ]

BONUS:

r) 2 963 → [ ]

s) 997 → [ ]

t) 3 982 → [ ]

5. Round the following numbers to the nearest **thousands** place. Underline the thousands digit first. Then put your pencil on the digit to the right (the hundreds digit):

a) 2̲ 757 → 3 000

b) 9 052 → [ ]

c) 6 831 → [ ]

d) 3 480 → [ ]

e) 5 543 → [ ]

f) 4 740 → [ ]

g) 8 193 → [ ]

h) 2 607 → [ ]

i) 6 107 → [ ]

j) 9 125 → [ ]

k) 5 114 → [ ]

l) 7 649 → [ ]

m) 1 336 → [ ]

n) 9 538 → [ ]

o) 4 226 → [ ]

p) 7 311 → [ ]

q) 8 644 → [ ]

r) 2 750 → [ ]

s) 9 928 → [ ]

NS4-37: Estimating

Anita collected 21 books for charity and Mark collected 28 books. They estimated how many books they collected altogether:

1. First they rounded the numbers to the nearest tens:

| 2 | 1 | → *round to the nearest tens* → | 2 | 0 |

| 2 | 8 | → *round to the nearest tens* → | 3 | 0 |

2. Then they added the results:

```
   20
 + 30
   50
```

Answer the following questions in a notebook.

1. Estimate how many books the children collected. (Round to the nearest tens.)

   a) Kishon collected 24 books and Jasjit collected 32 books.

   b) Mumtaz collected 75 books and Elizabeth collected 18 books.

   c) Annisha collected 31 books and Christina collected 56 books.

2. a) Class 4A collected 243 books and class 4B collected 456 books for charity.
   About how many books did 4A and 4B collect altogether? (Round to the nearest hundreds.)

   b) Class 4C collected 645 books and class 4D collected 129 books.
   About how many books did the classes collect altogether?

   c) About how many more books did 4C collect than 4D?

   d) About how many books did all the Grade 4s (4A, 4B, 4C, 4D) collect altogether?

3. A store has the following items for sale:

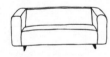

A. Sofa – $472   **B.** Arm Chair – $ 227   **C.** Table - $ 189   **D.** Desk - $382   **E.** Lamp - $ 112

   a) What could you buy if you had $800 to spend? Estimate to find out.
   Then add the actual prices.

   b) List a different set of items you could buy.

-----

4. Estimate the following sums and differences.
   Then add or subtract to find the actual sum or difference. How far off was your estimate?

   a) 376 + 212   b) 875 – 341   c) 907 – 588

ME4-1: Estimating Lengths in Centimetres

1. A **centimetre** (cm) is a unit of measurement for **length** (or **height** or **thickness**).

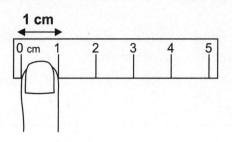

Your index finger is approximately one centimetre wide:

Measure the following objects using your index finger (or the finger closest to 1 cm):

a) My pencil is approximately _____ cm long.   b) My shoe is about _____ cm long.

2. Pick another object in the room to measure with your index finger:

_____ is approximately _____ cm.

3.

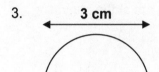

A toonie is about 3 cm wide.

How many toonies would you need to line up to make:
HINT: Skip count by 3s.

a) 15 cm? _____   b) 18 cm? _____   c) 30 cm? _____

4. Hold up your hand to a ruler. Line up your thumb at the zero (0) marker, as shown here. Then line your little finger up to the 10 cm mark:

How far do you have to spread your fingers to make your hand 10 cm wide?

Now measure the following objects in your room using your (measured) spread out hand:

a) My bed is approx. _____ cm long.

b) My arm is approx. _____ cm long.

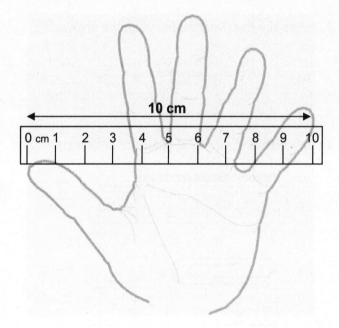

5. Pick other objects in your home to measure with your hand:

a) _____ is approximately _____ cm long.

b) _____ is approximately _____ cm long.

Measurement 1

Midori counts the number of centimetres between the arrows by counting the number of "hops" it takes to move between them:

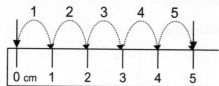

_____5_____ cm

- -

1. Measure the distance between the two arrows:

a) 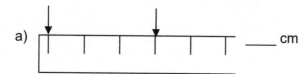 _____ cm   b) 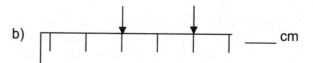 _____ cm

2. Measure the distance between the arrows. (Count carefully as the first arrow is not at the beginning of the ruler.)

a)  _____ cm   b) 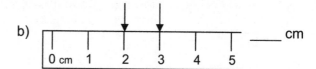 _____ cm

3. Measure the distance between the arrows:

a) 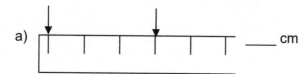 _____ cm   b) 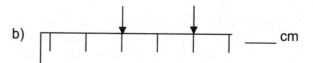 _____ cm

4. Measure the length of each line or object:

a) 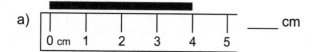 _____ cm   b)  _____ cm

c) 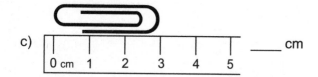 _____ cm   d)  _____ cm

5. Measure the length of the line and object below:

a)  _____ cm   b) 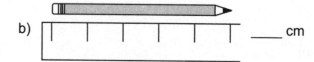 _____ cm

ME4-3: Drawing and Measuring in Centimetres

1. Measure the length of each line using a ruler:

    a) 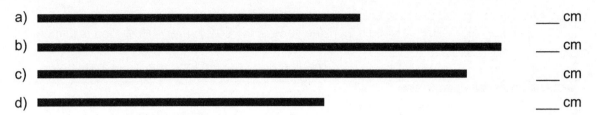 ___ cm

    b) ___ cm

    c) ___ cm

    d) ___ cm

2. Measure the length of each object using a ruler:

    a) 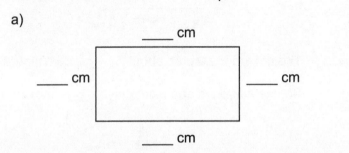 _____ cm

    b) 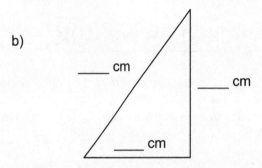 _____ cm

3. Measure all the sides of each shape:

    a)

    ___ cm

    ___ cm   ___ cm

    ___ cm

    b)

    ___ cm

    ___ cm

    ___ cm

4. Draw two arrows on each ruler the given distance apart. The first question is done for you:

    a) Two arrows 4 cm apart.   b) Two arrows 3 cm apart.   c) Two arrows 5 cm apart.

    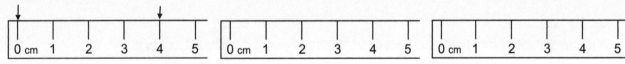

5. Using a straight edge, draw a line that is:

    a) 1 cm long   b) 4 cm long   c) 2 cm long

    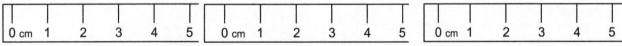

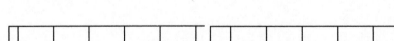**Answer the remaining questions in a notebook.**

6. Draw a line:
    a) 3 cm long
    b) 5 cm long
    c) 10 cm long

7. Draw each object to the exact measurement given:
    a) A caterpillar, 4 cm long
    b) A leaf, 11 cm long
    c) A feather, 8 cm long

8. On grid paper, draw a rectangle with a length of 5 cm and a width of 2 cm.

If you look at a ruler with millimetre measurements, you can see that 1 cm is equal to 10 mm:

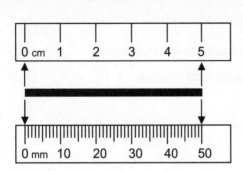

How long is the line in mm? How long is it in cm?

The line is _____ cm long, or _____ mm long.

To convert a measurement from cm to mm, we have to multiply the measurement by _____ .

----

1. Your index finger is about 1 cm – or 10 mm – wide. Measure the objects below using your index finger. Then convert your measurement to mm:

   a)

   CHEWING GUM

   The gum measures about ___5___ index fingers.

   So, the gum is approximately ___50___ mm long.

   b)

   The crayon measures about _____ index fingers.

   So, the crayon is approximately _____ mm long.

   c)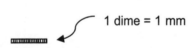

   The pencil measures about _____ index fingers.

   So, the pencil is approx. _____ mm long.

   d)

   The tack measures about _____ index fingers.

   So, the tack is approx. _____ mm long.

2. A dime is about 1 mm high. So a stack of 10 dimes would be about 1 cm high:

   1 dime = 1 mm   10 dimes = 10 mm = 1 cm

   How many dimes would be in a stack:

   a) 2 cm high?   b) 3 cm high?   c) 5 cm high?   d) 10 cm high?

   _____   _____   _____   _____

3. Jamelia has 4 stacks of dimes. Each stack is about 1 cm high.
   About how much money does Jamelia have?
   Explain.

4. A toonie is about 2 mm thick.
   Josie has a stack of toonies 10 mm high.
   How much money does Josie have?

ME4-5: Millimetres and Centimetres

Mei-Ling wants to measure a line that is 23 mm long.

Rather than counting every millimetre, Mei-Ling counts by tens until she reaches 20. Then she counts on by ones:

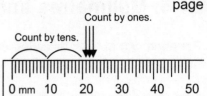

1. What is the distance between the two arrows?

   a)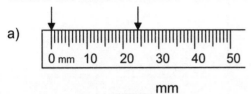

   _____ mm

   b)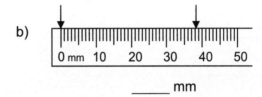

   _____ mm

2. Find the length of each line:

   a)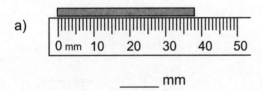

   _____ mm

   b)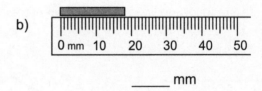

   _____ mm

3. Using a straight edge, draw a line starting from the "0" mark of the ruler and ending at the given length:

   a) Draw a line 16 mm long.

   b) Draw a line 41 mm long.

   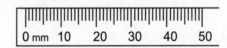

4. For each line below, estimate whether the length is **less** than 30 mm or **more** than 30 mm. Place a checkmark in the appropriate column:

	Less than 30 mm	More than 30 mm
a)		
b)		
c)		
d)		
e)		

5. How good were your estimates? For each estimate you made in Question 4, measure the length of the line and record your measurement in millimetres:

   a) _____ mm   b) _____ mm   c) _____ mm   d) _____ mm   e) _____ mm

Measurement 1

6. For each pair of lines below **estimate** whether the distance between them is **less** than 20 mm or **more** than 20 mm. Then measure the **actual** distance in millimetres.

	Less than 20 mm	More than 20 mm	Actual Distance
a)			
b)			
c)			
d)			

7. Measure the following lines using both centimetres and millimetres:

a) _____

_____ cm

_____ mm

b)

_____ cm

_____ mm

c)

_____ cm

_____ mm

d) _____

_____ cm

_____ mm

8. Measure the sides of the rectangles in cm. Then measure the distance between the two diagonal corners in cm and mm. (The dotted line is a guide for where you should place your ruler.)

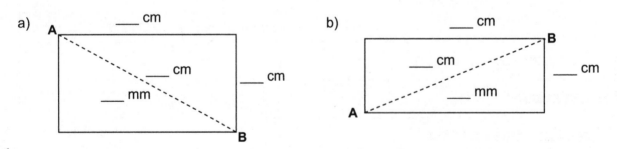

a) ____ cm   ____ cm   ____ mm   ____ cm

b) ____ cm   ____ cm   ____ mm   ____ cm

9. In a notebook, use a ruler to draw the following objects to the exact millimetre:

   a) Draw a line 20 mm long.   b) Draw a line 27 mm long.   c) Draw a line 52 mm long.

   d) Draw a beetle 30 mm long.   e) Draw a pencil 70 mm long.   f) Draw a bicycle 28 mm long.

10. On grid paper, draw a rectangle with a length of 60 mm and a width of 2 cm.

ME4-6: Comparing Centimetres & Millimetres

1. How many millimetres (mm) are there in one centimetre (cm)? _____

2. To change a measurement from centimetres (cm) into millimetres (mm), what should you multiply the measurement by? _____

3. Fill in the numbers missing from the following charts:

mm	cm
	4
	57
	5

mm	cm
	7
	12
	35

mm	cm
	112
	170
	293

mm	cm
	8
	257
	32

4. To change a measurement from mm to cm, what number do you have to divide by? _____

a) $40 \div 10 =$ _____ 　　b) $60 \div 10 =$ _____ 　　c) $2100 \div 10 =$ _____ 　　d) $90 \div 10 =$ _____

e) 320 mm = _____ cm 　f) 30 mm = _____ cm 　g) 910 mm = _____ cm 　h) 650 mm = _____ cm

5. Fill in the following tables:

mm	cm
5	
	80
	140

mm	cm
19	
1	
	10

mm	cm
12	
	2700
	180

mm	cm
7	
	91
	11 020

6. Convert the measurement in cm to mm (show your work). Then circle the greater measurement:

a) 　5 cm 　　70 mm 　　b) 　83 cm 　　910 mm 　　c) 　45 cm 　　53 mm

d) 　2 cm 　　12 mm 　　e) 　60 cm 　　6200 mm 　　f) 　72 cm 　　420 mm

7. Estimate the width and length (in cm) of each rectangle. Then measure each quantity exactly in mm using a ruler:

a) 　

b)

1. Using a ruler, draw a second line so that the pair of lines are the distance apart given in the table. Then complete the chart:

		Distance Apart	
		in cm	in mm
a)		4	40
b)		3	
c)			80
d)		7	

2. Draw a line with length:

   a) between 3 and 4 cm   How long is your line in mm? _____

   b) between 4 and 5 cm   How long is your line in mm? _____

   c) between 5 and 6 cm   How long is your line in mm? _____

3. Write a measurement in mm that is between:

   a) 6 and 7 cm _____   b) 7 and 8 cm _____   c) 12 and 13 cm _____

4. Write a measurement in cm that is between:

   a) 67 mm and 75 mm _____   b) 27 mm and 39 mm _____

   c) 52 mm and 7 cm _____   d) 112 mm and 13 cm _____

Answer the remaining questions in a notebook.

5. Draw a line that is a whole number of centimetres long and is between:
   a) 45 and 55 mm
   b) 65 and 75 mm
   c) 17 and 23 mm

6. Peter says 5 mm are longer than 2 cm because 5 is greater than 2.
   Is he right?
   Explain.

ME4-8: Problems and Puzzles

1. Each leaf has a different length.

    Elm: 4 cm   **Maple: 5 cm**   **Juniper: 6 cm**   **Oak: 7 cm**

    Measure the lengths to identify each leaf:

_____

_____

_____

_____

2. Which line is longer: A or B?

    a)

    A

    B

    b)

    A

    B

    c)

    A

    B

ME4-9: Decimetres

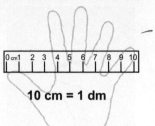

10 cm = 1 dm

If you spread your fingers wide, your hand is about 10 cm wide:
10 centimetres are equal to 1 decimetre (dm).

So there are 10 **cm** in 1 **dm**.

(Similarly, 10 **mm** is equal to 1 **cm**.)

---

1. Place a checkmark in the correct column:
   HINT: Remember that 1 dm = 10 cm.

	Less than 1 dm	More than 1 dm
My arm		
A paperclip		
A pencil		
The height of the door to my room		

2. To change a measurement from decimetres (dm) to centimetres (cm), what should you multiply the measurement by? _____

3. To change a measurement from cm to dm what should you divide by? _____

4. Find the numbers missing from the following charts:

   a)
cm	dm
150	15
	23
	32

   b)
cm	dm
90	
	510
400	

   c)
cm	dm
610	
	1
780	

5. Draw a line that is between 1 and 2 decimetres long:

   a) How long is your line in cm?_____   b) How long is your line in mm?_____

6. Write a measurement in cm that is between:

   a) 4 and 5 dm _____   b) 3 and 4 dm _____   c) 7 and 8 dm _____

7. Write a measurement in dm that is between:

   a) 72 and 82 cm _____   b) 27 and 35 cm _____   c) 68 and 74 cm _____

8. How many dm are in 100 cm? _____

9. There are 10 mm in 1 cm. There are 10 cm in 1 dm. How many mm are in 1 dm?_____
   How do you know? How could you check your answer? Answer in a notebook.

A **metre** (m) is a unit of measurement for **length** (or **height** or **thickness**) equal to 100 cm.

A metre stick is 100 cm long: |⊥⊥⊥⊥⊥⊥⊥⊥⊥⊥⊥⊥⊥⊥⊥⊥⊥⊥⊥⊥⊥⊥|

- -

You can estimate metres using parts of your body:

- A giant step is about a metre long.

- A four or five year old child is about a metre tall.

- If you stretch your arms out the distance between the tips of your fingers is about one metre.
(This distance is called your *arm span*.)

1. Take a giant step and ask a friend to measure your step with a piece of string.
Hold the string up to a metre stick.

   Is your step more or less than a metre? _____

2. Ask a friend to measure your arm span using a piece of string.

   Is your arm span more or less than a metre? _____

3. Measure your height in cm using a metre stick:

   Your height is _____ cm.   Are you taller than 1 metre? _____

4. Estimate the following distances. Then measure the actual distance with a metre stick or measuring tape.

   a) The length of the bed in your room: Estimate - ____ m _____ cm

   Actual - ____ m _____ cm

   b) The length of a table in your home: Estimate - ____ m _____ cm

   Actual - ____ m _____ cm

   c) The distance from the floor to the door handle: Estimate - ____ m _____ cm

   Actual - ____ m _____ cm

5. A small city block is about 100 m long. Write the name of a place you can walk to from your home (a store, a park, your school).
Approximately how far away from your home is the place you named?

   _____

   _____

Measurement 1

1. See if you can figure out the pattern in the following table. Then finish the table on your own:

m	1	2	3	4	5	6
dm	10	20				
cm	100	200				
mm	1000	2000				

2. a) 1 cm = _____ mm   b) 1 m = _____ cm   c) 1 m = _____ mm

3. Convert the following measurements:

a)

m	cm
1	
14	
80	

b)

m	mm
2	
19	
21	

c)

cm	mm
3	
65	
106	

4. Sheena measured her bedroom window with both a metre stick and a measuring tape.
   - When she measured with the metre stick, the height of the window was 2 m with 15 cm extra.
   - When she measured with the measuring tape, she got a measurement of 215 cm.

   Was there a difference in the two measurements? Explain:

   _____

   _____

5. Convert the measurement given in cm to a measurement using multiple units:

   a) 513 cm = __5__ m __13__ cm   b) 217 cm = _____ m _____ cm

   c) 367 cm = _____ m _____ cm   d) 481 cm = _____ m _____ cm

   e) 706 cm = _____ m _____ cm   f) 303 cm = _____ m _____ cm

6. Convert the following multiple units of measurements to a single unit:

   a) 3 m 71 cm = __371__ cm   b) 4 m 51 cm = _____ cm   c) 3 m 45 cm = _____ cm

   d) 8 m 2 cm = _____ cm   e) 9 m 7 cm = _____ cm   f) 7 m 50 cm = _____ cm

A **kilometre** is a unit of measurement for **length** equal to 1 000 metres.

1. a) Count by 100s to find out how many times you need to add 100 to make 1 000:

100 , _____ , _____ , _____ , _____ , _____ , _____ , _____ , _____ , _____

b) A football field is about 100 m long.
How many football fields long is a kilometre?

2. a) Skip count by 50s to find out how many times you need to add 50 to make 1 000:

__50__ , _____ , _____ , _____ , _____ , _____ , _____ , _____ , _____ , _____

_____ , _____ , _____ , _____ , _____ , _____ , _____ , _____ , _____ , _____

b) An Olympic swimming pool is 50 m long.
How many pools long is a kilometre?

3. Count by 10s to find the number of times you need to add 10 to make each number:

a) 100 = _____ tens

b) 200 = _____ tens

c) 300 = _____ tens

d) 400 = _____ tens

e) 500 = _____ tens

f) 600 = _____ tens

4. Using the pattern in Question 3, how many times would you need to add 10 to make 1 000?

_____

5. A school bus is about 10 m long. How many school buses, lined up end to end, would be:

a) close to a kilometre? _____

b) close to 2 km? _____

6. You can travel 1 km if you walk for 15 minutes at a regular speed. Can you name a place (a store, a park, your friend's house) that is about 1 km from your home?

_____

The numbers beside each line marks the length of the road between those cities (in kilometres).

Use the map to answer the questions below:

1. The driving distance between:

   a) Corner Brook and Port aux Basques is _____ km.

   b) Corner Brook and Gander is _____ km.

   c) Port aux Basques and Gander is _____ km.

   d) Gander and St. John's is _____ km.

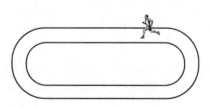

2. How far would you travel if you drove:

   a) from Corner Brook to Port aux Basques to Gander? _____ km.

   b) from Port aux Basques to Gander to St. John's? _____ km.

   c) from St. John's to Gander to Corner Brook? _____ km.

   d) from Gander to Port aux Basques to Corner Brook and back to Gander? _____ km.

3. This chart lists the lengths of some Canadian rivers and the provinces in which they are located. Order them from longest (1) to shortest (5):

River	Length
Clearwater (Sask.)	187 km
Bloodvein (Man.)	200 km
Kicking Horse (B.C.)	67 km
Jacques Cartier (Que.)	128 km
Athabasca (Atla.)	168 km

   1. _____

   2. _____

   3. _____

   4. _____

   5. _____

4. A track is 400 m long:

   a) If Khalid runs 2 times around the track, how many metres would he have travelled?

   b) Would he have travelled a km?

   c) Khalid plans to run the 1500 m race at the Metro Finals. About how many times around the track must he run?

   d) How many times around the track must Khalid run to cover 2 km?

Measurement 1

For the questions below, you will need to choose the appropriate unit of measurement:

REMEMBER: You can refer to the guidelines provided:

| the thickness of a dime is about **1 mm** | the width of your index finger is about **1 cm** | the width of your hand is about **1 dm** | the height of a 4 or 5 year old child is about **1 m** | The distance you can walk in 15 min is about **1 km** |

1. Match the word with the symbol:

    a)

    | cm | metre |
    | m | centimetre |

    b)

    | cm | centimetre |
    | m | kilometre |
    | km | metre |

    c)

    | mm | kilometre |
    | km | centimetre |
    | cm | millimetre |

2. Match the object with the most appropriate unit of measurement:

    a)

    | metre | height of a child |
    | centimetre | length of a nail |

    b)

    | metre | length of a worm |
    | kilometre | height of a door |
    | centimetre | length of a subway track |

3. Match the word with the symbol. Then match the object with the most appropriate unit of measurement. The first one has been done for you:

    a)

    | mm | kilometre | height of a book |
    | cm | centimetre | length of a street |
    | m | millimetre | height of a room |
    | km | metre | length of an ant |

    b)

    | km | metre | door height |
    | cm | millimetre | distance to Montreal |
    | m | kilometre | pencil length |
    | mm | centimetre | postage stamp width |

4. Order the following items from shortest to longest (1 = shortest, 2 = next shortest, 3 = longest). What unit would you use to measure each?

    a)

    #____   #____   #____

    Unit: _____   Unit: _____   Unit: _____

    b)

    #____   #____   #____

    Unit: _____   Unit: _____   Unit: _____

ME4-14: Ordering Units: Metres and Centimetres

1. How many centimetres are in a metre? _____

2. Change the following measurements into centimetres:

    a) 4 m = _____ cm   b) 6 m = _____ cm   c) _____ cm = 1 m   d) 3 m = _____ cm

3. Circle the greater amount:
    HINT: Change the measurement in metres (m) to centimetres (cm). Show your work in the box provided.

    a) 1 m   or   60 cm

    _____ cm

    b) 7 m   or   82 cm

    _____ cm

    c) 410 cm   or   5 m

    _____ cm

    d) 3 m   or   340 cm

    _____ cm

    e) 280 cm   or   4 m

    _____ cm

    f) 7 m   or   680 cm

    _____ cm

4. Mark the measurements on the number line. (First change all measurements to cm.)

    A. 150 cm

    B. 2 m

    C. 1 m

    ```
    ├────────┼────────┼────────┼────────┤
    0 cm    50 cm   100 cm   150 cm   200 cm
    ```

5. This chart shows the lengths
    of some snakes at the zoo:

Snake	Length
Garter Snake - **G**	150 cm
Coral Snake - **C**	50 cm
Fox Snake - **F**	100 cm
Boa Snake - **B**	2 m

Mark the lengths of **G**, **C**, **F** and **B** on the number line:

```
├──────────────────┼──────────────────┤
0 cm             100 cm             200 cm
```

1. What would the best unit of measurement be for:

   a) The length of a chalkboard eraser:

   _____

   b) The length of a subway car:

   _____

   c) The distance travelled on a plane flight from Halifax to Moncton:

   _____

2. Which unit of measurement would make the statement correct?

   a) The thickness of a piece of construction paper is about 1 _____ .

   b) Schools might close if more than 50 _____ of snow has fallen overnight.

   c) An average adult bicycle is about 2 _____ long.

   d) It is more than 500 _____ from Toronto to Montreal.

3. For the following questions, circle the unit of measurement that makes the statement correct:

   a) The bedroom door is about 2 **cm** / **m** high.

   b) The length of your shoe is close to 1 **m** / **dm**

   c) The thickness of your JUMP Math workbook is about 10 **mm** / **cm**.

   d) The height of the CN Tower is about 553 **km** / **m**.

4. What would you use to measure the following distances – metres (m) or kilometres (km)?
   REMEMBER: A kilometre is about 10 football fields (or short blocks) long.

   a) From your bedroom to the kitchen: _____   b) From your home to school: _____

   c) Between Toronto and Ottawa: _____   d) From your school to the CN Tower: _____

   e) Between your home and the local
      public library: _____

   f) Between your home and your best
      friend's home: _____

   g) Between your home and your nearest
      grocery store: _____

   h) Around the school yard: _____

(continued)

5. Some BIG and SMALL facts about Canada! Choose which (km, m, or cm) belongs to complete each sentence:

    PARENT: Read these questions out loud to your child before you assign them.

    a) The Red Deer River flows from Alberta to Saskatchewan.

       It is 724 _____ long.

    b) The sea otter can reach a length of 150 _____.

    c) The city of Stewart, in British Columbia, gets a lot of snowfall.

       It receives about 660 _____ of snowfall every year.

    d) The CN Tower, at 553 _____, is the world's tallest free-standing structure.

    e) The Douglas Fir tree can grow to a height of 100 _____.

    f) An Atlantic cod is about 1 _____ long and can swim in water that is 305 _____ deep.

    g) The width of a maple leaf is approximately 16 _____.

6. Which unit of measurement would you use for the following:

    a) Length of a postage stamp

       _____

    b) Distance from your home to school

       _____

    c) Length of a subway car

       _____

    d) Length of your hair

       _____

    e) The distance travelled on a plane flight from Halifax to Moncton

       _____

7. Find any object in your room.
   Write down what unit of measure would be best for measuring it.
   Explain why it would be the best unit of measure.

ME4-16: Perimeter

ME4-16: Perimeter

Maria makes a figure using toothpicks:

She counts the number of toothpicks around the outside of the figure:

1 2 3 4 5

The distance around the outside of a shape is called the **perimeter** of the shape. The perimeter of Maria's figure, measured in toothpicks, is **5 toothpicks**.

- -

1. Count the number of toothpicks around the outside of the figure. (Mark the toothpicks as you count, so you don't miss any!) Write your answer in the circle provided:

   a) ◯   b) ◯   c) ◯

2. Count the number of edges around the **outside** of the figure, marking the edges as you count:

   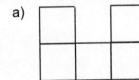 edge

   a) _____   b) _____   c) _____

3. Each edge in the figure is 1 cm long. Find the perimeter in cm:

   a) 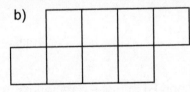   b)   c)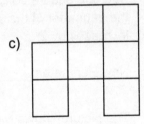

   _____ cm   _____ cm   _____ cm

4. The picture shows the designs for two gardens. Find the perimeter of each garden by writing an addition statement:

   a)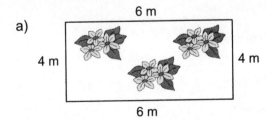
   6 m
   4 m   4 m
   6 m

   b)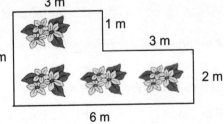
   3 m
   1 m
   3 m   3 m
   2 m
   6 m

   _____   _____

5. Write the perimeter of each figure in the sequence (assume each edge is 1 unit):

a) How does the perimeter change each time a square is added? _____

b) If the sequence were continued, what would the perimeter of the 5th figure be? _____

c) If the sequence were continued, what would the perimeter of the 6th figure be? _____

d) If the sequence were continued, what would the perimeter of the 7th figure be? _____

6. Write the perimeter of each figure in the sequence below:

a) How does the perimeter change each time a hexagon is added? _____

b) If the sequence were continued, what would the perimeter of the 5th figure be? _____

c) If the sequence were continued, what would the perimeter of the 6th figure be? _____

d) If the sequence were continued, what would the perimeter of the 7th figure be? _____

7. a) Perimeter: _____

Add one square so that the perimeter of the shape increases by 2:

New Perimeter: _____

b) Perimeter: _____

Add one square so that the perimeter of the shape stays the same:

New Perimeter: _____

8. The picture shows two ways (A and B) to make a rectangle using 4 squares:

a) Which figure has the shorter perimeter? How do you know?

b) Are there any other ways to make a rectangle using 4 squares?

9. On grid paper, show all the ways you can make a rectangle using:

a) 6 squares   b) 10 squares   c) 9 squares

d) Which of the rectangles in b) above has the greatest perimeter? What is the perimeter?

1. Each edge is 1 cm long. Write the total length of each side beside the figure (one side is done for you). Then write an addition statement and find the perimeter:

a)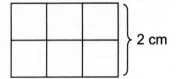

Perimeter: _____

b)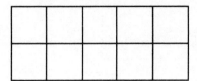

Perimeter: _____

c)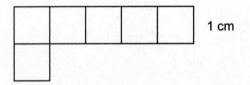

Perimeter: _____

d)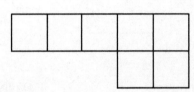

Perimeter: _____

2. Each edge is 1 unit long. Write the length of each side beside the figure (don't miss any edges!). Then use the side lengths to find the perimeter:

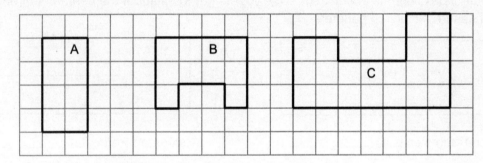

3. Draw your own figure and find the perimeter:

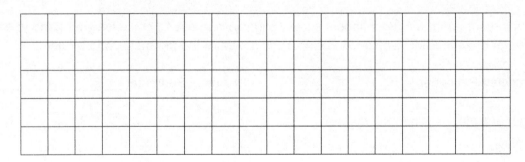

4. On grid paper, draw your own figures and find their perimeters. Try making letters or other shapes!

PARENT:
Your child will enjoy this activity. Let them spend time inventing shapes and finding their perimeters.

ME4-18: Measuring Perimeter

1. Measure the perimeter of each figure in cm using a ruler:

   a)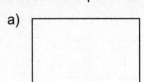

   _____

   b)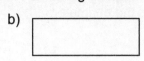

   _____

   c)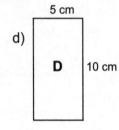

   _____

2. Find the perimeter of each shape (include the units) from greatest to least perimeter:

   a)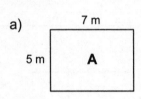

   b)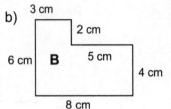

   c)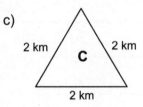

   d)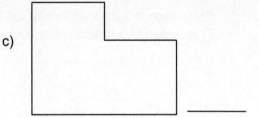

   Perimeter: _____   Perimeter: _____   Perimeter: _____   Perimeter: _____

   e) Write the letters of the shapes in order from greatest to least perimeter (watch the units!):

   _____ , _____ , _____ , _____

3. The width of your index finger is about 1 cm. Use your finger to estimate the perimeter of each shape in cm. Then measure the actual perimeter:

   a)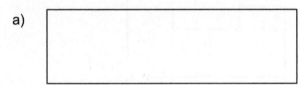

   Estimated Perimeter_____

   Actual Perimeter_____

   b)

   Estimated Perimeter_____

   Actual Perimeter_____

4. The width of your hand, with your fingers spread slightly, is about 10 cm. Use your hand to estimate the perimeter of your JUMP workbook in cm. Then measure the perimeter with a ruler:

   Estimated Perimeter _____   Actual Perimeter _____

5. The length of a bicycle is about 2 metres:

   a) About how many bicycles, parked end to end, would fit along the width of your home? _____

   b) About how wide is your home? **HINT: Use your answer in a) and count by 2s.** _____

   c) About how long is your home? _____

   d) What is the approximate perimeter of your home? _____

6. The length of a square room is about 3 ½ bicycles:
   REMEMBER: A bike is about 2 m long.

   a) About how many metres long is the room? _____

   b) What is the approximate perimeter of the room? _____

7. What units (cm, m, or km) would you use to measure the perimeter of:

   a) a house? ____   b) a book? ____   c) a school yard? ____   d) a provincial park? ____

       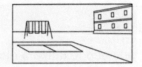

   e) a calculator? ____   f) a city? ____   g) a basketball court? ____   h) a country? ____

Answer the remaining questions in a notebook.

8. Estimate the perimeter of a room in your home. Explain how you estimated the perimeter.

9. How could you find the perimeter of a square with sides 5 cm without drawing a picture?

10. Sally arranges 4 squares (each with sides 1 m) to make a poster:

   1 m {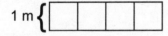

   She wants to make a border for her poster out of ribbon:

   Ribbon costs 15¢ for each meter.
   How much will the border cost?

11. How could you measure the perimeter of a round object (like a plate or a can) using a piece of string and a ruler?

12. In a notebook, explain the meaning of perimeter.

13. Can two different shapes have the same perimeter? Explain your thinking on grid paper.

1. Write the name and value of each coin:

a) 1 ¢   Name _____   Value _____

b) 5 ¢   Name _____   Value _____

c) 10 ¢   Name _____   Value _____

d) 25 ¢   Name _____   Value _____

2. Answer the following questions:

a) How many pennies do you need to make a nickel? _____

b) How many pennies do you need to make a dime? _____

c) How many nickels do you need to make a dime? _____

d) How many nickels do you need to make a quarter? _____

e) How many pennies do you need to make a quarter? _____

f) How many dimes do you need to make a quarter if you already have one nickel? _____

3. Count by 5s starting from the given numbers:

a) 80, _____, _____, _____   b) 40, _____, _____, _____   c) 60, _____, _____, _____

d) 70, _____, _____, _____   e) 105, _____, _____, _____   f) 120, _____, _____, _____

4. Count on by 5s from the given number:

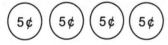   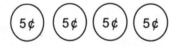   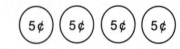

a) 55, ____, ____, ____, ____   b) 75, ____, ____, ____, ____   c) 85, ____, ____, ____, ____

5. Count by 10s starting from the given numbers:

a) 30, _____, _____, _____   b) 60, _____, _____, _____   c) 80, _____, _____, _____

d) 70, _____, _____, _____   e) 100, _____, _____, _____   f) 120, _____, _____, _____

6. Count on by 10s from the given number:

a) 55, ____, ____, ____, ____   b) 70, ____, ____, ____, ____   c) 85, ____, ____, ____, ____

ME4-19: Counting Coins (continued)

7. Count by the first number given, then by the second number after the vertical line:

a) __5__ , ___ , ___ , ___ , ___ | ___ , ___ , ___

       Count by 5s | *Continue counting by 1s*

b) __5__ , ___ , ___ , ___ | ___ , ___ , ___

       Count by 5s | *Continue counting by 1s*

8. Count by the first number given, then by the second number after the vertical line:

(10¢) (10¢) | (5¢) (5¢) (5¢) (5¢) (5¢)   (10¢) (10¢) (10¢) | (5¢) (5¢) (5¢) (5¢)

a) __5__ , ___ , ___ | ___ , ___ , ___ , ___ , ___

      Count by 10s | *Continue counting by 5s*

b) ___ , ___ , ___ | ___ , ___ , ___ , ___

      Count by 10s | *Continue counting by 5s*

9. Complete each pattern by counting by the 25s, then by the second number after the vertical line:

(25¢) (25¢) (25¢) (10¢) (10¢)   (25¢) (25¢) (25¢) (5¢) (5¢)

a) ___ , ___ , ___ | ___ , ___

    Count by 25s | *Count by 10s*

b) ___ , ___ , ___ | ___ , ___

    Count by 25s | *Count by 5s*

10. Count by the first number given, then by the following numbers given:

a) __25__ , __50__ , __75__ | __80__ , __85__ | __86__

     Count by 25s | *Count by 5s* | *Count by 1s*

b) ___ , ___ | ___ , ___ | ___ , ___ , ___

     Count by 25s | *Count by 10s* | *Count by 5s*

c) ___ , ___ | ___ , ___ | ___ , ___

     Count by 25s | *Count by 10s* | *Count by 5s*

d) ___ , ___ , ___ | ___ , ___ | ___ , ___

     Count by 25s | *Count by 10s* | *Count by 1s*

BONUS:

e) ___ , ___ | ___ , ___ , ___ | ___ , ___ | ___ , ___

     Count by 25s | *Count by 10s* | *Count by 5s* | *Count by 1s*

11. Count by the first coin value given, then by the others as the coin type changes. The first one is done for you:

(10¢) (10¢) (10¢) (5¢) (5¢) (1¢)   (5¢) (5¢) (5¢) (10¢) (10¢) (1¢)

a) __10__ , __20__ , __30__ , __35__ , __40__ , __41__

b) ___ , ___ , ___ , ___ , ___ , ___

BONUS:

(25¢) (25¢) (25¢) (25¢) (10¢) (10¢) (5¢) (5¢) (5¢) (1¢) (1¢) (1¢) (1¢)

c) ___ , ___ , ___ , ___ , ___ , ___ , ___ , ___ , ___ , ___ , ___ , ___ , ___

12. Complete each pattern:

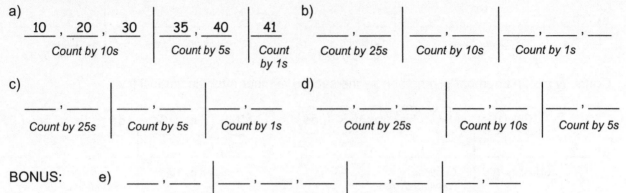

a)

____10____ , __20__ , __30__ | __35__ , __40__ | __41__
Count by 10s | Count by 5s | Count by 1s

b)

____ , ____ | ____ , ____ | ____ , ____ , ____
Count by 25s | Count by 10s | Count by 1s

c)

____ , ____ | ____ , ____ | ____ , ____
Count by 25s | Count by 5s | Count by 1s

d)

____ , ____ , ____ | ____ , ____ | ____ , ____
Count by 25s | Count by 10s | Count by 5s

BONUS: e)   ____ , ____ | ____ , ____ , ____ | ____ , ____ | ____ , ____

Count by 25s | Count by 10s | Count by 5s | Count by 1s

13. Write the total amount of money in cents for the number of coins given in the charts below:

   HINT: Count by the greatest amount first.

a)

Nickels	Pennies
7	4

Total amount =

b)

Quarters	Dimes
4	2

Total amount =

c)

Quarters	Nickels
6	6

Total amount =

BONUS:

d)

Quarters	Nickels	Pennies
3	1	2

Total amount =

e)

Quarters	Dimes	Nickels
2	2	5

Total amount =

f)

Quarters	Dimes	Nickels	Pennie
2	1	2	6

Total amount =

g)

Quarters	Dimes	Nickels	Pennie
5	3	4	9

Total amount =

14. Count the given coins and write the total amount. **Hint: Count by the greatest amount first.**

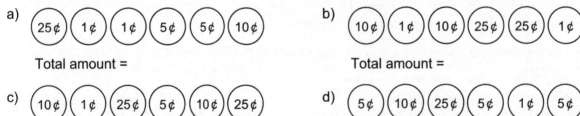

a) 25¢ 1¢ 1¢ 5¢ 5¢ 10¢

Total amount =

b) 10¢ 1¢ 10¢ 25¢ 25¢ 1¢

Total amount =

c) 10¢ 1¢ 25¢ 5¢ 10¢ 25¢

Total amount =

d) 5¢ 10¢ 25¢ 5¢ 1¢ 5¢

Total amount =

BONUS:

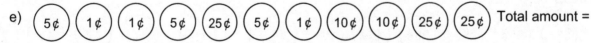

e) 5¢ 1¢ 1¢ 5¢ 25¢ 5¢ 1¢ 10¢ 10¢ 25¢ 25¢   Total amount =

PARENT:

Allow your child to practise the skill in Question 14 with play money. Do not move on until they can add up any combination of coins up to a dollar.

ME4-20: Counting by Different Denominations

1. Fill in the missing amounts, counting by 5s:

a) 14, ____ , 24 , 29   b) 30, ____ , ____ , 45   c) 67, ____ , ____ , 82

d) 18, ____ , ____ , 33   e) 71, ____ , ____ , 86   f) 45, ____ , ____ , 60

2. Fill in the missing amounts, counting by 10s:

a) 63, ____ , 83   b) 24, ____ , ____ , 54   c) 39, ____ , ____ , 69

3. For each of the questions below, write in the missing coin to complete the addition statement.
   The possibilities for each question are listed:

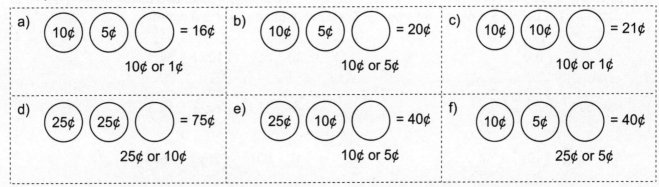

4. For each question, draw in the number of additional **nickels** needed to make the total:

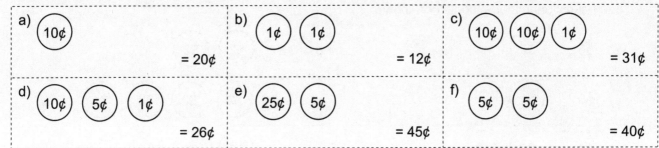

5. For each question, draw in the number of additional **dimes** needed to make the total:

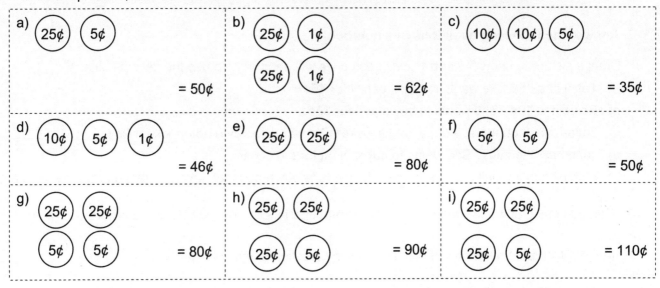

6. For each question, draw in the additional **coins** needed to make each total:

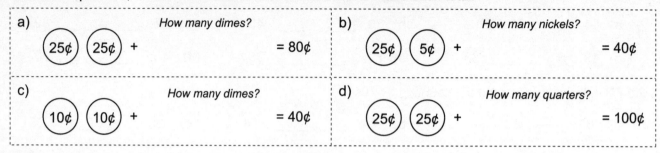

a)   *How many dimes?*

(25¢) (25¢) +   = 80¢

b)   *How many nickels?*

(25¢) (5¢) +   = 40¢

c)   *How many dimes?*

(10¢) (10¢) +   = 40¢

d)   *How many quarters?*

(25¢) (25¢) +   = 100¢

BONUS:

7. Draw the additional coins needed to make each total. You can only use **two** coins for each question, such as: (i) a penny & a nickel, (ii) a penny & a dime or (iii) a nickel & a dime:

a) 21¢ (10¢)

b) 35¢ (10¢) (5¢)

c) 50¢ (25¢) (10¢)

d) 17¢ (5¢) (1¢)

e) 31¢ (10¢) (1¢)

f) 65¢ (25¢) (25¢)

8. Draw the number of additional coins needed to make each total. You can only use **two** coins for each question, either a loonie or a toonie:

a) $5 ($2)

b) $7 ($2) ($2)

c) $3 ($1)

d) $10 ($2) ($2) ($2) ($1)

e) $8 ($2) ($2)

f) $6 ($2) ($1)

Answer the following questions in a notebook.

9. Draw a picture to show the **extra** coins each child will need. Try to use the fewest coins:

   a) Tashi has 25¢. He wants to buy a pencil for 45¢.

   b) Rosie has 19¢. She wants to buy a pen for 35¢.

   c) Zoltan has 3 quarters, a dime, and a nickel. He wants to buy a notebook for 98¢.

   d) Jane has 3 toonies. She wants to buy a plant for ten dollars.

   e) Marzuk has 2 toonies and a loonie. He wants to buy a book for seven dollars and twenty five cents.

10. Can you make 80¢ using only: a) dimes and quarters?   b) nickels and quarters?   Explain.

11. Make up a problem like one of the problems in Question 9 and solve it.

Measurement 1

ME4-21: Least Number of Coins

1. Use the least number of coins to make the totals:

   HINT: Start by seeing how many dimes you need.

   a) 12¢   (10¢)(1¢)(1¢) *correct*
            (5¢)(5¢)(1¢)(1¢) *incorrect*

   b) 16¢

   c) 22¢

   d) 23¢

2. Use the least number of coins to make the totals:

   a) 15¢

   b) 20¢

3. Use the least number of coins to make the totals:

   HINT: Start by seeing how many dimes you need (if any), then nickels and then pennies.

   a) 17¢

   b) 24¢

   c) 11¢

   d) 15¢

   e) 19¢

   f) 17¢

4. Fill in the amounts: a) 2 quarters = _____ ¢   b) 3 quarters = _____ ¢   c) 4 quarters = _____ ¢

5. What is the greatest amount you could pay in quarters without exceeding the amount? (Draw the quarters to show your answer.)

Amount	Greatest amount you could pay in quarters	Amount	Greatest amount you could pay in quarters
a) 35¢		b) 53¢	
c) 78¢		d) 83¢	
e) 59¢		f) 64¢	
g) 49¢		h) 31¢	
i) 82¢		j) 95¢	
k) 29¢		l) 72¢	

Measurement 1

6. Find the greatest amount you could pay in quarters. (Represent the amount remaining using the least number of coins.)

Amount	Amount Paid in Quarters	Amount Remaining	Amount Remaining in Coins
a) 83¢	75¢	83¢ - 75¢ = 8¢	5¢ 1¢ 1¢ 1¢
b) 56¢			
c) 33¢			
d) 85¢			
e) 97¢			

7. Use the **least** number of coins to make the totals. The first one is done for you:

   HINT: Start by finding the greatest amount you can make in quarters, as in Question 6.

a) 30¢ 10 10 10 *incorrect* 25 5¢ *correct*	b) 76¢
c) 40¢	d) 53¢

  Answer the remaining questions in a notebook.

8. Show how you could make 55¢ using the least number of coins. Use play money to help you.

9. Trade coins to make each amount with the least amount of coins.   Draw a picture to show your final answer:

a) 5¢ 5¢ 5¢ 10¢	b) 25¢ 25¢ 25¢ 25¢	c) 5¢ 5¢ $1 $1
d) 10¢ 10¢ 5¢ $1	e) 25¢ 10¢ 5¢ $2 25¢ 10¢ 25¢ 25¢	
f) 10¢ 10¢ 5¢ $1 $1 $1 $1 1¢ 1¢ 1¢ 1¢ 1¢		

10. Show how you could trade the amounts for the least number of coins:

   a) 5 quarters   b) 4 dimes and 2 nickels   c) 6 loonies

   d) 7 loonies and 5 dimes   e) 9 loonies, 6 dimes, 2 nickels and 5 pennies

The charts show how to represent money in cent notation and in dollar notation.

	Cent Notation	Dollar (Decimal) Notation
Sixty-five cents	65¢	$0.65
		dimes *pennies*

	Cent Notation	Dollar (Decimal) Notation
Seven cents	7¢	$0.07
		dimes *pennies*

A dime is a **tenth** of a dollar. A penny is a **hundredth** of a dollar.

----

1. Write the total amount of money in cent and in dollar (decimal) notation:

a)

dimes	pennies
3	4

= __34__ ¢ = $ __0.34__

b)

dimes	pennies
0	5

= _____ ¢ = $ _____

c)

dimes	pennies
4	3

= _____ ¢ = $ _____

d)

dimes	pennies
8	7

= _____ ¢ = $ _____

e)

dimes	pennies
5	4

= _____ ¢ = $ _____

f)

dimes	pennies
0	9

= _____ ¢ = $ _____

g)

dimes	pennies
0	2

= _____ ¢ = $ _____

h)

dimes	pennies
7	5

= _____ ¢ = $ _____

i)

dimes	pennies
0	1

= _____ ¢ = $ _____

2. Count the given coins and write the total amount in cents and in dollar (decimal) notation:

a) 10¢ 10¢ 5¢ 5¢ 1¢ 1¢ 1¢

Total amount = _____ ¢ = $ _____

b) 25¢ 10¢ 10¢ 1¢ 1¢

Total amount = _____ ¢ = $ _____

c) 25¢ 25¢ 10¢ 10¢ 5¢ 1¢

Total amount = _____ ¢ = $ _____

d) 25¢ 25¢ 25¢ 10¢

Total amount = _____ ¢ = $ _____

e) 25¢ 10¢ 10¢ 10¢ 10¢ 5¢ 1¢

Total amount = _____ ¢ = $ _____

f) 25¢ 10¢ 10¢ 5¢ 5¢ 1¢ 1¢

Total amount = _____ ¢ = $ _____

BONUS:

g) 25¢ 25¢ 10¢ 10¢ 10¢ 5¢ 1¢ 1¢ 1¢

Total amount = _____ ¢ = $ _____

ME4-23: More Dollar and Cent Notation

1. Complete the chart:

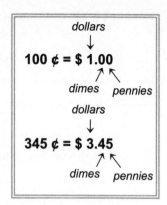

	Amount in ¢	Dollars	Dimes	Pennies	Amount in $
a)	143¢	1	4	3	$ 1.43
b)	47¢				
c)	325¢				
d)	3¢				
e)	816¢				

2. Write each amount in cent notation. The first one is done for you:

a) $3.00 = ___300¢___   b) $0.60 = _____   c) $0.08 = _____   d) $1.00 = _____

e) $7.00 = _____   f) $12.00 = _____   g) $15.00 = _____   h) $14.00 = _____

i) $1.99 = _____   j) $1.11 = _____   k) $1.51 = _____   l) $1.37 = _____

m) $0.98 = _____   n) $0.55 = _____   o) $0.03 = _____   p) $0.08 = _____

3. Write each amount in dollar notation. The first is done for you:

a) 254¢ = ___$2.54___   b) 103¢ = _____   c) 216¢ = _____   d) 375¢ = _____

e) 300¢ = _____   f) 4¢ = _____   g) 7¢ = _____   h) 90¢ = _____

i) 600¢ = _____   j) 1000¢ = _____   k) 1200¢ = _____   l) 1600¢ = _____

m) 64¢ = _____   n) 99¢ = _____   o) 3¢ = _____   p) 56¢ = _____

4. Complete each pattern by counting by the type of coin or paper money pictured. Write your answers in cent notation and in dollar notation:

a)   b)

___25¢___ , _____ , _____ , _____ , _____   ___200¢___ , _____ , _____ , _____ , _____

___$ .25___ , _____ , _____ , _____ , _____   ___$ 2.00___ , _____ , _____ , _____ , _____

c)   d)

_____ , _____ , _____   _____ , _____ , _____ , _____

_____ , _____ , _____   _____ , _____ , _____ , _____

Dollar notation and **cent notation** are related in the following way:

$1.00 = 100¢ $0.50 = 50¢ $0.05 = 5¢ $3.82 = 382¢

----

1. Change the amount in dollar notation to cent notation. Then circle the greater amount of money in each pair:

   a) 175¢   or $1.73   b) $1.00   or   101¢   c) 6¢   or $0.04

   d) $5.98   or   597¢   e) 650¢   or $6.05   f) $0.87   or   187¢

2. Write each amount in dollar notation. Then circle the greater amount of money in each pair:

   a) three dollars and eighty five cents   or   three dollars and twenty eight cents

   _____   _____

   b) nine dollars and seventy cents   or   nine dollars and eighty two cents

   _____   _____

   c) eight dollars and seventy five cents   or   863¢

   _____   _____

   d) twelve dollars and sixty cents   or $12.06

   _____   _____

3. How much money would you have if you had the following coins? Write your answer in cent notation then in dollar notation. The first question is done for you:

   a) 7 pennies = __7¢__ = __$ .07__   b) 4 nickels = _____ = _____   c) 6 dimes = _____ = _____

   d) 4 pennies = _____ = _____   e) 13 pennies = _____ = _____   f) 1 quarter = _____ = _____

   g) 5 nickels = _____ = _____   h) 3 quarters = _____ = _____   i) 8 dimes = _____ = _____

   j) 6 toonies = _____ = _____   k) 4 loonies = _____ = _____   l) 7 loonies = _____ = _____

4. Which is a greater amount of money: 168¢ or $1.65? Explain: _____

   _____

1. Calculate the change owing for each purchase. Subtract the amounts by counting up on your fingers if necessary:

   a) Price of a pencil = 42¢
      Amount paid = 50¢

      Change = _____

   b) Price of an eraser = 34¢
      Amount paid = 50¢

      Change = _____

   c) Price of a sharpener = 81¢
      Amount paid = 90¢

      Change = _____

   d) Price of a ruler = 56¢
      Amount paid = 60¢

      Change = _____

   e) Price of a marker = 78¢
      Amount paid = 80¢

      Change = _____

   f) Price of a notebook = 63¢
      Amount paid = 70¢

      Change = _____

   g) Price of a folder = 67¢
      Amount paid = 70¢

      Change = _____

   h) Price of a juice box = 49¢
      Amount paid = 50¢

      Change = _____

   i) Price of a freezie = 26¢
      Amount paid = 30¢

      Change = _____

2. Count up by 10s to find the change owing from a dollar (100¢):

Price Paid	Change	Price Paid	Change	Price Paid	Change
a) 90¢		d) 40¢		g) 20¢	
b) 70¢		e) 10¢		h) 60¢	
c) 50¢		f) 30¢		i) 80¢	

3. Find the change owing for each purchase:
   HINT: Count up by 10s.

   a) Price of a lollipop = 50¢
      Amount paid = $1.00

      Change = _____

   b) Price of an eraser = 60¢
      Amount paid = $1.00

      Change = _____

   c) Price of an apple = 30¢
      Amount paid = $1.00

      Change = _____

   d) Price of a banana = 60¢
      Amount paid = $1.00

      Change = _____

   e) Price of a patty = 80¢
      Amount paid = $1.00

      Change = _____

   f) Price of a pencil = 20¢
      Amount paid = $1.00

      Change = _____

   g) Price of a gumball = 10¢
      Amount paid = $1.00

      Change = _____

   h) Price of a juice = 40¢
      Amount paid = $1.00

      Change = _____

   i) Price of a popsicle = 70¢
      Amount paid = $1.00

      Change = _____

4. Find the smallest 2-digit number ending in zero (i.e. 10, 20, 30, 40, ...) that is **greater** than the number given. Write your answer in the box provided:

   a) 72 [80]   b) 54 [   ]   c) 47 [   ]   d) 26 [   ]   e) 58 [   ]   f) 7 [   ]

5. Make change from $1.00 for the numbers written below. Follow the steps shown for 17¢:

Step 1:   Find the smallest multiple of 10 greater than 17¢.   17¢ ⟶ 20¢

Step 2:   Find the differences: 20 – 17 *and* 100 – 20   17¢ —³→ 20¢ —⁸⁰→ 100¢

Step 3:   Add the differences: 3¢ + 80¢   **Change = 83¢**

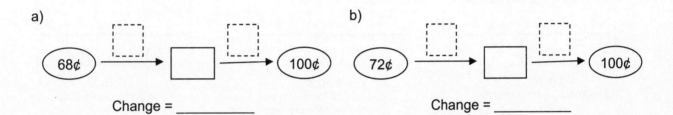

a) 68¢ ⟶ ☐ ⟶ 100¢

Change = _____

b) 72¢ ⟶ ☐ ⟶ 100¢

Change = _____

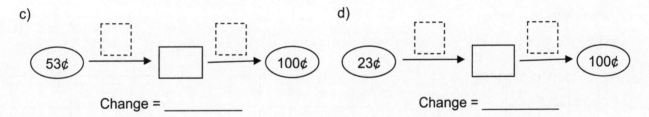

c) 53¢ ⟶ ☐ ⟶ 100¢

Change = _____

d) 23¢ ⟶ ☐ ⟶ 100¢

Change = _____

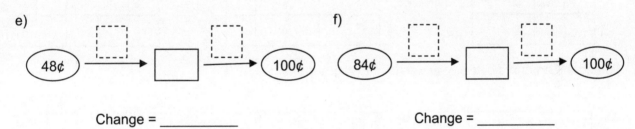

e) 48¢ ⟶ ☐ ⟶ 100¢

Change = _____

f) 84¢ ⟶ ☐ ⟶ 100¢

Change = _____

6. Find change from 100¢ for the following. Try to do the work in your head:

a) 58¢ _____   b) 64¢ _____   c) 27¢ _____   d) 36¢ _____   e) 52¢ _____

f) 29¢ _____   g) 97¢ _____   h) 14¢ _____   i) 89¢ _____   j) 91¢ _____

BONUS:

7. Find the change for the following amount in your head:

a) Price: 37¢   Amount paid: 50¢

    Change required: _____

b) Price: 58¢   Amount paid: 75¢

    Change required: _____

ME4-26: Adding Money

1. Add:

a) 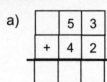 b) 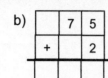 c) 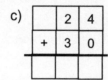 d) 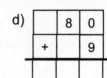 e)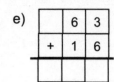

2. Shelly spent $12.50 on a blouse and $4.35 on a pair of socks.
To find out how much she spent, she added the amounts using the following steps:

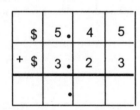 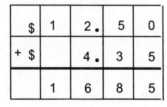 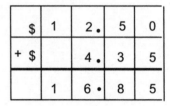

Step 1:
She lined up the numerals.

Step 2:
She added the numerals, starting with the pennies.

Step 3:
She added a decimal point to show the amount in dollars.

Find the total by adding:

a) $5.45 + $3.23   b) $22.26 + $15.23   c) $18.16 + $20.32

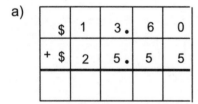 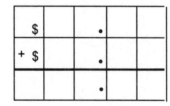 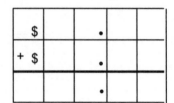

3. To add the amounts below, you will have to regroup:

a) 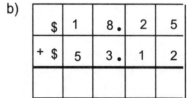 b) 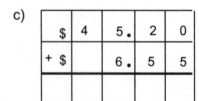 c)

d) 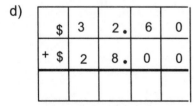 e) 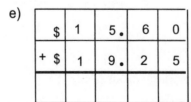 f)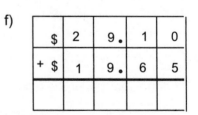

Answer the following questions in a notebook.

4. Ari paid 23¢ for a doughnut and 35¢ for an apple.
   How much did he spend in total?

5. Alan bought a book for $14.25 and a box of candles for $10.14.
   How much did he spend in total?

6. Add: a) $14.72 + $15.29   b) $23.75 + $32.18   c) $67.60 + $22.53

7. From her babysitting job, Meera saved 6 toonies, 5 dimes and 3 pennies.
   Kyle saved a 5 dollar bill, 3 toonies, 2 dimes and 4 pennies from his.
   Who saved more money?

8. Four children bought dogs at an animal shelter. The chart shows the price of each dog (with tax):

   ✓ Anthony paid for his dog with 2 twenty dollar bills, 1 toonie, 1 loonie, 2 quarters and 1 nickel.

   ✓ Mike paid with 2 ten dollar bills, 8 toonies and 1 quarter.

   ✓ Sandor paid with 1 twenty and 1 ten dollar bill, 1 loonie and 3 quarters.

   ✓ Tory paid with 2 twenty dollar bills, 4 toonies, 1 loonie and 3 dimes.

   Find the amount each child paid. Then match their names with the dog they bought:

Dog A	Dog B	Dog C	Dog D	Dog E	Dog F
$ 31.75	$ 49.30	$42.68	$ 44.34	$ 36.25	$ 43.55

9. Mansa has $18.

   a) If she spends $12.00 on a movie, can she buy a magazine, for $3.29?

   b) If she buys a book for $7.50 and a cap for $9.00, can she buy a subway ticket for $2.25?

10. Try to find the answer mentally:

   a) How much do 3 roses cost at $1.25 each?

   b) How many lemons costing 30¢ could you buy with $1.00?

   c) Sketch pads cost $5.25. How many could you buy if you had $26.00?

1. Find the remaining amount by subtracting:

a)
$	2 .	8	4
− $	1 .	3	1

b)
$	7 .	2	9
− $	4 .	0	5

c)
$	9 .	6	7
− $	4 .	2	6

d)
$	7 .	8	6
− $	5 .	2	3

e)
$	5 .	5	4
− $	3 .	3	4

2. Subtract the given money amounts by regrouping once or twice:

Example:

Step 1
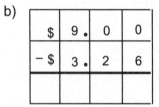

Step 2
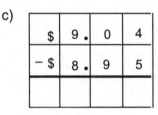

a)
$	7 .	0	0
− $	4 .	4	5

b)
$	9 .	0	0
− $	3 .	2	6

c)
$	9 .	0	4
− $	8 .	9	5

d)
$	5	3 .	0	0
− $	2	2 .	3	1

e)
$	4	7 .	4	5
− $	3	8 .	4	5

f)
$	2	7 .	4	8
− $	1	3 .	6	6

 Answer the following questions in a notebook.

3. Val has $1.85. He lends $1.45 to his friend.
   How much money does he have left?

4. Chris spent $4.23 on his lunch.
   He paid with a five dollar bill. Calculate his change.

5. Betty has $6.75 and Karen has $4.23.
   How much more money does Betty have than Karen?

6. Anya went to a grocery store with $10.00.
   Can she buy bread for $2.50, juice for $4.00 and cereal for $4.50?
   If not, by how much is she short?

7. Mark has $25.00.
   He wants to buy a shirt for $14.95 and pants for $16.80.
   How much extra money does he need to buy the pants and shirt?

PARENT:
Review the meaning of the terms "less than," "greater than," "odd," "even," "multiples of 2," and "multiples of 3" before your child completes this worksheet.

REMEMBER:
Zero is an even number and is also a multiple of any number.

----

1. Write the numbers from 0 to 9 in order:

2. Write all the numbers from 0 to 9 that are:

   a) greater than 5

   b) greater than 4

   c) less than 5

   d) less than 7

   e) greater than 7

   f) less than 8

   g) even numbers

   h) odd numbers

   i) multiples of 4

   j) multiples of 2

   k) multiples of 3

   l) multiples of 7

3. Make two lists to find the numbers from 0 to 9 that are:

   a) **even numbers smaller than 7**

      (i) even numbers: (0) , (2) , (4) , (6) , 8

      (ii) numbers less than 7: (0) , 1, (2) , 3, (4) , 5, (6)

      Answer: **0, 2, 4, 6**

   b) **odd numbers greater than 4**

      (i) odd numbers:

      (ii) numbers greater than 4:

      Answer:

Show your work for the remaining questions in a notebook.

   c) odd numbers less than 8

   d) even numbers less than 9

   e) even numbers greater than 3

   f) multiples of 4

   g) odd numbers that are multiples of 3

   h) odd numbers greater than 4 and less than 8

Logic and Systematic Search

Many problems in mathematics and science have more than one solution.

If a problem involves two quantities, list the values of one quantity in increasing order.
Then you won't miss any solutions.

For instance, to find all the ways you can make 35¢ with dimes and nickels, start by assuming you have no dimes, then 1 dime, and so on up to 3 dimes (4 would be too many).

In each case, count on by 5s to 35 to find out how many nickels you need to make 35¢:

Step 1:

dimes	nickels
0	
1	
2	
3	

Step 2:

dimes	nickels
0	7
1	5
2	3
3	1

----

1. Fill in the amount of pennies, nickels, or dimes you need to:

a) make 19¢

dimes	pennies
0	
1	
2	

b) make 45¢

dimes	nickels
0	
1	
2	
3	
4	

c) make 24¢

nickels	pennies
0	
1	
2	
3	
4	

d) make 35¢

dimes	nickels
0	
1	
2	
3	

e) make 80¢

quarters	nickels
0	
1	
2	
3	

f) make 95¢

quarters	nickels
0	
1	
2	
3	

2.

quarters	nickels
0	
1	
2	

Kyle wants to find all the ways he can make 55¢ using quarters and nickels. He lists the number of quarters in increasing order. Why did he stop at 2 quarters?

_____

_____

No unauthorized copying   **Logic and Systematic Search**

3. Fill in the amount of pennies, nickels, dimes, or quarters you need to:

   HINT: You may not need to use all of the rows.

a) make 13¢

dimes	pennies

b) make 35¢

dimes	nickels

c) make 80¢

quarters	nickels

PARENT:

Give your child practice at questions like the one below before you allow them to continue.

4. Birds have 2 legs, cats have 4 legs, and ants have 6 legs. Complete the charts to find out how many legs each combination of 2 animals has:

a)

birds	cats	total number of legs
0	2	
1	1	
2	0	

b)

birds	ants	total number of legs
0	2	
1	1	
2	0	

5. Fill in the charts to find the solution to each problem:

a)

birds	dogs	total number of legs

2 pets have a total of 6 legs.
Each pet is either a bird or a dog.
How many birds and dogs?

b)

birds	cats	total number of legs

3 pets have a total of 8 legs.
Each pet is either a bird or cat.
How many birds and cats?

1. Pick two numbers, one from each of the boxes to the right, so that:

    a) the product of the two numbers is smallest: _____ × _____ = _____

    b) the product is the greatest: _____ × _____ = _____

    c) the product is closest to 20: _____ × _____ = _____

    d) the difference between the numbers is smallest: _____ – _____ = _____

2. A frog takes two long jumps (of equal length) and
    two shorter jumps (of equal length):

    What lengths could the first and last jumps be if the frog jumps a total distance of:

    a) 10 metres? _____

    b) 16 metres? _____

Answer the remaining questions in a notebook.

3. Show all the ways you can colour the flag with red (R), green (G), and blue (B), using one block of
    each colour:

4. Using the numbered boxes above, show all the ways you can make a stack of **two** boxes so that a
    box with a lower number never sits on top of a box with a higher number:

    | 1 | | 2 | | 3 | | 4 |

5. Crayons come in boxes of 4 or 5. Can you buy a combination of boxes that contain:
    NOTE: For some of these questions, you needn't buy boxes of both types. **Show your work.**

    a) 8 crayons?

    b) 10 crayons?

    c) 11 crayons?

    d) 14 crayons?

    e) 17 crayons?

    f) 18 crayons?

    g) 19 crayons?

    h) 21 crayons?

No unauthorized copying **Logic and Systematic Search**

Marie is on a bicycle tour 300 km from home. She can cycle 75 km each day.

She starts riding towards home on Tuesday morning.
How far away from home will she be by Thursday evening?

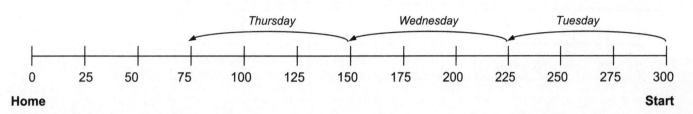

On Thursday evening, Marie will be 75 km from home.

- -

1. On Wednesday morning, Ryan's campsite is 20 km from Mount Currie in British Columbia.

    He plans to walk 6 km towards the mountain each day.

    How far from the mountain will he be on Thursday evening? _____

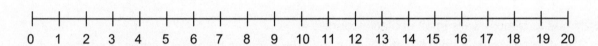

2. Jane is camping 50 km from her home. She can cycle 15 km every hour.

    How far from home will she be after 3 hours? _____

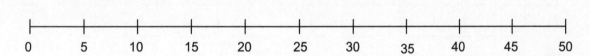

Draw and label a number line in the grid to solve the following problems.

3. Midori is 16 blocks from home. She can bike 4 blocks in a minute.

    How far from home will she be after 3 minutes? _____

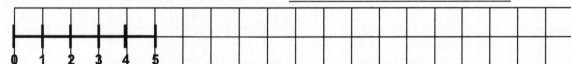

4. Tom lives 12 blocks from the park. He can rollerblade 2 blocks per minute.

    How many minutes will it take him to rollerblade to the park? _____

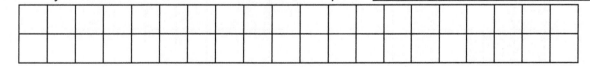

In the questions below, you will have to decide on a scale for your number lines.

1. James has entered a 250 km bicycle race. He can cycle 75 km each day.

   How far from the finish will he be after 3 days? _____

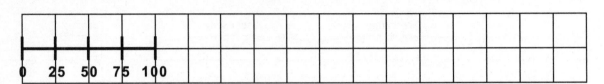

   0   25   50   75   100

2. Sudha is typing an essay. It is 250 words long. She can type 25 words per minute.

   How long does she take to type the whole assignment? _____

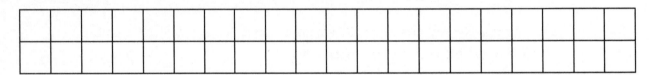

3. Wendy has to climb 5 walls in an obstacle course.

   The 1st wall is 100 metres from the start. After that, each wall is 50 metres further than the last.

   How far from the start is the 3rd wall? _____

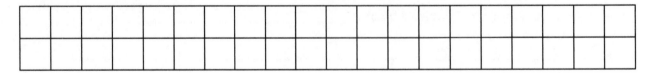

4. Daniel plants 5 rose bushes in a row.

   The nearest bush is 10 metres from his house. The bushes are 5 m apart.

   How far away from Daniel's house is the last bush? _____

   HINT: Put Daniel's house at zero on the number line.

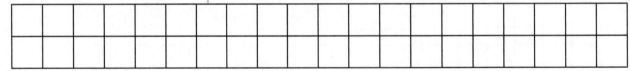

5. A painter's ladder has 12 steps. The painter spills red paint on every second step and blue paint on every third step. Which steps have red and blue paint on them?

PA4-14: Describing and Creating Patterns

In this sequence, each number is greater than the one before it.
The sequence is always **increasing**:

7 , 8 , 10 , 15 , 21

In this sequence, each number is less than the one before it.
The sequence is always **decreasing**:

25 , 23 , 18 , 11 , 8

In this sequence, the numbers **increase** and **decrease**.
The **+** signs show where the sequence increases.
The **−** signs show where it decreases:

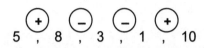

5 , 8 , 3 , 1 , 10

----

1. Write a **+** sign in the circle to show where the sequence **increases**.
   Write a **−** sign to show where it **decreases**.

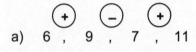

a) 6 , 9 , 7 , 11   b) 1 , 5 , 7 , 2   c) 10 , 7 , 6 , 8

d) 2 , 5 , 1 , 7   e) 5 , 3 , 9 , 8   f) 2 , 5 , 9 , 12

g) 2 , 7 , 4 , 9   h) 11 , 15 , 18 , 13   i) 18 , 13 , 11 , 23

j) 28 , 36 , 49 , 52   k) 17 , 38 , 29 , 85   l) 53 , 64 , 96 , 98

2. Write a **+** sign in the circle to show where the sequence **increases**.
   Write a **−** sign to show where it **decreases**. Then write:

> an **A** beside the sequence if it **increases**
>
> a **B** beside the sequence if it **decreases**
>
> a **C** beside the sequence if it **increases** and **decreases**.

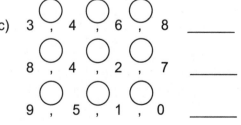

a) 4 , 8 , 3 , 7   _C_

2 , 8 , 9 , 11 _____

10 , 9 , 4 , 1 _____

c) 3 , 4 , 6 , 8 _____

8 , 4 , 2 , 7 _____

9 , 5 , 1 , 0 _____

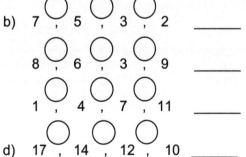

b) 7 , 5 , 3 , 2 _____

8 , 6 , 3 , 9 _____

1 , 4 , 7 , 11 _____

d) 17 , 14 , 12 , 10 _____

20 , 24 , 15 , 29 _____

23 , 29 , 34 , 40 _____

Patterns & Algebra 2

1. Find the **amount** by which the sequence **increases** or **decreases**.
    (Write a number with a **+** sign if the sequence increases, and a **–** sign if it decreases.)

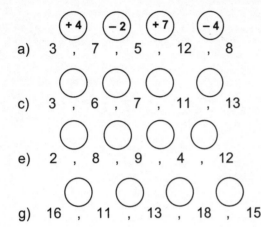

a) 3 , 7 , 5 , 12 , 8   (+4)(−2)(+7)(−4)

b) 2 , 5 , 4 , 8 , 5

c) 3 , 6 , 7 , 11 , 13

d) 4 , 2 , 6 , 2 , 9

e) 2 , 8 , 9 , 4 , 12

f) 18 , 15 , 11 , 13 , 12

g) 16 , 11 , 13 , 18 , 15

h) 28 , 31 , 24 , 31 , 38

2. Match each sequence with the sentence that describes it. This sequence:

a) A   increases by 3 each time.
    B   increases by different amounts.

    ____   9 , 12 , 15 , 18 , 21

    ____   7 , 10 , 13 , 14 , 19

b) A   increases by 4 each time.
    B   increases by different amounts.

    ____   6 , 10 , 14 , 17 , 21

    ____   5 , 9 , 13 , 17 , 21

c) A   decreases by 5 each time.
    B   decreases by different amounts.

    ____   35 , 30 , 25 , 20 , 15

    ____   30 , 25 , 20 , 15 , 5

d) A   decreases by different amounts.
    B   decreases by the same amount.

    ____   10 , 9 , 8 , 6 , 5

    ____   11 , 10 , 9 , 8 , 7

BONUS:

e) A   increases by 5 each time.
    B   decreases by different amounts.
    C   increases by different amounts.

    ____   17 , 22 , 28 , 32 , 34

    ____   17 , 14 , 10 , 9 , 6

    ____   14 , 19 , 24 , 29 , 34

f) A   increases and decreases.
    B   increases by the same amount.
    C   decreases by different amounts.
    D   decreases by the same amount.

    ____   21 , 19 , 15 , 13 , 9

    ____   10 , 13 , 9 , 7 , 5

    ____   19 , 17 , 15 , 13 , 11

    ____   9 , 12 , 15 , 18 , 21

3. Write a rule for each pattern. Use the words **add** or **subtract**, and be sure to say what number the pattern starts with:

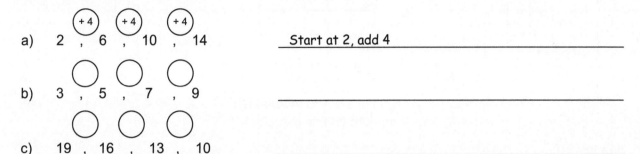

a)   2 , 6 , 10 , 14   <u>Start at 2, add 4</u>

b)   3 , 5 , 7 , 9   _____

c)   19 , 16 , 13 , 10   _____

4. Write a rule for each pattern:
   NOTE: One sequence doesn't have a rule – see if you can find it.

   a)   8 , 11 , 14 , 17   _____

   b)   14 , 10 , 6 , 2   _____

   c)   25 , 21 , 18 , 17 , 11   _____

   d)   61 , 65 , 69 , 73   _____

5. Describe each pattern as **increasing**, **decreasing** or **repeating**:

   a) 1 , 4 , 7 , 10 , 13 , 16   _____   b) 1 , 5 , 8 , 1 , 5 , 8   _____

   c) 9 , 8 , 7 , 6 , 5 , 4   _____   d) 2 , 4 , 6 , 8 , 10 , 12   _____

   e) 3 , 8 , 3 , 8 , 3 , 8   _____   f) 21 , 16 , 10 , 7 , 5 , 1   _____

Answer the following questions in a notebook.

6. Write the first 5 numbers in each of the patterns described:
   a) Start at 6, add 3   b) Start at 26, subtract 4   c) Start at 39, add 5

7. Create an increasing number pattern. Give the rule for your pattern.

8. Create a decreasing number pattern. Give the rule for your pattern.

9. Create a repeating pattern using: a) letters   b) shapes   c) numbers

10. Create a pattern and ask a friend to find the rule for your pattern.

1.

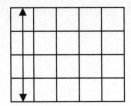 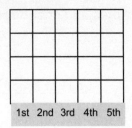 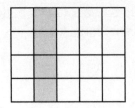

Columns run up and down.

Columns are numbered left to right (in this exercise).

The 2nd column is shaded.

Shade:

a)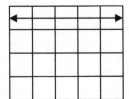

the 1st column.

b)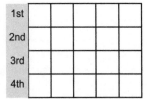

the 5th column.

c)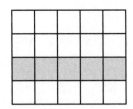

the 3rd column.

d)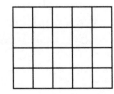

the 4th column.

2.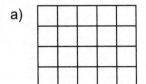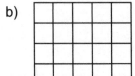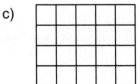

Rows run sideways.

Rows are numbered from top to bottom (in this exercise).

The 3rd row is shaded.

Shade:

a)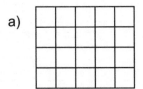

the 2nd row.

b)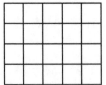

the 4th row.

c)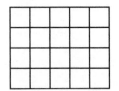

the 1st row.

d)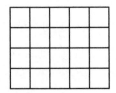

the 3rd row.

3. Shade:

a)

2	4	6
8	10	12
14	16	18

the 2nd row.

b)

2	4	6
8	10	12
14	16	18

the 1st column.

c)

2	4	6
8	10	12
14	16	18

the 3rd column.

d)

2	4	6
8	10	12
14	16	18

the diagonals.
(one is shaded)

 4. In a notebook, describe the pattern in the numbers you shaded for each part of Question 3.

Describe the patterns you see in each chart below
(remember to look horizontally, vertically and diagonally).

You should use the words "rows," "columns" and
"diagonals" in your answers:

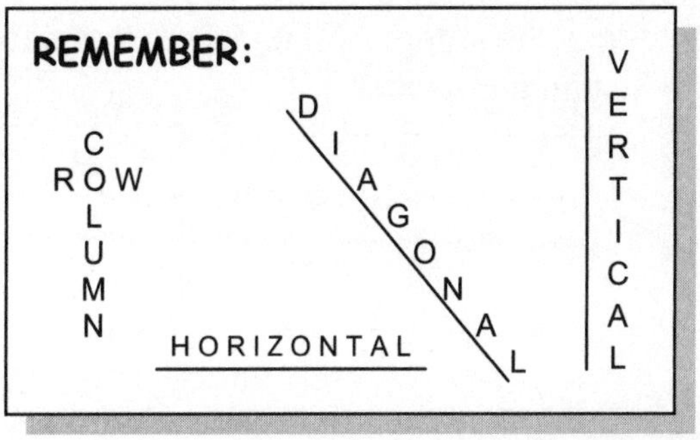

REMEMBER:

C
R O W
O
L
U
M
N

HORIZONTAL

D
I
A
G
O
N
A
L

V
E
R
T
I
C
A
L

5.

2	4	6
4	6	8
6	8	10

6.

12	15	18	21
9	12	15	18
6	9	12	15
3	6	9	12

7. Complete the multiplication chart.

×	1	2	3	4	5	6
1	1	2				
2		4				
3		6				
4						
5						
6						

Describe the patterns you see in the rows, columns and
diagonals of the chart:

1. Place the letters A, B and C so that each row and each column has exactly one A, one B and one C in it (in any order):

2. Place the letters A and B so that each row and each column has two As and two Bs in it:

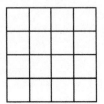

3.

Row 1	L	R	T	T	L
Row 2	R	T	T		
Row 3					
Row 4					
Row 5					
Row 6					
Row 7					

A gardener plants roses (R), lilies (L) and tulips (T) in rows in the pattern shown to the left:

a) Complete the chart.

b) In which row will the pattern in the second row be repeated?

_____

4. a) Shade every third square on a hundreds chart. **(These are the multiples of 3.)**
   How can you describe the position of the squares you shaded?

   b) Mark every fifth square on the same chart with an "X." **(These are the multiples of 5.)**

   c) Write out the numbers between 1 and 100 that are **multiples** of 3 and 5.
   Describe the pattern in the tens digits and in the ones digits of the numbers.

5. The "multiples of 3" are also called the numbers that are "divisible by 3."
   Complete the chart below by inserting the whole numbers from 1 to 20 into the correct boxes:

	Less than 11	Greater than or equal to 11
Divisible by 3		
Not divisible by 3		

6. Here are some number pyramids:

   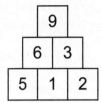

Can you find the rule by which the patterns in the pyramids were made? Describe it here:

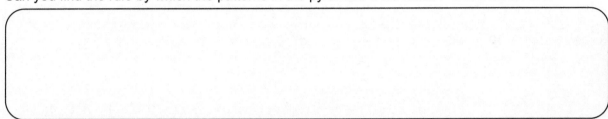

7. Using the rule you described in Question 6, find the missing numbers:

a)   b)   c)   d)   e)

f) 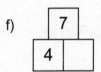   g)   h) 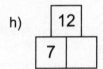   i)   j)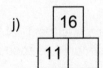

k) 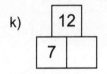   l)   m)   n)   o)

BONUS:

p) 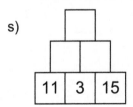   q) 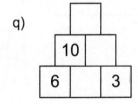   r)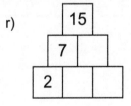

s) 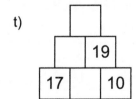   t) 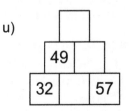   u)

1. In the sequences below, the step or gap between the numbers increases. Can you see a pattern in the way the gap increases? Use the pattern to extend the sequence:

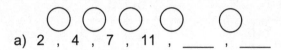

a) 2 , 4 , 7 , 11 , ___ , ___

b) 3 , 4 , 6 , 9 , 13 , ___ , ___

c) 11 , 14 , 19 , 26 , ___ , ___

d) 6 , 8 , 12 , 18 , 26 , ___ , ___

e) 17 , 16 , 14 , 11 , ___ , ___

f) 32 , 30 , 26 , 20 , ___ , ___

g) 31 , 30 , 27 , 22 , ___ , ___

h) 110 , 105 , 95 , 80 , 60 , ___ , ___

2. Complete the T-table for the 3rd and 4th figures. Then use the pattern in the gap to predict the number of squares needed for the 5th and 6th figures:

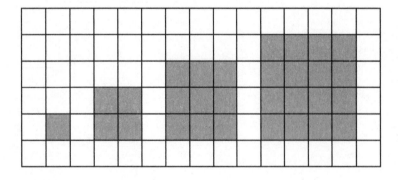

Figure	Number of Squares
1	1
2	4
3	
4	
5	
6	

Write the number of squares added each time here

3. In a notebook, make a T- table to predict how many squares will be needed for the 5th figure:

Figure 1   Figure 2   Figure 3

PA4-19: Advanced Patterns

1. Ahmed made a pattern starting at 2:

    2, 4, 8, 16, ____, ____, ____, ____

    a) What number did Ahmed multiply each term by to get the next term? _____

    b) Continue Ahmed's pattern.

    c) Find the gap between the numbers. What do you notice? _____

2. Olivia and Krishna save the amounts shown in the chart below:

Week	Olivia	Krishna
1	$1	$15
2	$2	$20
3	$4	$25
4	$8	$30
5		
6		
7		

    a) What is the pattern rule for the amount Krishna saves?

    _____

    b) What is the pattern rule for the amount Olivia saves?

    _____

    c) Who do you think will save more by the end of the
        seven weeks?

    _____

    d) Continue the patterns in the chart. Were you right?

    _____

3. **3 , 6 , 4 , 7 , 5 , 8 , _____ , _____ , ____**

    a) Describe how the gap changes in the pattern above: _____

    _____

    b) Fill in the blanks to continue the pattern.

 Answer the remaining questions in a notebook.

4. Make a T-table to predict how many dots will
    be needed for the 6th figure:

    Figure 1   Figure 2   Figure 3

5. Jane runs for 10 minutes on Monday. Each day after that she trains for 2 minutes longer.
    How many minutes in all did she run in the first four days?

PA4-20: Patterns with Larger Numbers

1. Use addition or multiplication to complete the following charts:
   REMEMBER: There are 60 seconds in a minute, 52 weeks in a year, and 365 days in a year.

a)

Minutes	Seconds
1	60
2	
3	
4	
5	

b)

Years	Weeks
1	52
2	
3	
4	

c)

Years	Days
1	365
2	
3	
4	

Using T-tables, solve the following problems in a notebook.

2. There are 12 months in a year.
   How many months are there in 4 years?

3. A rabbit's heart beats 200 times a minute.
   How many times will it beat in 5 minutes?

4. A blue goose can fly 1500 km in 2 days.
   How far can it fly in 6 days?

5. Miguel earns $18 for the first hour he works.
   He earns $16 for each hour after that.
   How much will he earn for 5 hours of work?

6. Halley's comet returns to Earth every 76 years. It was last seen in 1986.
   List the next three dates it will return to Earth.

7. Use multiplication or a calculator to find the first few products. Look for a pattern. Use the pattern to fill in the rest of the numbers:

a)   999 × 2 = _____

   999 × 3 = _____

   999 × 4 = _____

   _____ = _____

   _____ = _____

b)   6 × 9 = _____

   6 × 99 = _____

   6 × 999 = _____

   _____ = _____

   _____ = _____

BONUS:
8. Using a calculator, can you discover any patterns like the ones in Question 7?

Patterns & Algebra 2

PA4-21: Problems and Puzzles

PARENT:
Give your child a copy of the hundreds charts and the calendars in the front of this book, and some grid paper for drawing number lines and T-tables. Let your child decide which tool they should use for each question.

Show your work for the questions below in a notebook.

1.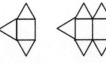

   Figure 1   Figure 2   Figure 3

   How many triangles will be needed for the 6th figure?

2. April 1st is a Monday.
   Andrea has a piano lesson every 5th day of the month, starting on April 5th.
   Peter has a lesson every Friday.
   On what dates in April do they have lessons together?

3. Sue makes ornaments using squares and triangles.
   She has 12 squares.

   a) How many triangles will she need to use to make ornaments with all 12 squares?

   b) How did you solve the problem? Did you use a T-table? A picture? A model?

4. Hank has to climb 7 walls in an obstacle course.
   The 1st wall is 200 metres from the start.
   After that, each wall is 50 metres further than the last.
   How far from the start is the 5th wall?

   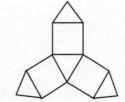

5. Continue the patterns:

   a) [rectangle] [hexagon] [rectangle] [hexagon] ____ ____

   b) K Q A 10 K Q A ____ ____ ____

   c) 001, 010, 100, 001, ____, ____, ____

   d) 000, 001, 011, 111, 000, ____, ____, ____

   e) 010, 020, 030, 010, ____, ____, ____

   f) AA, AB, AC, AD, ____, ____, ____, ____

   g) M O M M O M M O M ____ ____ ____

   h) 2 T 22 T 222 ____ ____ ____ ____ ____

Patterns & Algebra 2

6. What strategy would you use to find the 23rd shape in this pattern? What is the shape?

7. Find the mystery number:

   a) I am greater than 21 and less than 26. I am a multiple of 3. What am I?

   b) I am greater than 29 and less than 33. I am a multiple of 4. What am I?

   c) I am less than 15. I am a multiple of 3 **and** a multiple of 4. What am I?

8. Extend each pattern:

   a) 3 427 , 3 527 , 3 627 , _____ , _____ , _____

   b) 4 234 , 5 235 , 6 236 , _____ , _____ , _____

   c) 1 234 , 2 345 , 3 456 , _____ , _____ , _____

9. Sam and Kiana run up 12 steps with muddy shoes.

   a) Sam steps on every 3rd step and Kiana steps on every 4th step.
      Which steps have both of their footprints on them?

   b) If Sam's right foot lands on the 3rd step, on which steps does his left foot land?

10. Make a pattern by shading squares in a hundreds chart.
    Describe any patterns you see in the numbers you have shaded.

11. Every 2nd person who arrives at a book sale receives a free pen.
    Every 3rd person receives a free book.
    Which of the first 15 people will receive a free pen and book?

12. Emma makes a staircase using stone blocks.

    How many blocks will she need to build
    a stairway 6 steps high?

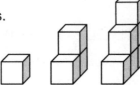

NS4-38: Sharing – Knowing the Number of Sets

Kate wants to share 16 cookies with three friends.
She sets out four plates (one for herself and one for each of her friends).

She puts one cookie at a time on the plates:

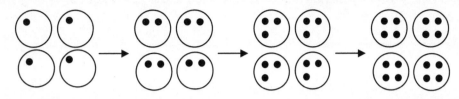

Each plate holds a **set** (or group) of 4 cookies.
When 16 cookies are **divided** (or shared equally) into 4 sets, there are 4 cookies **in each set**.

---

1. Put an equal number of cookies on each plate. Draw circles for the plates and dots for the cookies.
    (Draw the plates, then place one cookie at a time.)

    a) 12 cookies; 3 plates

    b) 12 cookies; 4 plates

2. Draw dots for the things being shared or divided equally. Draw circles for the sets:

    a) 2 vans; 8 people
        How many people in each van?

    b) 3 kids; 9 stickers
        How many stickers for each kid?

    c) 20 flowers; 5 plants
        How many flowers on each plant?

    d) 12 grapefruits; 6 boxes
        How many grapefruits in each box?

Solve the following question in a notebook.

3. 5 friends picked 20 cherries. How many cherries does each friend get?

4. Eileen shared 12 stickers among 3 friends and herself. How many stickers does each person get?

5. There are 16 apples in 8 trees. How many apples are in each tree?

Number Sense 2

Saud has 30 apples. He wants to give 5 apples to each of his friends.

To find out how many friends he can give apples to, he counts out **sets** or **groups** of 5 apples until he has used all 30 apples:

He can give apples to 6 friends. When 30 apples are divided into sets of 5 apples, there are 6 sets.

----

1. Put the correct number of dots in each set. The first one has been done for you:

   a)   b) • • • • • • • • • •   c) • • • • • • • • • • • •

   4 dots in each set   5 dots in each set   3 dots in each set

2. Draw circles to divide these arrays into:

   a) groups of 3   b) groups of 4   c) groups of 3   d) groups of 4

   • • •   • • • •   • • • • •   • • • •
   • • •   • • • •   • • • • •   • • • •
   • • •   • • • •   • • • • •   • • • •
                                                                       • • • •

3. Draw dots for the things being shared or divided equally. Draw circles for the sets:

   a) 15 apples; 5 apples in each box.   b) 10 stickers; 5 stickers for each kid.
       How many boxes?   How many kids?

   _____ boxes   _____ kids

Solve the problems below in a notebook. Use counters or pictures to model the problem.

4. Shelly has 18 cookies. She gives 3 cookies to each of her siblings.
    How many siblings does she have?

5. Vinaya has 14 stamps. He puts 2 stamps on each envelope.
    How many envelopes does he have?

Elisa has 12 glasses of water. A tray holds 3 glasses.

There are 4 trays:

What has been shared or divided into **sets** or **groups**?   *(Glasses)*

How many sets are there?   *(There are 4 sets of glasses.)*

How many of the things being divided are in each set?   *(There are 3 glasses in each set.)*

----

1. a)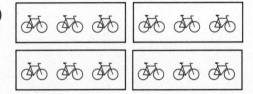

b)

What has been shared or divided into sets?

_____

How many sets? _____

How many in each set? _____

What has been shared or divided into sets?

_____

How many sets? _____

How many in each set? _____

2. Using circles for **sets** and dots for **things**, draw a picture to show:

a) 4 sets
6 things in each set

b) 6 groups
3 things in each group

c) 6 sets
2 things in each set

d) 4 groups
5 things in each group

3.

	What has been shared or divided into sets?	How many sets?	How many in each set?

a) 20 toys
   4 toys for each child
   5 kids
	20 toys	5	4

b) 7 friends
   21 pencils
   3 pencils for each friend			

c) 16 students
   4 desks
   4 students at each desk			

d) 8 plants
   24 flowers
   3 flowers on each plant			

e) 6 grapefruits in each box
   42 grapefruits
   7 boxes			

f) 3 school buses
   30 children
   10 children in each school bus			

g) 6 puppies in each litter
   6 litters
   36 puppies			

BONUS:

4. In a notebook, draw a picture for Questions 3 a), b) and c) using **circles** for sets and **dots** for the things being divided.

NS4-41: Two Ways of Sharing

Samuel has 15 cookies. There are two ways he can share or **divide** his cookies equally:

I • He can decide how many **sets** (or **groups**) of cookies he wants to make:

For example:

Samuel wants to make 3 sets of cookies. He draws 3 circles:

He puts one cookie at a time into the circles until he has placed 15 cookies.

II • He can decide how many cookies he wants to put **in each set**:

For example:

Samuel wants to put 5 cookies in each set. He counts out 5 cookies:

He counts out sets of 5 cookies until he has placed 15 cookies in the sets.

- -

1. Share **20** dots equally. How many dots are in each set? **HINT: Place one dot at a time.**

   a) 4 sets:

   b) 5 sets:

   There are _____ dots in each set.   There are _____ dots in each set.

2. Share the triangles equally among the sets. **HINT: Count the triangles first.**

   a)   b)

3. Share the squares equally among the sets:

4. Group the lines so that there are 3 lines in each set:

   a) | | | | | | | | | b) | | | | | | | | | | | | c) | | | | | |

   There are _____ sets.   There are _____ sets.   There are _____ sets.

5. Group **12** dots so that:

   a) there are 6 dots in each set.   b) there are 4 dots in each set.

6. In each question fill in what you know. Write a question mark for what you don't know:

	What has been shared or divided into sets?	How many sets?	How many in each set?
a) Vanessa has 25 pencils. She puts 5 pencils in each box.	25 pencils	?	5
b) 30 children are in 10 boats	30 children	10	?
c) Ben has 36 stickers. He gives 9 stickers to each of his friends.			
d) Donald has 12 books. He puts 3 on each shelf.			
e) 15 girls sit at 3 tables.			
f) 30 students are in 2 school buses.			
g) 9 fruit bars are shared among 3 children.			
h) 15 chairs are in 3 rows.			
i) 20 boys sit at 5 tables.			

NS4-42: Division

1. Draw a picture using dots and circles to solve each question:

a) 15 dots; 5 sets

_____ dots in each set

b) 16 dots; 8 dots in each set

_____ sets

c) 15 dots; 5 dots in each set

_____ sets

d) 8 dots; 4 sets

_____ dots in each set

e) 10 children are in 2 boats

How many children are in each boat? _____

f) Paul has 12 pencils.
He puts 3 pencils in each box.

How many boxes does he have? _____

g) 4 friends share 12 tickets.

How many tickets does each friend get? _____

h) Pamela has 10 apples.
She gives 2 apples to each friend.

How many apples does each friend get? _____

i) 6 children go sailing in 2 boats.

How many children are in each boat? _____

j) Alan has 10 stickers.
He puts 2 on each page.

How many pages does he use? _____

Number Sense 2

When 15 things are divided into 5 sets, there are 3 things in each set: **15 ÷ 5 = 3**

We could also describe the picture as follows:

When 15 things are divided into sets of size 3, there are 5 sets: **15 ÷ 3 = 5**

- -

2. Fill in the blanks. Then write two division statements:

a)

_____ lines _____ sets

_____ lines in each set

_____ ÷ _____ = _____

_____ ÷ _____ = _____

b)

_____ lines _____ sets

_____ lines in each set

_____

_____

c)

_____ lines _____ sets

_____ lines in each set

_____

_____

3. Fill in the blanks. Then write two division statements. **HINT: Count the figures first.**

a)

_____ sets

_____ squares in each set

_____

_____

b)

_____ sets

_____ triangles in each set

_____

_____

c)

_____ sets

_____ stars in each set

_____

_____

4. Solve the problem by drawing a picture. Then write a division statement for your answer:

a) 12 triangles; 4 sets

_____

How many triangles in each set? _____

b) 6 squares; 3 squares in each set

_____

How many sets? _____

5. Solve each problem by drawing a picture. Write a division statement for your answer.
   HINT: Use dots or lines for things and circles or boxes for sets.

   a) 20 people; 5 cars
      How many people in each car?

   b) 12 children; 3 boats
      How many children in each boat?

Every **division** statement implies an **addition** statement.

For example, the statement "15 divided into sets of size 3 gives 5 sets" is equivalent to the statement "adding 3 five times gives 15":

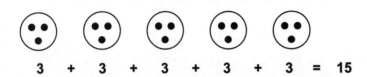

3 + 3 + 3 + 3 + 3 = 15

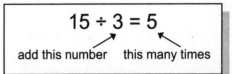

$$15 \div 3 = 5$$

add this number   this many times

Hence the division statement $15 \div 3 = 5$ can be read as "add three five times."

----

1. Draw a picture and write an **addition** statement for each **division** statement, as shown in a):

   a) $8 \div 2 = 4$ b) $10 \div 5 = 2$ c) $8 \div 4 = 2$

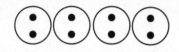

   2 + 2 + 2 + 2 = 8

2. Draw a picture and write a **division** statement for each **addition** statement:

   a) $4 + 4 + 4 = 12$ b) $7 + 7 + 7 = 21$

   $12 \div 4 = 3$

   c) $6 + 6 + 6 = 18$ d) $8 + 8 = 16$

   e) $3 + 3 + 3 + 3 = 12$ f) $9 + 9 = 18$

1. You can solve the division problem **15 ÷ 3 = ?** by skip counting on the number line:

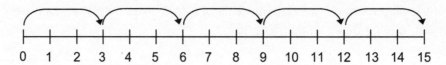

The number line shows that it takes 5 skips of size 3 to get 15:

$$3 + 3 + 3 + 3 + 3 = 15 \quad \text{so...} \quad 15 ÷ 3 = 5$$

Use the number line to find the answer to the division statement. (Draw arrows to show your skip counting.)

a)

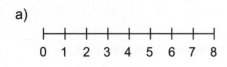

8 ÷ 2 = _____

b)

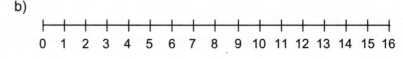

16 ÷ 8 = _____

2. What division statement does the picture represent?

a)

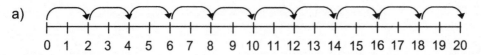

_____

b)

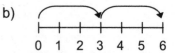

_____

3. You can also find the answer to a division question by skip counting on your fingers.

   Example: Skip count by 9s until you reach 45

   The number of fingers you have up when you stop is the answer.

   45 ÷ 9

   So 45 ÷ 9 = 5

   Find the answers by skip counting on your fingers:

   a) 14 ÷ 2 = _____   b) 18 ÷ 6 = _____   c) 24 ÷ 8 = _____   d) 21 ÷ 7 = _____   e) 35 ÷ 5 = _____

   f) 45 ÷ 5 = _____   g) 32 ÷ 4 = _____   h) 40 ÷ 5 = _____   i) 24 ÷ 3 = _____   j) 16 ÷ 4 = _____

   k) 36 ÷ 9 = _____   l) 28 ÷ 7 = _____   m) 12 ÷ 3 = _____   n) 18 ÷ 3 = _____   o) 35 ÷ 7 = _____

4. Seven friends share 28 tickets to a fair. How many tickets does each friend get?

5. 30 students sit in 6 rows. How many students are in each row?

Daniel bought 12 fish from a pet store: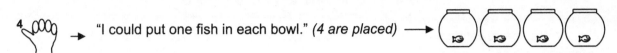

Daniel has 4 fish bowls. How many fish can he put in each fish bowl? Daniel counts by 4s to find out:

4 → "I could put one fish in each bowl." *(4 are placed)* →

8 / **4** → "I could put one more in each bowl." *(8 are placed)* →

8 12 / **4** → "I could put one more in each bowl." *(12 are placed)* →

He has raised 3 fingers, so he knows that **12 ÷ 4 = 3**. He puts 3 fish in each fish bowl.

---

6. Draw circles to divide the objects in the number of equal sets given.
    HINT: Divide the number of objects by the number of sets to find the number of objects in each set.

a) | | | | | | | | | | | |

3 equal sets

b) ♡ ♡ ♡ ♡ ♡ ♡ ♡ ♡ ♡ ♡

5 equal sets

c) ✦ ✦ ✦ ✦ ✦ ✦ ✦ ✦

2 equal sets

d) ✿ ✿ ✿ ✿ ✿ ✿ ✿ ✿ ✿ ✿ ✿ ✿

4 equal sets

e) ● ● ● ● ● ● ● ● ● ● ● ● ● ●

7 equal sets

f) ▯▯▯▯▯▯▯▯▯▯▯▯▯▯▯▯

2 equal sets

g) ◇ ◇ ◇ ◇ ◇ ◇ ◇ ◇ ◇ ◇ ◇ ◇

3 equal sets

h) ○○○○○○○○○○○○

6 equal sets

BONUS:

i)

3 equal sets

j)

5 equal sets

k)

4 equal sets

7. Azul has 16 fish and 4 fish bowls. How many fish can he put in each bowl?

Write a division statement for your answer: _____

Every division statement implies a multiplication statement. The statement:

"10 divided into sets of size 2 gives 5 sets" (or **10 ÷ 2 = 5**)

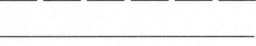

can be rewritten as: "5 sets of size 2 equals 10" (**5 × 2 = 10 or 2 × 5 = 10**)

- -

1. Write two multiplication statements and two division statements for each picture:

a)

_____

_____

_____

_____

b)

_____

_____

_____

_____

c)

_____

_____

_____

How many fish? _____

How many sets? _____

How many fish in each set? _____

d)

_____

_____

_____

How many snails? _____

How many sets? _____

How many snails in each set? _____

2. Find the answer to the division problem by first finding the answer to the multiplication statement:

a) 4 × **5** = 20

   20 ÷ 4 = **5**

b) 6 × ☐ = 12

   12 ÷ 6 = ☐

c) 5 × ☐ = 20

   20 ÷ 5 = ☐

d) 6 × ☐ = 30

   30 ÷ 6 = ☐

e) 9 × ☐ = 45

   45 ÷ 9 = ☐

f) 7 × ☐ = 21

   21 ÷ 7 = ☐

g) 3 × ☐ = 24

   24 ÷ 3 = ☐

h) 6 × ☐ = 24

   24 ÷ 6 = ☐

Ori wants to share 7 cookies with 2 friends. He sets out 3 plates, one for himself and one for each of his friends. He puts one cookie at a time on a plate:

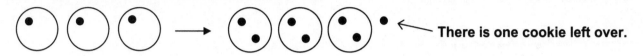

There is one cookie left over.

7 cookies cannot be shared equally into 3 sets. Each friend gets 2 cookies, but one is left over.

$$7 \div 3 = 2 \text{ Remainder } 1 \quad \text{OR} \quad 7 \div 3 = 2 \text{ R } 1$$

- -

1. Can you share 5 cookies equally onto 2 plates? Show your work using dots and circles for plates:

2. Share the dots as equally as possible among the circles:
   IMPORTANT: In one question, the dots can be shared equally (so there's no remainder).

   a) 7 dots in 2 circles

   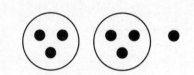

   _____ dots in each circle; _____ dots remaining

   b) 10 dots in 3 circles

   _____ dots in each circle; _____ dots remaining

   c) 10 dots in 5 circles

   _____ dots in each circle; _____ dots remaining

   d) 9 dots in 4 circles

   _____ dots in each circle; _____ dots remaining

   e) 12 dots in 5 circles

   _____ dots in each circle; _____ dots remaining

   f) 13 dots in 4 circles

   _____ dots in each circle; _____ dots remaining

3. Share the dots as equally as possible. Draw a picture and write a division statement:

a) 7 dots in 3 circles

$7 \div 3 = 2 \text{ R}$

b) 11 dots in 3 circles

c) 14 dots in 3 circles

d) 10 dots in 6 circles

e) 10 dots in 4 circles

f) 13 dots in 5 circles

4. Three friends want to share 7 oranges. How many oranges will each friend receive? How many will be left over? Show your work:

5. Find two different ways to share 13 cookies into equal groups so that one is left over:

6. Fred, George and Paul have less than 10 oranges and more than 3 oranges. They share the oranges evenly. How many oranges do they have? Is there more than one answer?

NS4-47: Long Division — 2-Digit by 1-Digit

Inez is preparing snacks for 4 classes. She needs to divide 93 apples into 4 groups.
She will use long division and a model to solve the problem:

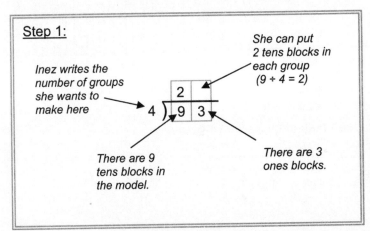

Step 1:

Inez writes the number of groups she wants to make here

She can put 2 tens blocks in each group (9 ÷ 4 = 2)

There are 9 tens blocks in the model.

There are 3 ones blocks.

$$4 \overline{)9 \; 3}$$ with 2 above

Inez makes a model of the problem:
93 = 9 tens + 3 ones

Inez can divide 8 of the 9 tens blocks into 4 equal groups of size 2:

---

1. Inez has written a division statement to solve a problem. How many groups does she want to make? How many tens blocks and how many ones would she need to model the problem?

a) $3 \overline{)85}$

groups ___3___

tens blocks ___8___

ones ___5___

b) $4 \overline{)92}$

groups _____

tens blocks _____

ones _____

c) $5 \overline{)86}$

groups _____

tens blocks _____

ones _____

d) $2 \overline{)87}$

groups _____

tens blocks _____

ones _____

2. How many tens blocks can be put in each group? Use division or skip counting to find the answers:

a) $3 \overline{)7 \; 5}$ with 2

b) $4 \overline{)9 \; 3}$

c) $5 \overline{)6 \; 2}$

d) $3 \overline{)9 \; 8}$

e) $4 \overline{)8 \; 2}$

f) $2 \overline{)8 \; 5}$

g) $3 \overline{)8 \; 7}$

h) $8 \overline{)9 \; 1}$

i) $6 \overline{)8 \; 3}$

j) $s \overline{)9 \; 2}$

3. How many groups have been made? How many tens are in each group?

a) $3 \overline{)7 \; 5}$ with 2

groups ___3___

number of tens in each group ___2___

b) $2 \overline{)9 \; 1}$

groups _____

number of tens in each group _____

c) $4 \overline{)9 \; 5}$

groups _____

number of tens in each group _____

d) $2 \overline{)7 \; 3}$

groups _____

number of tens in each group _____

Step 2:

There are 2 tens blocks in each group

There are 4 groups

$$4 \overline{) \, 9 \, 3} \quad \begin{array}{c} 2 \end{array}$$

So $2 \times 4 = 8$ tens blocks have been placed.

In the model:

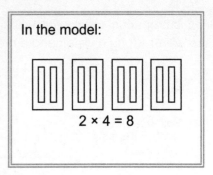

$2 \times 4 = 8$

4. For each question, find how many tens have been placed by multiplying:

a)
$$3 \overline{) \, 8 \, 7} \quad \begin{array}{c} 2 \\ 6 \end{array}$$

How many groups? _____

How many tens? _____

How many tens in each group? _____

How many tens placed altogether? _____

b)
$$4 \overline{) \, 9 \, 6} \quad \begin{array}{c} 2 \\ 8 \end{array}$$

How many groups? _____

How many tens? _____

How many tens in each group? _____

How many tens placed altogether? _____

5. Use skip counting to find out how many tens can be placed in each group. Then use multiplication to find out how many tens have been placed:

a) $2 \overline{) \, 7 \, 3}$

b) $3 \overline{) \, 8 \, 2}$

c) $2 \overline{) \, 9 \, 5}$

d) $5 \overline{) \, 9 \, 8}$

e) $7 \overline{) \, 8 \, 1}$

f) $6 \overline{) \, 6 \, 3}$

g) $2 \overline{) \, 7 \, 1}$

h) $3 \overline{) \, 7 \, 5}$

i) $4 \overline{) \, 9 \, 3}$

j) $8 \overline{) \, 8 \, 5}$

k) $2 \overline{) \, 8 \, 1}$

l) $3 \overline{) \, 7 \, 2}$

m) $9 \overline{) \, 9 \, 5}$

n) $7 \overline{) \, 9 \, 3}$

o) $6 \overline{) \, 8 \, 0}$

p) $2 \overline{) \, 5 \, 3}$

q) $3 \overline{) \, 7 \, 8}$

r) $4 \overline{) \, 9 \, 0}$

s) $5 \overline{) \, 5 \, 0}$

t) $6 \overline{) \, 7 \, 3}$

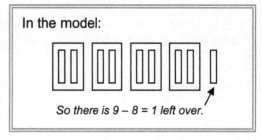

Step 3: There are 9 tens blocks and Inez has placed 8.

She subtracts to find out how many are left over (9 − 8 = 1).

In the model:

So there is 9 − 8 = 1 left over.

6. For each question, carry out the first 3 steps of the long division:

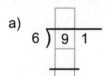 a) $6 \overline{)\,9\ 1}$ b) $3 \overline{)\,7\ 6}$ c) $2 \overline{)\,4\ 1}$ d) $4 \overline{)\,8\ 3}$ 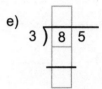 e) $3 \overline{)\,8\ 5}$

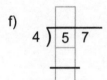 f) $4 \overline{)\,5\ 7}$ g) $8 \overline{)\,9\ 3}$ h) $2 \overline{)\,9\ 9}$ i) $3 \overline{)\,7\ 1}$ 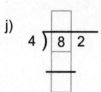 j) $4 \overline{)\,8\ 2}$

Step 4: There is one tens block left over and 3 ones. So there are 13 ones left over. Inez writes the 3 beside the 1 to show this.

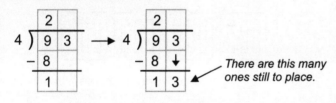

There are this many ones still to place.

In the model:

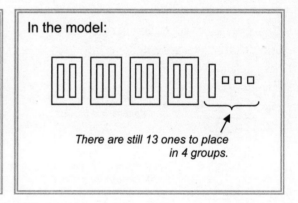

There are still 13 ones to place in 4 groups.

7. Carry out the first four steps of the division:

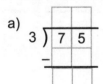 a) $3 \overline{)\,7\ 5}$ b) $2 \overline{)\,5\ 7}$ 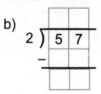 c) $2 \overline{)\,9\ 3}$ d) $4 \overline{)\,8\ 3}$ 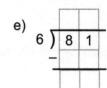 e) $6 \overline{)\,8\ 1}$

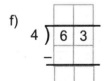 f) $4 \overline{)\,6\ 3}$ 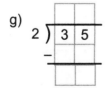 g) $2 \overline{)\,3\ 5}$ h) $7 \overline{)\,8\ 8}$ i) $8 \overline{)\,9\ 1}$ j) $9 \overline{)\,9\ 3}$

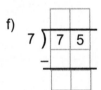

13 ÷ 4 = 3

She can put 3 ones blocks in each group.

In the model:

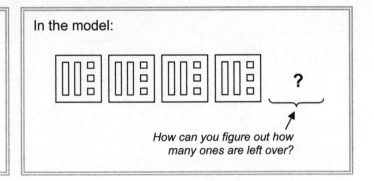

?

How can you figure out how many ones are left over?

8. Carry out the first five steps of the division:

a) 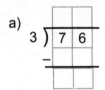 $3 \overline{) 7\ 6}$

b) 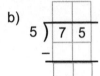 $5 \overline{) 7\ 5}$

c) $2 \overline{) 5\ 5}$

d) 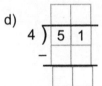 $4 \overline{) 5\ 1}$

e) 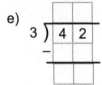 $3 \overline{) 4\ 2}$

f) $7 \overline{) 7\ 5}$

g) $2 \overline{) 9\ 1}$

h) $3 \overline{) 9\ 6}$

i) 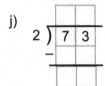 $9 \overline{) 9\ 2}$

j) $2 \overline{) 7\ 3}$

Steps 6 and 7:

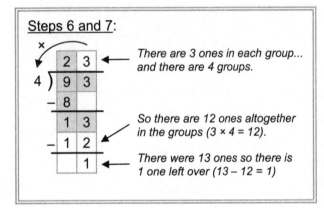

There are 3 ones in each group... and there are 4 groups.

So there are 12 ones altogether in the groups (3 × 4 = 12).

There were 13 ones so there is 1 one left over (13 − 12 = 1)

In the model:

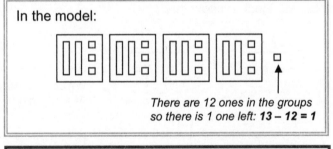

*There are 12 ones in the groups so there is 1 one left: **13 − 12 = 1***

The division statement and the model both show that Inez can give each class 23 apples with one left over.

9. Carry out all 7 steps of the division:

a) 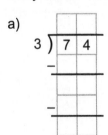 $3 \overline{) 7\ 4}$

b) 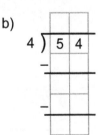 $4 \overline{) 5\ 4}$

c) 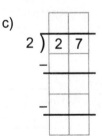 $2 \overline{) 2\ 7}$

d) 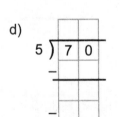 $5 \overline{) 7\ 0}$

e) 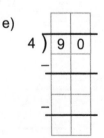 $4 \overline{) 9\ 0}$

f)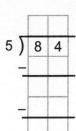
$5 \overline{)\, 8 \; 4}$

g)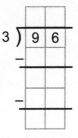
$4 \overline{)\, 6 \; 4}$

h)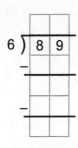
$3 \overline{)\, 9 \; 6}$

i)
$6 \overline{)\, 8 \; 9}$

j)
$7 \overline{)\, 9 \; 7}$

k)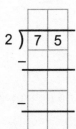
$2 \overline{)\, 7 \; 5}$

l)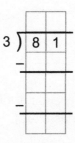
$3 \overline{)\, 8 \; 1}$

m)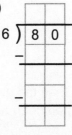
$6 \overline{)\, 8 \; 0}$

n)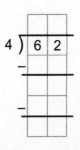
$4 \overline{)\, 6 \; 2}$

o)
$8 \overline{)\, 9 \; 7}$

10. Sandra put 62 tomatoes into cartons of 5. How many tomatoes did she have left over?

11. How many weeks are there in 84 days?

12. A pentagon has a perimeter of 95 cm. How long is each side?

13. Shawn can hike 8 km in a day. How many days will it take him to hike 96 km?

Answer the remaining questions in a notebook.

14. A boat can hold 6 kids. How many boats will 84 kids need?

15. Alexa put 73 apples in bags of 6. Mike put 46 apples in bags of 4. Who had more apples left over?

1. Write a division statement for each question:

a) 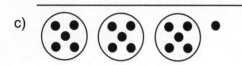 •

_____

c) 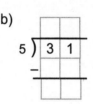 •

_____

b)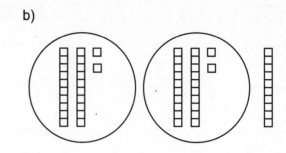

_____

2. In each question below there are fewer tens than the number of groups. Write a 0 in the tens position and then perform the division (as if the tens had been regrouped as ones):

a)

```
        0  5
   5 ) 2  7
     - 2  5
           2
```

← 5 ones can be placed in each group

← 25 ones have been placed

← 2 ones are left over

b)

```
   5 ) 3  1
     -
```

c)

```
   4 ) 2  7
     -
```

d)

```
   8 ) 5  2
     -
```

Answer the remaining questions in a notebook.

3. Estimate each quotient by first rounding each number to the nearest ten.
   Then find the actual answer by long division.

   a) 87 ÷ 9   b) 78 ÷ 8   c) 91 ÷ 8   d) 126 ÷ 9

4. When you divide a number by 1, what is the result? Explain.

In Questions 5 to 8, you will have to interpret what the remainder means.

5. A canoe can hold 3 kids.
   How many canoes will 44 kids need?

6. Anne reads 5 pages before bed every night.
   She has 63 pages left to read in her book.
   How many nights will it take her to finish her book?

7. Ed wants to give 65 hockey cards to 4 friends.
   How many cards will each friend get?

8. Daniel wants to put 97 hockey cards into a scrap book. A page can hold 9 cards.
   How many pages will he need?

1. Write one multiplication statement and two division statements in the same fact family as:

   $$6 \times 8 = 48$$

2. Find the mystery numbers:

   a) I am a multiple of 4. I am greater than 25 and less than 31.

   b) I am divisible by 3. I am between 20 and 26. I am an even number.

3. 92 kids attend a play on 4 buses. There are an equal number of kids on each bus.

   a) How many kids are on each bus?

   b) A ticket for the play costs $6. 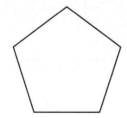 How much will it cost for one busload of kids to attend the play?

4. Find two different ways to share 14 apples in equal groups so there are 2 apples left over.

   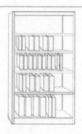

5. Find three numbers that give the same remainder when divided by 3.

6. A queen ant can lay one egg every ten seconds. How many eggs can she lay in:

   a) 1 minute?   b) 2 minutes?   c) an hour?

   How did you find your answers?

7. Six friends read 96 books for a read-a-thon. Each friend reads the same number of books.

   How many books did each friend read?

8. Jennifer plants 84 pansies in 4 flower beds.

   How many pansies are in each flower bed?

9. A square park has perimeter 680 m. How long is each side of the park?

10. A square park has sides of length 236 m. What is the perimeter of the park?

11. A pentagon with equal sides has perimeter 75 cm. How long is each side?

12. A robin lays **at least** 3 eggs and **no more than** 6 eggs:

    a) What is the least number of eggs 3 robins' nests would hold (if there were eggs laid in each nest)?

    b) What is the greatest number of eggs 3 robins' nests would hold?

    c) Three robins' nests contain 13 eggs.

       Draw a picture to show 2 ways the eggs could be shared among the nests.

NS4-50: Naming of Fractions

The pie is cut into 4 equal parts. 3 parts out of 4 are shaded:

$\frac{3}{4}$ of a pie is shaded.

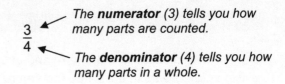

The **numerator** (3) tells you how many parts are counted.

$\frac{3}{4}$

The **denominator** (4) tells you how many parts in a whole.

----

1. Name the fraction shown by the shaded part of each image:

a)  b)   c)  d)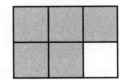

e) 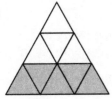 f) 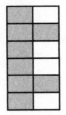 g) 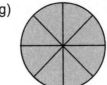 h)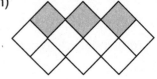

2. Shade the fractions named:

a) $\frac{3}{6}$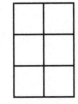

b) $\frac{2}{5}$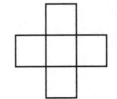

c) $\frac{5}{9}$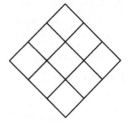

3. Use one of the following words to describe the parts in the figures below:

halves   thirds   fourths   fifths   sixths   sevenths   eighths   ninths

a)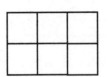

_____

b)

_____

c)

_____

d)

_____

e)

_____

f)

_____

No unauthorized copying   **Number Sense 2**

1. Use a **ruler** to divide each line into equal parts:

   a) 5 equal parts   b) 3 equal parts   c) 4 equal parts

   _____   _____   _____

   d) 7 equal parts   e) 9 equal parts

   _____   _____

2. Use a **ruler** to divide each box into equal parts:

   a) 4 equal parts   b) 5 equal parts

   c) 3 equal parts   d) 6 equal parts

3. Using a **ruler**, find what fraction of each of the following boxes is shaded:

   a)

   _____ is shaded   b)   _____ is shaded

   c)   d)

   _____ is shaded   _____ is shaded

4. Using a **ruler**, complete the following figures to make a whole:

   a) $\frac{1}{2}$ b) $\frac{1}{3}$ c) $\frac{1}{4}$

 Answer the remaining questions in a notebook.

5. Sketch a pie cut in:

   a) thirds   b) quarters (or fourths)   c) eighths

6. You have $\frac{3}{5}$ of a pie:

   a) What does the bottom (denominator) of the fraction tell you?

   b) What does the top (numerator) of the fraction tell you?

7. Explain why each picture does (or does not) show $\frac{1}{4}$:

   a)    b)   c)   d)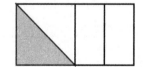

Fractions can name parts of a set: $\frac{3}{5}$ of the figures are triangles, $\frac{1}{5}$ are squares and $\frac{1}{5}$ are circles:

---

1. Fill in the blanks:

a)

_____ of the figures are circles.

_____ of the figures are shaded.

b)

_____ of the figures are shaded.

_____ of the figures are triangles.

c)

_____ of the figures are triangles.

_____ of the figures are shaded.

_____ of the figures are squares.

_____ of the figures are unshaded.

2. Fill in the blanks:

$\frac{4}{8}$ of the figures are _____

$\frac{3}{8}$ of the figures are _____

$\frac{1}{8}$ of the figures are _____

3. Write 4 fraction statements for the picture:

(i) _____

(ii) _____

(iii) _____

(iv) _____

4.

Can you describe this picture in two different ways using the fraction $\frac{3}{5}$?

_____

_____

5. A soccer team wins 5 games and loses 3 games:

   a) How many games did the team play? _____

   b) What **fraction** of the games did the team win? _____

6. A basketball team wins 7 games, loses 2 games and ties 3 games. What fractions of the games did the team:

   a) win? _____   b) lose? _____   c) tie? _____

7. A box contains 4 blue markers, 3 black markers and 3 red markers.
   What fraction of the markers are **not** blue? _____

 Answer the remaining questions in a notebook.

8. Julie lives 3 km from her school.
   She has biked 1 km towards her school.
   What fraction of the distance to her school does she still have to bike?

9. Pia is 9 years old.
   She lived in Calgary for 4 years, before she moved to Regina.
   What fraction of her life did she live in Calgary?

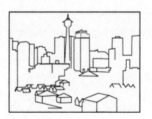

10. Draw a picture to solve the puzzle:

   a) There are 5 circles and squares.

      $\frac{3}{5}$ of the figures are squares.

      $\frac{2}{5}$ of the figures are shaded.

      Two circles are shaded.

   b) There are 5 triangles and squares.

      $\frac{3}{5}$ of the figures are shaded.

      $\frac{2}{5}$ of the figures are triangles.

      One square is shaded.

1. What fraction is shaded? How do you know?

2. 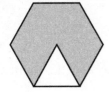 Draw lines from the point in the centre of the hexagon to the vertices of the hexagon.

How many triangles cover the hexagon? _____

3. What fraction of each figure is the shaded part?

a)    b) 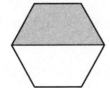   c)   d)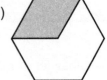

_____   _____   _____   _____

4. What fraction of the figure is the shaded piece?

a)   b)   c)    d)

_____   _____   _____   _____

PARENT: For the remaining questions, your child will need patterns blocks.

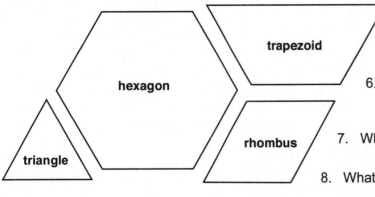

5. What fraction of the trapezoid is the triangle? (How many triangles will fit in the trapezoid?)

6. What fraction of the hexagon is the trapezoid?

7. What fraction of the hexagon is the rhombus?

8. What fraction of the hexagon is the triangle?

9. What fraction of two hexagons is the triangle?

1. 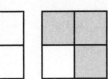 What fraction has a greater numerator, $\frac{1}{4}$ or $\frac{3}{4}$?

   Which fraction is greater?

   REMEMBER:

   $\frac{3}{4}$ ← numerator

   ← denominator

   Explain your thinking: _____

   _____

2. Circle the greater fraction in each pair:

   a) $\frac{3}{14}$ or $\frac{6}{14}$ b) $\frac{4}{12}$ or $\frac{7}{12}$ c) $\frac{2}{9}$ or $\frac{5}{9}$ d) $\frac{4}{7}$ or $\frac{5}{7}$

   e) $\frac{7}{27}$ or $\frac{4}{27}$ f) $\frac{13}{98}$ or $\frac{20}{98}$ g) $\frac{47}{125}$ or $\frac{46}{125}$ h) $\frac{88}{287}$ or $\frac{42}{287}$

3. Write the fractions in order from least to greatest:

   a) $\frac{2}{3}$, $\frac{1}{3}$, $\frac{3}{3}$ b) $\frac{2}{10}$, $\frac{1}{10}$, $\frac{7}{10}$, $\frac{9}{10}$ c) $\frac{5}{17}$, $\frac{9}{17}$, $\frac{8}{17}$, $\frac{16}{17}$

4. Write a fraction that is:

   a) greater than $\frac{3}{7}$ and less than $\frac{6}{7}$: _____

   b) greater than $\frac{1}{8}$ and less than $\frac{4}{8}$: _____

   c) greater than $\frac{3}{10}$ and less than $\frac{7}{10}$: _____

   d) greater than $\frac{8}{15}$ and less than $\frac{11}{15}$: _____

   e) greater than $\frac{14}{57}$ and less than $\frac{19}{57}$: _____

   f) greater than $\frac{58}{127}$ and less than $\frac{63}{127}$: _____

5. Two fractions have the same **denominators** (bottoms) but different **numerators** (tops). How can you tell which fraction is greater?

   _____

   _____

1. a) Trace and cut out this square. Then cut the square in half.

    What fraction of the square is each part?

    b) Next, cut each of these parts in half.

    What fraction of the square is each new part?

    c) As the denominator (bottom) of the fraction **increases**, what happens to the size of each piece?

    _____

2. Circle the **greatest** fraction in each pair:

    a) $\frac{1}{5}$ or $\frac{1}{7}$ b) $\frac{3}{15}$ or $\frac{3}{7}$ c) $\frac{2}{197}$ or $\frac{2}{297}$ d) $\frac{17}{52}$ or $\frac{17}{57}$

3. Circle the **greatest** fraction in each pair:

    a) $\frac{1}{3}$ or $\frac{1}{9}$ b) $\frac{7}{11}$ or $\frac{7}{13}$ c) $\frac{6}{15}$ or $\frac{6}{18}$ d) $\frac{3}{27}$ or $\frac{3}{42}$

4. Write the fractions in order from least to greatest:

    a) $\frac{1}{5}$, $\frac{1}{2}$, $\frac{1}{4}$ b) $\frac{1}{5}$, $\frac{1}{8}$, $\frac{1}{7}$ c) $\frac{2}{3}$, $\frac{2}{5}$, $\frac{2}{7}$

    _____   _____   _____

    BONUS:

    d) $\frac{5}{7}$, $\frac{5}{5}$, $\frac{5}{11}$ e) $\frac{3}{11}$, $\frac{3}{4}$, $\frac{3}{8}$ f) $\frac{5}{8}$, $\frac{5}{11}$, $\frac{7}{8}$

    _____   _____   _____

5. Which fraction is greater, $\frac{1}{2}$ or $\frac{1}{100}$?   Explain your thinking:

    _____

    _____

6. Fraction A and Fraction B have the same **numerators** (tops) but different **denominators** (bottoms). How can you tell which fraction is greater?

    _____

    _____

1. Using a ruler, divide each line into 2 equal parts:

    a) _____

    b) _____

    c) _____

    d) _____

2. Divide each line into 3 equal parts:

    a) _____

    b) _____

    c) _____

3. Draw the whole:

    a)

    $\frac{1}{2}$

    b)

    $\frac{1}{2}$

    c)

    $\frac{1}{3}$

4. Fill in the blanks:

    a) $\frac{1}{2}$ and ⬚ make 1 whole

    b) $\frac{1}{3}$ and ⬚ make 1 whole

    c) $\frac{1}{5}$ and ⬚ make 1 whole

    d) $\frac{3}{7}$ and ⬚ make 1 whole

Answer the remaining questions in a notebook.

5.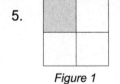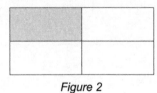

   Figure 1   Figure 2

   Is $\frac{1}{4}$ of Figure 1 the same as $\frac{1}{4}$ of Figure 2?

   Explain why or why not.

6. Is it possible for $\frac{1}{4}$ of a pie to be bigger than $\frac{1}{3}$ of another pie? Show your thinking with a picture.

7. Ken ate $\frac{3}{5}$ of a pie. Karen ate the rest. Who ate more pie? Explain.

NS4-57: Mixed Fractions

Alan and his friends ate the amount of pie shown:

They ate two and one quarter pies altogether (or $2\frac{1}{4}$ pies).

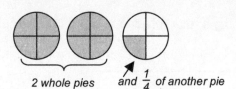

2 whole pies   and $\frac{1}{4}$ of another pie

NOTE: $2\frac{1}{4}$ is called a **mixed fraction** because it is a mixture of a whole number and a fraction.

----

1. Write how many **whole** pies are shaded:

a)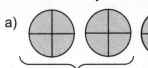

2

_____ whole pies

b)

_____ whole pies

c)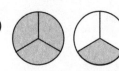

_____ whole pie

2. Write the fractions as **mixed fractions**:

a)

b)

c)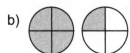

d)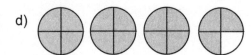

e)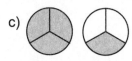

f)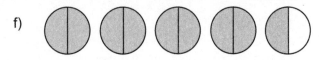

g)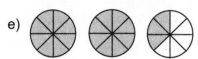

3. Shade the amount of pie given in bold:
    NOTE: There may be more pies than you need.

a) $2\frac{1}{2}$

b) $3\frac{1}{2}$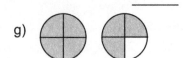

c) $1\frac{1}{2}$

d) $2\frac{2}{3}$

e) $3\frac{3}{4}$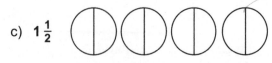

f) $1\frac{4}{5}$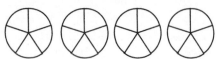

4. In a notebook, sketch:

a) $2\frac{1}{2}$ pies   b) $3\frac{1}{2}$ pies   c) $2\frac{1}{4}$ pies   d) $3\frac{2}{3}$ pies

Number Sense 2

Improper Fraction: *Mixed Fraction:*

$$\frac{9}{4} \qquad = \qquad 2\frac{1}{4}$$

Alan and his friends ate **9** quarter-sized pieces of pizza. Altogether they ate $\frac{9}{4}$ pizzas.

NOTE: When the numerator of a fraction is larger than the denominator, the fraction represents **more than** a whole. Such fractions are called **improper fractions**.

----

1. Write these fractions as **improper** fractions.

a)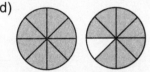

b)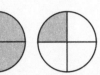

c)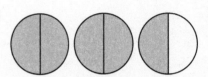

d)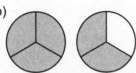

e)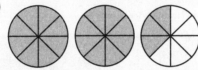

f)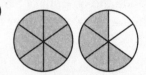

g)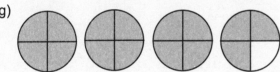

h)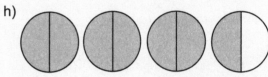

2. Shade one piece at a time until you have shaded the amount of pie given in bold:

a) $\frac{5}{2}$

b) $\frac{7}{2}$

c) $\frac{8}{3}$

d) $\frac{13}{4}$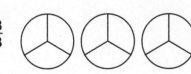

 Answer the remaining questions in a notebook.

3. Sketch: a) $\frac{3}{2}$ pies   b) $\frac{9}{2}$ pies   c) $\frac{10}{4}$ pies   d) $\frac{10}{3}$ pies

4. Which fractions are more than a whole? How do you know?   a) $\frac{3}{4}$ b) $\frac{9}{4}$ c) $\frac{7}{5}$

1. Write these fractions as **mixed** fractions and as **improper** fractions:

a)

b)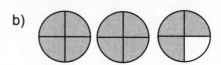

c)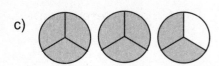

d)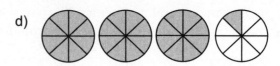

e)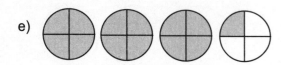

f)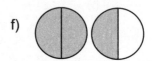

2. Shade the amount of pie given in bold.
    Then write an **improper** fraction for the amount of pie:

a) $2\frac{1}{2}$

Improper Fraction: _____

b) $3\frac{1}{4}$

Improper Fraction: _____

c) $2\frac{1}{6}$

Improper Fraction: _____

d) $2\frac{5}{8}$

Improper Fraction: _____

3. Shade one piece at a time until you have shaded the amount of pie given in bold.
    Then write a **mixed** fraction for the amount of pie:

a) $\frac{7}{3}$

Mixed Fraction: _____

b) $\frac{13}{6}$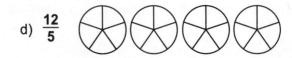

Mixed Fraction: _____

c) $\frac{7}{4}$

Mixed Fraction: _____

d) $\frac{12}{5}$

Mixed Fraction: _____

NS4-60: Mixed Fractions (Advanced)

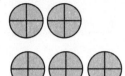 There are 4 quarter pieces in 1 pie.

There are 8 (2 × 4) quarters in 2 pies.

There are 12 (3 × 4) quarters in 3 pies.

How many quarter pieces are in $3\frac{3}{4}$ pies?

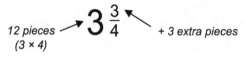

12 pieces → $3\frac{3}{4}$ ← *+ 3 extra pieces*
(3 × 4)

So there are 15 quarter pieces altogether.

---

1. Find the number of **halves** in each amount:

   a) 1 pie = _____ halves

   b) 2 pies = _____ halves

   c) 3 pies = _____ halves

   d) $1\frac{1}{2}$ pies = _____ halves

   e) $2\frac{1}{2}$ pies = _____ halves

   f) $3\frac{1}{2}$ pies = _____

2. Find the number of **thirds** in each amount:

   a) 1 pie = _____ thirds

   b) 2 pies = _____ thirds

   c) 3 pies = _____ thirds

   d) $1\frac{1}{3}$ pies = _____ thirds

   e) $2\frac{2}{3}$ pies = _____

   f) $3\frac{1}{3}$ pies = _____

3. Find the number of **quarters** (or fourths) in each amount:

   a) 1 pie = _____ quarters

   b) 2 pies = _____ quarters

   c) 3 pies = _____ quarters

   d) $2\frac{1}{4}$ pies = _____ quarters

   e) $2\frac{3}{4}$ pies = _____

   f) $3\frac{3}{4}$ pies = _____

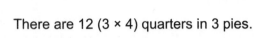 4. A box holds 4 cans:

   a) 2 boxes hold _____ cans

   b) $3\frac{1}{4}$ boxes hold _____ cans

   c) $4\frac{3}{4}$ boxes hold _____ cans

5. A box holds 6 cans:

   a) $2\frac{1}{6}$ boxes hold _____ cans

   b) $2\frac{5}{6}$ boxes hold _____ cans

   c) $3\frac{1}{6}$ boxes hold _____ cans

6. Pens come in packs of 8. Dan used $1\frac{5}{8}$ packs. How many pens did he use? _____

7. Bottles come in packs of 6. How many bottles are in $2\frac{1}{2}$ packs? _____

Number Sense 2

NS4-61: Mixed and Improper Fractions (Advanced)

How many whole pies are there in $\frac{13}{4}$ pies?

There are 13 pieces altogether. ← $\frac{13}{4}$ → *Each pie has 4 pieces.*

So you can find the number of whole pies by dividing 13 by 4:

13 ÷ 4 = 3 Remainder 1

There are 3 whole pies and 1 quarter left over. So: $\frac{13}{4} = 3\frac{1}{4}$

----

1. Find the number of whole pies in each amount by dividing:

   a) $\frac{4}{2}$ pies = _____ whole pies   b) $\frac{6}{2}$ pies = _____ whole pies   c) $\frac{10}{2}$ pies = _____ whole pies

   d) $\frac{6}{3}$ pies = _____ whole pies   e) $\frac{12}{3}$ pies = _____ whole pies   f) $\frac{8}{4}$ pies = _____ whole pies

2. Find the number of whole pies and the number of pieces remaining by dividing:

   a) $\frac{5}{2}$ pies = ___2___ whole pies and ___1___ half pie = __$2\frac{1}{2}$__ pies

   b) $\frac{7}{2}$ pies = _____ whole pies and _____ half pies = _____ pies

   c) $\frac{7}{3}$ pies = _____ whole pies and _____ third pies = _____ pies

   d) $\frac{10}{3}$ pies = _____ whole pies and _____ third pies = _____ pies

   e) $\frac{11}{4}$ pies = _____ whole pies and _____ quarter pies = _____ pies

3. Write the following improper fractions as mixed fractions:

   a) $\frac{3}{2}$ =   b) $\frac{9}{2}$ =   c) $\frac{8}{3}$ =   d) $\frac{15}{4}$ =   e) $\frac{22}{5}$ =

4. Write a mixed and improper fraction for the number of litres:

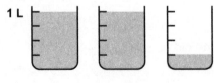

   Mixed _____   Improper _____

5. Write a mixed and improper fraction for the length of the rope:

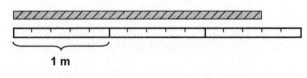

   Mixed _____   Improper _____

Number Sense 2

George shades $\frac{4}{6}$ of the squares in an array:

He then draws heavy lines around the squares to group them into 3 equal groups:

He sees that $\frac{2}{3}$ of the squares are shaded.

Four sixths are equal to two thirds: $\frac{4}{6} = \frac{2}{3}$ Four sixths and two thirds are **equivalent fractions**.

----

1. Write an equivalent fraction:

a)

$$\frac{3}{6} = \frac{}{2}$$

b)

$$\frac{6}{8} = \frac{}{4}$$

c)

$$\frac{6}{9} = \frac{}{3}$$

2. Group the squares (by drawing heavy lines) to show:

a) Two eighths equals one fourth ($\frac{2}{8} = \frac{1}{4}$)   b) Four eighths equals one half ($\frac{4}{8} = \frac{1}{2}$)

   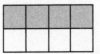

3. Group the squares to make an equivalent fraction:

a)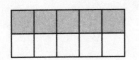

$$\frac{5}{10} = \frac{}{2}$$

b)

$$\frac{2}{6} = \frac{}{3}$$

c)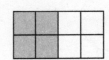

$$\frac{4}{8} = \frac{}{2}$$

d)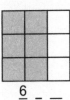

$$\frac{6}{9} = \frac{}{}$$

e)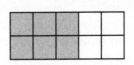

$$\frac{6}{10} = \frac{}{}$$

f)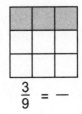

$$\frac{3}{9} = \frac{}{}$$

4. Shade squares to make an equivalent fraction:

a)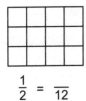

$$\frac{1}{2} = \frac{}{12}$$

b)

$$\frac{1}{3} = \frac{}{12}$$

c)

$$\frac{1}{4} = \frac{}{12}$$

Number Sense 2

Candice has a set of grey and white buttons.
Four of the six buttons are grey.

Candice groups buttons to show that
two thirds of the buttons are grey:

$$\frac{4}{6} \quad = \quad \frac{2}{3}$$

----

1. Group the buttons to make an equivalent fraction:

a)

$$\frac{2}{6} = \frac{}{3}$$

b)

$$\frac{2}{4} = \frac{}{2}$$

c)

$$\frac{3}{6} = \frac{}{2}$$

d)

$$\frac{6}{9} = \frac{}{3}$$

e)

$$\frac{8}{10} = \frac{}{5}$$

f)

$$\frac{3}{9} = \frac{}{\ \ }$$

g)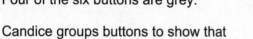

$$\frac{2}{10} = \frac{}{\ \ }$$

2. Group the pieces to make an equivalent fraction.
   The grouping in the first question has already been done for you:

a)

$$\frac{2}{8} = \frac{}{4}$$

b)

$$\frac{2}{6} = \frac{}{3}$$

c)

$$\frac{2}{10} = \frac{}{5}$$

d)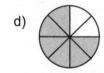

$$\frac{6}{8} = \frac{}{\ \ }$$

e)

$$\frac{4}{6} = \frac{}{\ \ }$$

f)

$$\frac{4}{10} = \frac{}{\ \ }$$

3. Cut each pie into smaller pieces to make an equivalent fraction:

a)

$$\frac{2}{3} = \frac{}{6}$$

b)

$$\frac{2}{3} = \frac{}{9}$$

c)

$$\frac{1}{2} = \frac{}{4}$$

Answer the remaining questions in a notebook.

4. Draw shaded and unshaded circles (as in Question 1) and group the circles to show:

   a) six eighths is equivalent to three quarters

   b) four fifths is equivalent to eight tenths

5. Dan says that $\frac{1}{2}$ is equivalent to $\frac{2}{4}$. Is he right? How do you know?

Number Sense 2

1. Complete the equivalent fractions:

a) 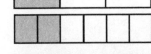 $\frac{1}{2} = \frac{}{4}$

b) 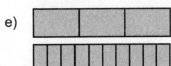 $\frac{1}{2} = \frac{}{6}$

c)  $\frac{1}{3} = \frac{}{6}$

d) $\frac{2}{3} = \frac{}{6}$

e) $\frac{3}{3} = \frac{}{10}$

f) $\frac{4}{10} = \frac{}{5}$

2. Use the picture to find the equivalent fractions:

1 whole							
$\frac{1}{2}$				$\frac{1}{2}$			
$\frac{1}{4}$		$\frac{1}{4}$		$\frac{1}{4}$		$\frac{1}{4}$	
$\frac{1}{8}$	$\frac{1}{8}$	$\frac{1}{8}$	$\frac{1}{8}$	$\frac{1}{8}$	$\frac{1}{8}$	$\frac{1}{8}$	$\frac{1}{8}$

a) $\frac{1}{4} = \frac{}{8}$ b) $\frac{1}{2} = \frac{}{8}$

c) $\frac{6}{8} = \frac{}{4}$ d) $\frac{2}{4} = \frac{}{2}$

3. Use the picture to find the equivalent fractions:

1 whole									
$\frac{1}{5}$		$\frac{1}{5}$		$\frac{1}{5}$		$\frac{1}{5}$		$\frac{1}{5}$	
$\frac{1}{10}$	$\frac{1}{10}$	$\frac{1}{10}$	$\frac{1}{10}$	$\frac{1}{10}$	$\frac{1}{10}$	$\frac{1}{10}$	$\frac{1}{10}$	$\frac{1}{10}$	$\frac{1}{10}$

a) $\frac{1}{5} = \frac{}{10}$ b) $\frac{6}{10} = \frac{}{5}$

c) $\frac{4}{5} = \frac{}{10}$ d) $\frac{5}{5} = \frac{}{10}$

4. Write two different fractions for each shaded set:

a)   b)   c)

_____   _____   _____

d) e) 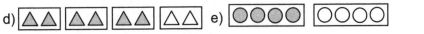   f)

_____   _____   _____

NS4-65: Sharing and Fractions

Dan has 6 cookies. He wants to give $\frac{2}{3}$ of his cookies to his friends. To do so, he shares the cookies equally onto 3 plates:

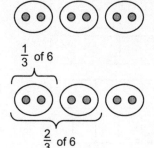

There are 3 equal groups, so each group is $\frac{1}{3}$ of 6.

There are 2 cookies in each group, so $\frac{1}{3}$ of 6 is 2.

There are 4 cookies in two groups, so $\frac{2}{3}$ of 6 is 4.

---

1. Write a fraction for the amount of dots shown. The first one has been done for you:

a)
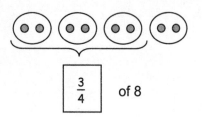

$\frac{3}{4}$ of 8

b)
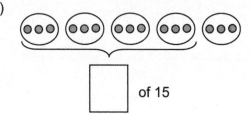

of 15

c)
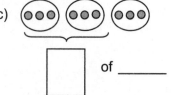

of _____

d)
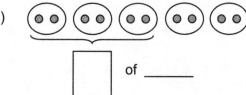

of _____

2. Fill in the missing numbers:

a) $\frac{1}{3}$ of 6 = _____

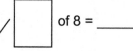

of _____ = _____

b) ☐ of 8 = _____

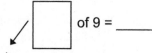

of _____ = _____

c) ☐ of 9 = _____

of _____ = _____

d)
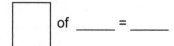

of _____ = _____

e)
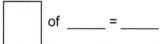

of _____ = _____

Number Sense 2

NS4-65: Sharing and Fractions (continued)

3. Draw a circle to show the given amount. The first one has been done for you:

a) $\frac{2}{3}$ of 6

b) $\frac{3}{4}$ of 8

c) $\frac{3}{5}$ of 10

d) $\frac{3}{4}$ of 12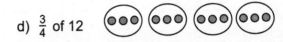

e) $\frac{4}{5}$ of 10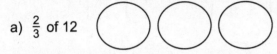

f) $\frac{2}{3}$ of 9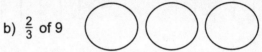

4. Fill in the correct number of dots in each circle, then draw a larger circle to show the given amount:

a) $\frac{2}{3}$ of 12

b) $\frac{2}{3}$ of 9

c) $\frac{1}{2}$ of 8

d) $\frac{3}{4}$ of 8

5. Find the fraction of the whole amount by sharing the cookies equally:
   HINT: Draw the correct number of plates, then place the cookies one at a time. Then circle the correct amount.

a) Find $\frac{1}{4}$ of 8 cookies.

   $\frac{1}{4}$ of 8 is _____

b) Find $\frac{1}{2}$ of 10 cookies.

   $\frac{1}{2}$ of 10 is _____

c) Find $\frac{2}{3}$ of 6 cookies.

   $\frac{2}{3}$ of 6 is _____

d) Find $\frac{3}{4}$ of 12 cookies.

   $\frac{3}{4}$ of 12 is _____

e) Find $\frac{1}{2}$ of 12 cookies.

   $\frac{1}{2}$ of 12 is _____

f) Find $\frac{3}{5}$ of 10 cookies.

   $\frac{3}{5}$ of 10 is _____

1. Gerome finds $\frac{1}{3}$ of 6 by dividing: 6 divided into 3 groups gives 2 in each group (6 ÷ 3 = 2).

    Find the fraction of each of the following numbers by writing an equivalent division statement:

    a) $\frac{1}{2}$ of 8 = 4   b) $\frac{1}{2}$ of 10   c) $\frac{1}{2}$ of 16   d) $\frac{1}{2}$ of 20

    _____ 8 ÷ 2 = 4 _____   _____   _____   _____

    e) $\frac{1}{3}$ of 9   f) $\frac{1}{3}$ of 15   g) $\frac{1}{4}$ of 12   h) $\frac{1}{6}$ of 18

    _____   _____   _____   _____

2. Circle $\frac{1}{2}$ of each set of lines:

    HINT: Count the lines and divide by 2.

    a) | | | | | | b) | | | | | | | | | | c) | | | |

    d) | | | | | | | | | | | | e) | | | | | | | | | | | | | |

3. Circle $\frac{1}{3}$ of each set of circles. Then circle $\frac{2}{3}$:

    a) ○ ○ ○ ○ ○ ○   b) ○ ○ ○ ○ ○ ○ ○ ○ ○ ○ ○ ○

    c) ○ ○ ○   d) ○ ○ ○ ○ ○ ○ ○ ○ ○

    e) ○ ○ ○ ○ ○ ○ ○ ○ ○ ○ ○ ○ ○ ○ ○

4. Circle $\frac{1}{4}$ of each set of triangles:

    a) △ △ △ △   b) △ △ △ △ △ △ △ △ △ △ △ △

    c) △ △ △ △ △ △ △ △ △ △ △ △ △ △ △ △

5. Shade $\frac{3}{5}$ of the boxes:

    HINT: First count the boxes and find $\frac{1}{5}$.

    a) 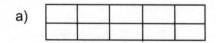   b)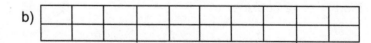

    c)

1. Fill in the missing mixed fractions on the number line:

a)

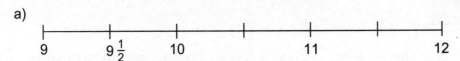

b)

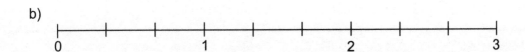

c)

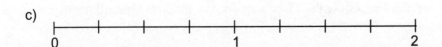

d)

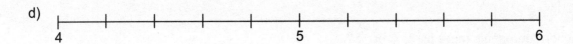

e)

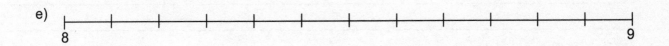

2. Continue the patterns:

a) $3\frac{2}{5}$, $3\frac{3}{5}$, $3\frac{4}{5}$, _____, _____

b) $4\frac{3}{7}$, $4\frac{4}{7}$, $4\frac{5}{7}$, _____, _____

3. Fill in the blanks:

a) $2\frac{1}{4}$ pies = _____ quarters

$2\frac{1}{4} = \frac{9}{4}$

b) $3\frac{3}{4}$ pies = _____ quarters

$3\frac{3}{4} =$

c) $4\frac{1}{4}$ pies = _____ quarters

$4\frac{1}{4} =$

d) $3\frac{1}{3}$ pies = _____ thirds

$3\frac{1}{3} =$

e) $4\frac{2}{3}$ pies = _____ thirds

$4\frac{2}{3} =$

f) $5\frac{1}{3}$ pies = _____ thirds

$5\frac{1}{3} =$

g) $2\frac{2}{5}$ pies = _____ fifths

$2\frac{2}{5} =$

h) $1\frac{4}{5}$ pies = _____ fifths

$1\frac{4}{5} =$

i) $3\frac{2}{5}$ pies = _____ fifths

$3\frac{2}{5} =$

1.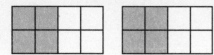

   Show two different ways to group the squares into equal amounts. Are the fractions four eighths ($\frac{4}{8}$), two fourths ($\frac{2}{4}$), and one half ($\frac{1}{2}$) the same or different? Explain:

   _____

   _____

2. 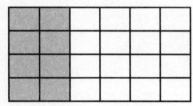   Write four equivalent fractions for the amount shaded here:

   _____ _____ _____ _____

3. Which fraction represents more pie? $\frac{5}{2}$ or $\frac{7}{2}$?

   How do you know?

   _____

   _____

Answer the following questions in a notebook.

4. Draw a picture to find out which fraction is greater:

   a) $3\frac{1}{2}$ or $2\frac{1}{2}$ b) $\frac{7}{4}$ or $\frac{5}{4}$ c) $3\frac{1}{2}$ or $\frac{5}{2}$ d) $2\frac{1}{3}$ or $\frac{8}{3}$

5. Write the following mixed fractions as improper fractions:

   a) $2\frac{1}{4}$ b) $3\frac{2}{3}$ c) $2\frac{3}{5}$ d) $4\frac{1}{2}$

6. Which is greater: $\frac{7}{3}$ or $\frac{5}{2}$?

   How do you know?

7. Which two whole numbers is $\frac{7}{4}$ between?

8.    Beth is making a black and white patchwork. Two thirds of the quilt has been completed (see diagram on left).

   How many black squares will be in the finished quilt?

NS4-69: Decimal Place Value

Fractions with denominators that are multiples of ten (tenths, hundredths) commonly appear in units of measurement:

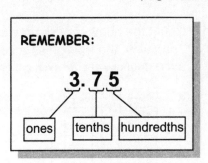

- A millimetre is a tenth of a centimetre (10 mm = 1 cm)
- A centimetre is a tenth of a decimetre (10 cm = 1 dm)
- A decimeter is a tenth of a metre (10 dm = 1 m)
- A centimetre is a hundredth of a metre (100 cm = 1 m)

Decimals are short forms for fractions. The chart shows the value of the decimal digits.

---

1. Write the place value of the underlined digit:

   a) 2.6<u>3</u> | hundredths | b) 3.<u>2</u>1 | | c) <u>7</u>.52 | |

   d) 5.<u>2</u>9 | | e) 9.9<u>8</u> | | f) <u>1</u>.05 | |

   g) <u>0</u>.32 | | h) 5.5<u>5</u> | | i) 6.<u>4</u>2 | |

2. Give the place value of the number 7 in each of the numbers below:

   a) 2.73 | | b) 9.73 | | c) 0.47 | |

   d) 2.07 | | e) 0.07 | | f) 7.83 | |

   g) 9.75 | | h) 2.37 | | i) 6.67 | |

3. Write the following numbers into the place value chart:

	Ones	Tenths	Hundredths
a) 6.02	6	0	2
b) 8.36			
c) 0.25			
d) 1.20			
e) 0.07			

No unauthorized copying   **Number Sense 2**

1. Count the number of shaded squares Write a fraction for the shaded part of the hundreds square.
   Then write the fraction as a decimal:

   HINT: Count by 10s for each column or row that is shaded.

   a)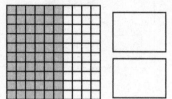

   b)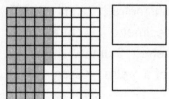

   c)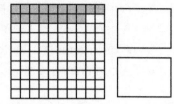

   d)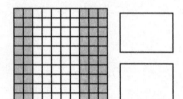

   e)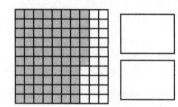

   f)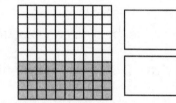

   g)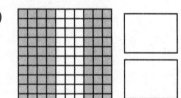

   h)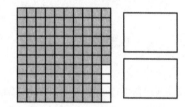

   i)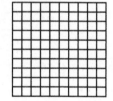

2. Convert the fraction to a decimal. Then shade:

   a) $\dfrac{38}{100}$ =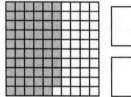

   b) $\dfrac{45}{100}$ =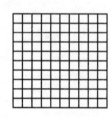

   c) $\dfrac{5}{100}$ =

3. Write a fraction and a decimal for
   each shaded part:

    _____ _____

    _____ _____

   ▦ _____ _____

4. Choose 3 designs of your own. Write a fraction
   and a decimal for each shaded part:

   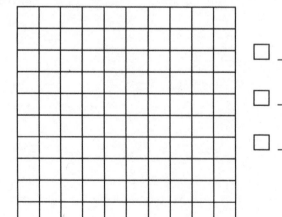

   ☐ _____ _____

   ☐ _____ _____

   ☐ _____ _____

Number Sense 2

NS4-71: Tenths and Hundredths

1. Write a fraction and a decimal to represent the number of shaded squares:

a)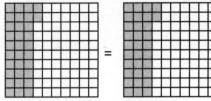

32 hundredths = 3 tenths ___ hundredths

$$\frac{32}{100} = .\underline{\ 3\ }\ \underline{\ 2\ }$$

b)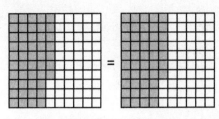

___ hundredths = ___ tenths ___ hundredths

$$\frac{}{100} = .\underline{\ \ }\ \underline{\ \ }$$

c)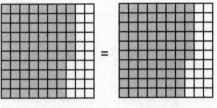

___ hundredths = ___ tenths ___ hundredths

$$\frac{}{100} = .\underline{\ \ }\ \underline{\ \ }$$

d)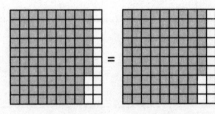

___ hundredths = ___ tenths ___ hundredths

$$\frac{}{100} = .\underline{\ \ }\ \underline{\ \ }$$

2. Fill in the blanks:

a) 71 hundredths = ___ tenths ___ hundredth

$$\frac{71}{100} = .\underline{\ 7\ }\ \underline{\ 1\ }$$

b) 28 hundredths = ___ tenths ___ hundredths

$$\frac{}{100} = .\underline{\ \ }\ \underline{\ \ }$$

c) 41 hundredths = ___ tenths ___ hundredth

$$\frac{}{100} = .\underline{\ \ }\ \underline{\ \ }$$

d) 60 hundredths = ___ tenths ___ hundredths

$$\frac{}{100} = .\underline{\ \ }\ \underline{\ \ }$$

e) 8 hundredths = ___ tenths ___ hundredths

$$\frac{}{100} = .\underline{\ \ }\ \underline{\ \ }$$

f) 2 hundredths = ___ tenths ___ hundredths

$$\frac{}{100} = .\underline{\ \ }\ \underline{\ \ }$$

3. Describe each decimal in two ways:

a) .52 = _5_ tenths _2_ hundredths

= ___52 hundredths___

b) .83 = ___ tenths ___ hundredths

= _____

c) .24 = ___ tenths ___ hundredths

= _____

d) .70 = ___ tenths ___ hundredths

= _____

e) .07 = ___ tenths ___ hundredths

= _____

f) .02 = ___ tenths ___ hundredths

= _____

Number Sense 2

1. Fill in the chart below. The first one has been done for you:

Drawing	Fraction	Decimal	Equivalent Decimal	Equivalent Fraction	Drawing
	$\frac{5}{10}$	0.5	0.50	$\frac{50}{100}$	

2. Write a fraction for the number of **hundredths**. Then count the shaded columns and write a fraction for the number of **tenths**:

a)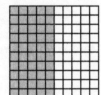

$$\frac{}{100} = \frac{}{10}$$

b)

$$\frac{}{100} = \frac{}{10}$$

c)

$$\frac{}{100} = \frac{}{10}$$

d)

$$\frac{}{100} = \frac{}{10}$$

3. Fill in the missing numbers. **REMEMBER:** $\frac{10}{100} = \frac{1}{10}$

a) $.2 = \frac{2}{10} = \frac{}{100} = .\_\_\_$

b) $.\_\_ = \frac{3}{10} = \frac{}{100} = .30$

c) $.\_\_ = \frac{7}{10} = \frac{}{100} = .70$

d) $.\_\_ = \frac{5}{10} = \frac{}{100} = .\_\_\_$

e) $.\_\_ = \frac{}{10} = \frac{60}{100} = .\_\_\_$

f) $.\_\_ = \frac{}{10} = \frac{90}{100} = .\_\_\_$

g) $.\_\_ = \frac{1}{10} = \frac{}{100} = .\_\_\_$

h) $.\_\_ = \frac{8}{10} = \frac{}{100} = .\_\_\_$

i) $.4 = \frac{}{10} = \frac{}{100} = .\_\_\_$

NS4-73: Decimals and Money

A **dime** is **one tenth** of a dollar. A **penny** is one **hundredth** of a dollar.

1. Express the value of each decimal in four different ways:

    a) .73

    _____7 dimes 3 pennies_____

    _____7 tenths 3 hundredths_____

    _____73 pennies_____

    _____73 hundredths_____

    b) .62

    _____

    _____

    _____

    _____

    c) .48

    _____

    _____

    _____

    _____

    d) .03

    _____

    _____

    _____

    _____

    e) .09

    _____

    _____

    _____

    _____

    f) .19

    _____

    _____

    _____

    _____

2. Express the value of each decimal in 4 different ways:
    HINT: First add a zero in the hundredths place.

    a) .6 ____ dimes ____ pennies

        ____ tenths ____ hundredths

        ____ pennies

        ____ hundredths

    b) .8 ____ dimes ____ pennies

        ____ tenths ____ hundredths

        ____ pennies

        ____ hundredths

3. Express the value of each decimal in four different ways. Then circle the greater number:

    .3 ____ dimes ____ pennies

        ____ tenths ____ hundredths

        ____ pennies

        ____ hundredths

    .18 ____ dimes ____ pennies

        ____ tenths ____ hundredths

        ____ pennies

        ____ hundredths

4. Fred says .32 is greater than .5 because 32 is greater than 5. Can you explain his mistake?

    _____

    _____

No unauthorized copying   **Number Sense 2**

1.   Fill in the missing numbers:

a) 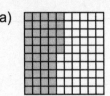   b) 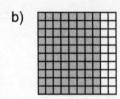   c) 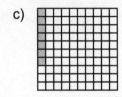   d)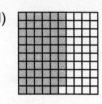

tenths	hundredths

tenths	hundredths

tenths	hundredths

tenths	hundredths

$\dfrac{}{100}$ = .____ ____
  tenths hundredths

$\dfrac{}{100}$ = .____ ____

$\dfrac{}{100}$ = .____ ____

$\dfrac{}{100}$ = .____ ____

2.   Write the following decimals as fractions:

a) .7 = $\dfrac{}{10}$ b) .3 = $\dfrac{}{10}$ c) .5 = $\dfrac{}{10}$ d) .1 = $\dfrac{}{10}$ e) .9 = $\dfrac{}{10}$

f) .23 = $\dfrac{}{100}$ g) .48 = $\dfrac{}{100}$ h) .66 = $\dfrac{}{100}$ i) .73 = $\dfrac{}{100}$ j) .29 = $\dfrac{}{100}$

k) .07 = $\dfrac{}{100}$ l) .02 = $\dfrac{}{100}$ m) .09 = $\dfrac{}{100}$ n) .01 = $\dfrac{}{100}$ o) .04 = $\dfrac{}{100}$

p) .7 = $\dfrac{}{10}$ q) .8 = $\dfrac{}{10}$ r) .05 = $\dfrac{}{100}$ s) .7 = $\dfrac{}{100}$ t) .07 = $\dfrac{}{100}$

u) .2 =   v) .35 =   w) .04 =   x) .8 =   y) .6 =

z) .02 =   aa) .72 =   bb) .4 =   cc) .23 =   dd) .25 =

3.   Change the following fractions to decimals:

a) $\dfrac{6}{10}$ = .___   b) $\dfrac{3}{10}$ = .___   c) $\dfrac{4}{10}$ = .___   d) $\dfrac{8}{10}$ = .___

e) $\dfrac{82}{100}$ = .___ ___   f) $\dfrac{7}{100}$ = .___ ___   g) $\dfrac{77}{100}$ = .___ ___   h) $\dfrac{9}{100}$ = .___ ___

4.   Circle the equalities that are incorrect:

a) .52 = $\dfrac{52}{100}$ b) .8 = $\dfrac{8}{10}$ c) .5 = $\dfrac{5}{100}$ d) $\dfrac{17}{100}$ = .17   e) $\dfrac{3}{100}$ = .03

f) .7 = $\dfrac{7}{100}$ g) .53 = $\dfrac{53}{10}$ h) .64 = $\dfrac{64}{100}$ i) .05 = $\dfrac{5}{100}$ j) .02 = $\dfrac{2}{10}$

10 is a tenth of 100, so a tens block represents a tenth of the whole. 1 is a hundredth of 100, so a ones block represents a hundredth of the whole:

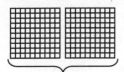 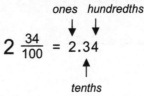

ones   hundredths

$2\frac{34}{100} = 2.34$

tenths

NOTE: A mixed fraction can be written as a decimal.

2 wholes   3 tenths   4 hundredths

----

1. Write a mixed fraction and a decimal for the base-ten models below:

a)

b)

c)

d)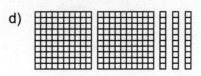

e)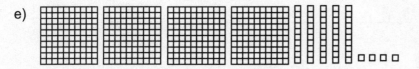

2. Draw a base-ten model for the following decimals:

a) 3.21

b) 1.62

3. Write a decimal and a mixed fraction for each of the pictures below:

a)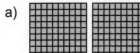

b)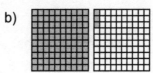

4. Write a decimal for each of the mixed fractions below:

a) $1\frac{32}{100} =$ b) $2\frac{71}{100} =$ c) $8\frac{7}{10} =$ d) $4\frac{27}{100} =$

e) $3\frac{7}{100} =$ f) $17\frac{8}{10} =$ g) $27\frac{1}{10} =$ h) $38\frac{5}{100} =$

Answer the remaining questions in a notebook.

5. Which decimal represents a greater number? Explain your answer with a picture.

a) 6 tenths or 6 hundredths?   b) .8 or .08?   c) 1.02 or 1.20?

This number line is divided into tenths.

The number represented by Point A is $2\frac{3}{10}$ or 2.3:

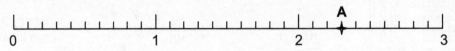

----

1. Write a decimal and a fraction (or mixed fraction) for each point:

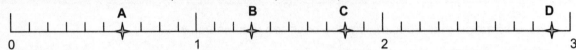

A: $\frac{6}{10}$ = .6   **B:**   **C:**   **D:**

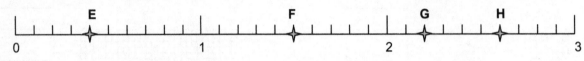

E: **F:**   **G:**   **H:**

2. Mark each point with an 'X' and label the points with the correct letter:

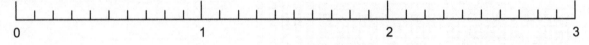

A. 1.1   **B.** 2.5   **C.** .60   **D.** 1.9

E. $1\frac{3}{10}$ **F.** $2\frac{1}{10}$ **G.** $1\frac{7}{10}$ **H.** $\frac{27}{10}$

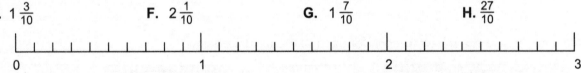

I. five tenths   **J.** one and six tenths   **K.** two and four tenths   **L.** two decimal nine

3. Write the name of each point as a fraction in words (e.g. seven tenths):

A. _____   **B.** _____   **C.** _____

4. Mark the approximate position of each point on the number line:

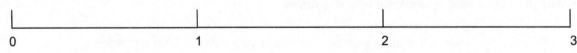

A. .5   **B.** $1\frac{1}{10}$ **C.** 1.7   **D.** 2.5   **E.** $2\frac{9}{10}$

1.

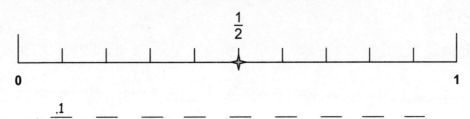

a) Write a decimal for each point marked on the number line. (The first decimal is written for you.)

b) Which decimal is equal to one half? $\frac{1}{2}$ =

2. Use the number line in Question 1 to say whether each decimal is closer to "zero," "a half" or "one":

a) .2 is closer to _____   b) .6 is closer to _____   c) .9 is closer to _____

d) .4 is closer to _____   e) .8 is closer to _____   f) .1 is closer to _____

3.

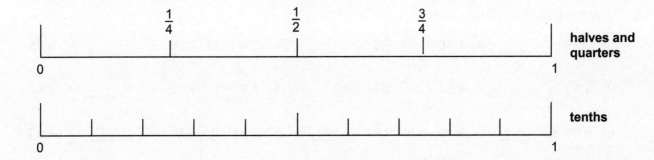

Using the number lines above to write "less than" or "greater than" between each pair of numbers:

a) 0.3 is _____ $\frac{1}{2}$ b) 0.9 is _____ $\frac{3}{4}$

c) 0.6 is _____ $\frac{1}{4}$ d) 0.3 is _____ $\frac{1}{2}$

e) 0.4 is _____ $\frac{1}{2}$ f) 0.7 is _____ $\frac{3}{4}$

4. Which whole number is each decimal or mixed fraction closest to: "zero," "one," "two," or "three"?

a) 1.2 is closest to _____   b) 1.7 is closest to _____   c) .1 is closest to _____

d) $2\frac{9}{10}$ is closest to _____   e) .7 is closest to _____   f) 2.7 is closest to _____

NS4-78: Difference of .1 and .01

1. Fill in the blanks:

   a) .53 + .1 = _____

   b) .23 + .1 = _____

   c) .07 + .1 = _____

   d) .59 + .1 = _____

   e) .84 + .01 = _____

   f) .30 + .01 = _____

   g) 3.75 + .01 = _____

   h) 4.63 + .1 = _____

   i) 5.98 + .01 = _____

2. Fill in the blanks:

   a) _____ is .1 more than .8

   b) _____ is .1 more than 3.7

   c) _____ is .1 more than .3

   d) _____ is .1 more than .52

   e) _____ is .1 more than .7

   f) _____ is .1 more than .29

3. Fill in the blanks:

   a) 1.35 + _____ = 1.36

   b) 2.3 + _____ = 2.4

   c) 3.06 − _____ = 3.05

   d) 4.95 − _____ = 4.94

   e) 3.7 + _____ = 4.7

   f) 7.85 + _____ = 7.95

   g) 9.08 + _____ = 9.18

   h) 2.31 − _____ = 2.21

   i) 5.01 − _____ = 5.00

4. Fill in the missing numbers on the number lines:

   a)
   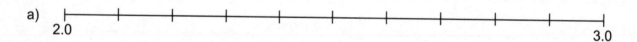
   2.0 .... 3.0

   b)

   5.7 .... 6.7

5. Continue the patterns:

   a) .3, .4, .5, _____, _____, _____

   b) 1.4, 1.5, 1.6, _____, _____, _____

   c) 2.6, 2.7, 2.8, _____, _____, _____

   d) 5.5, 5.6, 5.7, _____, _____, _____

6. Fill in the blanks:

   a) 2.9 + .1 = ____

   b) 7.9 + .1 = ____

   c) 6.95 + .1 = _____

1. Write the numbers in order by first changing each decimal to a fraction with a denominator of 10:
    NOTE: Show your work beside each number.

a) 0.7 $\frac{7}{10}$ 0.3   0.5

b) $\frac{1}{10}$ 0.3   0.9

c) 0.2   0.6 $\frac{3}{10}$

☐ ☐ ☐   ☐ ☐ ☐   ☐ ☐ ☐

d) 1.2 $1\frac{2}{10}$ 3.5   3.1

e) 1.5   1.2   1.7

f) $1\frac{1}{10}$ .7   3.5

☐ ☐ ☐   ☐ ☐ ☐   ☐ ☐ ☐

g) $1\frac{3}{10}$ 1.2   1.1

h) 4.5   3.2 $1\frac{7}{10}$

i) 2.3   2.9 $2\frac{1}{2}$

☐ ☐ ☐   ☐ ☐ ☐   ☐ ☐ ☐

2. Karen says: "To compare .6 and .42, I add a zero to .6:

    .6 = 6 tenths = 60 hundredths = .60

    60 (hundredths) is greater than 42 (hundredths).

    So .6 is greater than .42."

Add a zero to the decimal expressed in tenths. Then circle the greater number in each pair:

a) .7   .52

b) .34   .6

c) .82   .5

3. Write each decimal as a fraction with denominator 100 by first adding a zero to the decimal:

a) .7 = .70 = $\frac{70}{100}$

b) .6 = ☐ = ☐

c) .5 = ☐ = ☐

4. Write the numbers in order from least to greatest by first changing all of the decimals to fractions with denominator 100:

a) .2   .8   .35

b) $\frac{27}{100}$ .9   .25

c) 1.3 $1\frac{22}{100}$ $1\frac{39}{100}$

☐ ☐ ☐   ☐ ☐ ☐   ☐ ☐ ☐

5. 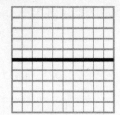 Shade $\frac{1}{2}$ of the squares. Write 2 fractions and 2 decimals for $\frac{1}{2}$:

   Fractions: $\frac{1}{2}$ $=$ $\overline{10}$ $=$ $\overline{100}$

   Decimals: $\frac{1}{2}$ $=$.____ $=$.____

6. 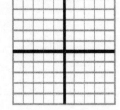 Shade $\frac{1}{5}$ of the boxes. Write 2 fractions and 2 decimals for $\frac{1}{5}$:

   Fractions: $\frac{1}{5}$ $=$ $\overline{10}$ $=$ $\overline{100}$

   Decimals: $\frac{1}{5}$ $=$.____ $=$.____

7. Write equivalent fractions:

   a) $\frac{2}{5}$ $=$ $\overline{10}$ $=$ $\overline{100}$

   b) $\frac{3}{5}$ $=$ $\overline{10}$ $=$ $\overline{100}$

   c) $\frac{4}{5}$ $=$ $\overline{10}$ $=$ $\overline{100}$

8. 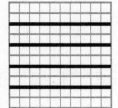 Shade $\frac{1}{4}$ of the squares. Write a fraction and a decimal for $\frac{1}{4}$:

   Fraction: $\frac{1}{4}$ $=$ $\overline{100}$ *Decimal:* $\frac{1}{4}$ $=$.____

9. Circle the greater number:
   HINT: First change all fractions and decimals to fractions with denominator 100.

   a) $\frac{1}{2}$ .37
      $\boxed{\frac{50}{100}}$ $\square$

   b) $\frac{1}{4}$ .52
      $\square$ $\square$

   c) $\frac{2}{5}$ .42
      $\square$ $\square$

   d) .7 $\frac{3}{5}$
      $\square$ $\square$

   e) .23 $\frac{1}{5}$
      $\square$ $\square$

   f) .52 $\frac{1}{2}$
      $\square$ $\square$

10. Write the numbers in order from least to greatest by first changing all fractions and decimals to fractions with denominator 100:

    a) .7   .32 $\frac{1}{2}$
       $\square$ $\square$ $\square$

    b) $\frac{1}{4}$ $\frac{3}{5}$ .63
       $\square$ $\square$ $\square$

    c) $\frac{2}{5}$ .35 $\frac{1}{2}$
       $\square$ $\square$ $\square$

NS4-80: Adding and Subtracting Tenths

1. 1.3 is one whole and 3 tenths. How many tenths is that altogether? _____

2. Fill in the blanks:

    a) 4.7 = _____ tenths

    b) 7. 1 = _____ tenths

    c) 3. 0 = _____ tenths

    d) _____ = 38 tenths

    e) _____ = 42 tenths

    f) _____ = 7 tenths

3. Add or subtract the decimals by writing them as whole numbers of tenths:

    a)   2.1   __21_ tenths
         + 1.0   __10_ tenths
         ┌─────┐
         │ 3.1 │ ← _31_ tenths
         └─────┘

    b)   1.3   ___ tenths
         + 1.1   ___ tenths
         ┌─────┐
         │   │ ← ___ tenths
         └─────┘

    c)   1.4   ___ tenths
         + 7.3   ___ tenths
         ┌─────┐
         │   │ ← ___ tenths
         └─────┘

    d)   2.5   ___ tenths
         − 1.0   ___ tenths
         ┌─────┐
         │   │ ← ___ tenths
         └─────┘

    e)   7.6   ___ tenths
         − 4.2   ___ tenths
         ┌─────┐
         │   │ ← ___ tenths
         └─────┘

    f)   8.9   ___ tenths
         − 1.4   ___ tenths
         ┌─────┐
         │   │ ← ___ tenths
         └─────┘

4. Find the sum or difference:

    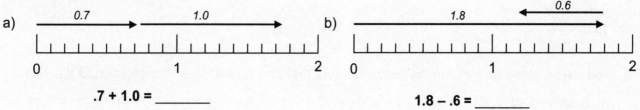

    a) .7 + 1.0 = _____

    b) 1.8 − .6 = _____

    Now draw your own arrows:

    c)

        2.5 + 1.2 = _____

    d)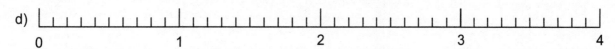

        2.7 − 1.9 = _____

5. Add or subtract:

    a)   3.5   b)   4.6   c)   5.4   d)   9.2   e)   3.7   f)   2.8
         − 1.2   + 3.2   + 1.7   − 4.9   + 4.9   − 1.9
         ┌─────┐   ┌─────┐   ┌─────┐   ┌─────┐   ┌─────┐   ┌─────┐
         │   │   │   │   │   │   │   │   │   │   │   │
         └─────┘   └─────┘   └─────┘   └─────┘   └─────┘   └─────┘

1. Write a fraction for each shaded part. Then add the fractions together and shade your answer. The first one has been done for you:

a) 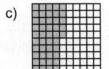 + =   b) + 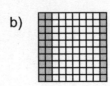 =

$$\frac{20}{100} \quad + \quad \frac{55}{100} \quad = \quad \frac{75}{100}$$

+ =

c) 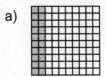 + =   d) + =

2. Write the decimals that correspond to the fractions in Question 1 above:

a) .20 + .55 = .75   b)

c)   d)

3. Add the decimals by lining up the digits. Be sure that your final answer is expressed as a decimal:

a) 0.32 + 0.57 =   b) 0.92 + 0.05 =   c) 0.54 + 0.27 =   d) 0.22 + 0.75 =

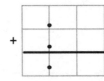

e) 0.7 + 0.25 =   f) 0.3 + 0.87 =   g) 0.72 + 0.31 =   h) 0.38 + 0.52 =

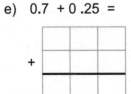   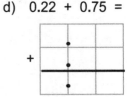   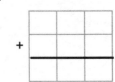

4. In a notebook, add the following decimals:

   a) 0.32 + 0.17 =   b) 0.64 + 0.23 =   c) 0.46 + 0.12=   d) 0.87 + 0.02 =

   e) 0.94 + 0.03 =   f) 0.19 + 0.61=   g) 0.67 + 0.2 =   h) 0.48 + 0.31 =

NS4-82: Subtracting Hundredths

1. Subtract by crossing out the correct number of boxes:

a)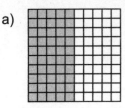

$$\frac{50}{100} - \frac{20}{100} =$$

b)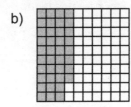

$$\frac{38}{100} - \frac{25}{100} =$$

c)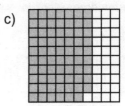

$$\frac{69}{100} - \frac{42}{100} =$$

2. Write the decimals that correspond to the fractions in Question 1 above:

a) .50 - .20 = .30   b)   c)

3. Subtract the decimals by lining up the digits. Regroup where necessary:

a) 0.53 − 0.21 =

0	5	3
− 0	2	1
0	3	2

b) 0.93 − 0.31 =

c) 0.87 − 0.26 =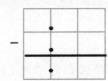

d) 0.39 − 0.11 =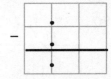

e) 0.67 − 0.59 =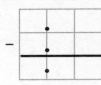

f) 0.23 − 0.19 =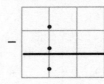

g) 0.74 − 0.59 =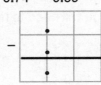

h) 0.93 − 0.18 =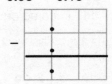

i) 1.00 − 0.46 =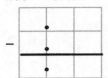

j) 1.00 − 0.26 =

k) 1.00 − 0.57 =

l) 1.00 − 0.89 =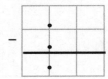

4. In a notebook, subtract the following decimals:

a) .52 − .43   b) .98 − .36   c) .75 − .47   d) .32 − .29

e) .58 − .5   f) .63 − .3   g) .89 − .07   h) .41 − .08

5. Find the missing decimal in each of the following:

a) 1 = .45 + ☐   b) 1 = .63 + ☐   c) 1 = .39 + ☐

1. Add by drawing a base ten model. Then, using the chart provided, line up the numbers and add:
   NOTE: Use a hundreds block for a whole and a tens block for one tenth.

   a) 1.23 + 1.12

   b) 1.14 + 1.21

ones	tenths	hundredths
+		

ones	tenths	hundredths
+		

2. Subtract by drawing a base ten model of the greater number as shown in part a):

   a) 2.35 – 1.12

   b) 3.24 – 2.11

   ⊠ ☐ ⊠|| ⊠ ⊠ ☐ ☐ ☐ = 1.23

3. Add. In some questions, you will need to regroup:

   a) 2 . 1 5
     + 1 . 2 4

   b) 3 . 4 2
     + 1 . 0 5

   c) 2 . 7 1
     + 1 . 4 2

   d) 3 . 8 7
     + 2 . 9 3

   e) 5 . 3 2
     + 3 . 1 9

   f) 3 . 3 7
     − 1 . 2 4

   g) 2 . 5 1
     − 1 . 4 0

   h) 4 . 2 5
     − 1 . 8 2

   i) 8 . 3 2
     − 1 . 5 3

   j) 9 . 7 5
     − 7 . 1 6

Show your work for the remaining questions in a notebook.

4. The largest animal heart measured belonged to a blue whale. It weighed 698.5 kg.
   How much would 2 hearts of that size weigh?

5. The world record for longest hair is 7.5 m. Julia's hair is .37 m long.
   How much longer than Julia's hair is the longest hair?

Number Sense 2

1. Read the numbers from left to right and circle the first place value where they differ.
   Then write the greater number in the box:

   a) 3 . 2 5
      3 . 3 8

      ☐ 3 . 3 8

   b) 7 . 0 4
      7 . 0 6

      ☐

   c) 8 . 5 3
      8 . 4 2

      ☐

   d) 9 . 2
      9 . 1 5

      ☐

   e) 6 . 3 5
      5 . 4

      ☐

2. Write < or > to show the greater number.

   a) 5 . 2 5 | > | 5 . 1 3

   b) 8 . 3 2 | ☐ | 8 . 1 5

   c) 7 . 0 5 | ☐ | 7 . 0 4

   d) 6 . 3 2 | ☐ | 5 . 7 0

   e) 4 . 3 | ☐ | 4 . 1 2

   f) 6 . 2 1 | ☐ | 6 . 4

3. Using the numbers 1, 2, 3, 4 create:

   a) the greatest number:

   b) the least number:

   ☐ ☐ . ☐ ☐   ☐ ☐ . ☐ ☐

4. Write 3 decimals greater than .4 and less than .5: _____ _____ _____

5. Round the numbers to the nereast whole number:

   a) 1 . 7   b) 2 . 1   c) 3 . 9   d) 4 . 3

   e) 8 . 1   f) 9 . 5   g) 4 . 9   h) 0 . 8

6. Continue the patterns:

   a) .2 , .4 , .6 , _____, _____   b) .3 , .6 , .9 , _____, _____

 Answer the remaining questions in a notebook.

7. Explain the error:

$$\begin{array}{r} 5.2 \\ + 3.42 \\ \hline 3.94 \end{array}$$

8. Explain why 1.02 is less than 1.20:

The size of a unit of measurement depends on which unit has been selected as the **whole**.

A millimetre is a **tenth** of a centimetre, but it is only a **hundredth** of a decimetre.
REMEMBER: A decimetre is 10 centimetres.

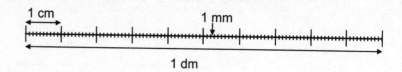

1 cm   1 mm

1 dm

1. Draw a picture in the space provided to show 1 tenth of each whole:

a)

1 whole   1 tenth

b)

1 whole   1 tenth

c)

1 whole   1 tenth

2. Write each measurement as a fraction, then as a decimal:
   REMEMBER: 1 centimetre is 1 hundredth of a metre.

a) 1 cm = $\frac{1}{100}$ m = ___.01___ m

b) 4 cm = _____ m = _____ m

c) 75 cm = _____ m = _____ m

d) 17 cm = _____ m = _____ m

e) 8 mm = $\frac{8}{10}$ cm = _____ cm

f) 7 mm = _____ cm = _____ cm

Answer the remaining questions in a notebook.

3. Add the measurements by first changing the **smaller unit** into a decimal in the **larger unit**:

a) 4 cm + 9.2 m = .04 m + 9.2 m = 9.24 m

b) 18 cm + 2.4 m

c) 6 cm + 8.2 m

d) 26 cm + 1.52 m

e) 423 cm + 1.75 m

4.

Plant	Height
Canada Golden Rod	1.5 m
Field Birdwell	1 m
White Sweet Clover	300 cm
Yellow Sorrel	0.5 m

a) How should Rick order the flowers so the shortest are at the front of his garden, and the tallest at the back?

b) How much taller will the clover grow than the sorrel?

5. Explain how you would change 1.72 m into cm. **HINT: How many centimetres are $\frac{72}{100}$ of a metre?**

6. $0.25 means 2 dimes and 5 pennies. Why do we use decimal notation for money? What is a dime a tenth of? What is a penny a hundredth of?

NS4-86: Unit Rates

A **rate** is a comparison of two quantities in different units.

In a **unit rate**, one of the quantities is equal to one.

For instance: "1 apple costs 30¢" is a unit rate.

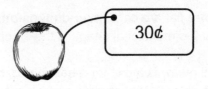

30¢

---

1. Fill in the missing information:

   a) 1 book costs $4

      2 books cost _____

      3 books cost _____

      4 books cost _____

   b) 1 ticket costs 5¢

      2 tickets cost _____

      3 tickets cost _____

      4 tickets cost _____

   c) 1 apple costs 20¢

      2 apples cost _____

      3 apples cost _____

      4 apples cost _____

   d) 20 km in 1 hour

      ____ km in 3 hours

   e) $12 allowance in 1 week

      ____ allowance in 4 weeks

   f) 1 teacher for 25 students

      3 teachers for ____

   g) 1 kg of rice for 10 cups of water   5 kgs of rice for _____ cups of water

2. In the pictures, 1 centimetre represents 3 metres. Use a ruler to find out how long each whale is:

   Length in cm ___

   Length in m ____

   Killer Whale

   Length in cm ___

   Length in m ____

   Baleen Whale

   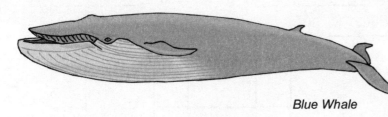

   Length in cm ___

   Length in m ____

   Blue Whale

3. Cho earns $8 an hour babysitting.
   How much will he earn in 4 hours?

   _____

4. Alice earns $10 an hour mowing lawns.
   How much will she earn in 8 hours?

   _____

5. Find the unit rate:

   a) 2 books cost $10

       1 book costs _____

   b) 4 mangoes cost $12

       1 mango costs _____

   c) 6 cans of juice cost $12

       1 can costs _____

No unauthorized copying   **Number Sense 2**

ME4-28: Area in Square Centimetres

Shapes that are flat are called **two-dimensional** (2-D) shapes.
The **area** of a 2-dimensional shape is the amount of space it takes up.

A square centimetre is a unit for measuring **area**.
A square with sides 1 cm has area one square centimetre.
The short form for a square centimetre is cm².

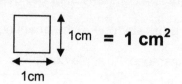

1cm **= 1 cm²**

1. Find the area of these figures in square centimetres:

a)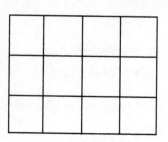

Area = _____ cm²

b)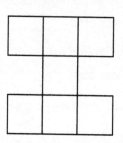

Area = _____ cm²

c)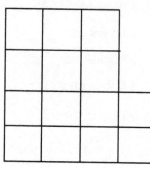

Area = _____ cm²

2. Using a ruler, join the marks lines to divide each rectangle into square centimetres:

a)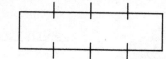

Area = _____ cm²

b)

Area = _____

c)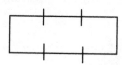

Area = _____

3. How can you find the area (in cm²) of each of the given shapes?

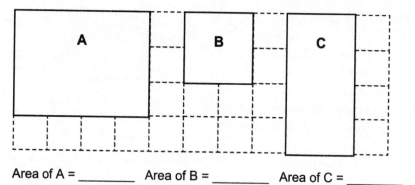

Area of A = _____   Area of B = _____   Area of C = _____

 Answer the following questions on grid paper.

4. Draw 3 different shapes that have an area of 8 cm² (the shapes don't have to be rectangles).

5. Draw several shapes and find their area and perimeter.

6. Draw a rectangle with an area of 8 cm² and perimeter of 12 cm.

Measurement 2

ME4-29: Area of Rectangles

1. Write a multiplication statement for each array:

a) 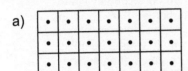 b) 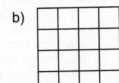 c) d)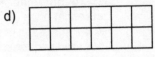

_____   _____   _____   _____

2. Draw a dot in each box.
   Then write a multiplication statement that tells you the number of boxes in the rectangle:

a) b) 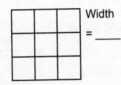 c)  d)

   ___3 × 7 = 21___   _____   _____   _____

3. Write the number of boxes along the width and length of each rectangle.
   Then write a multiplication statement for the area of the rectangle (in square units):

a) 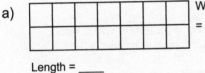 Width
   = ____

   Length = ____

b) 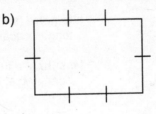 Width
   = ____

   Length = ____

c)  Width
   = ____

   Length = ____

_____   _____   _____

4. Using a ruler, join the marks to divide each rectangle into squares.
   Write a multiplication statement for the area of the boxes in cm²:
   NOTE: You will have to mark two of the boxes in centimetres yourself, using a ruler.

a) 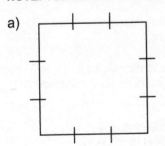 b) 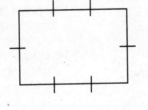 c)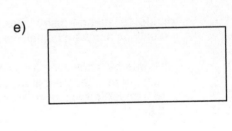

d) 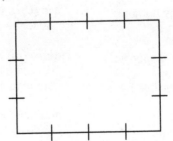 e)

5. If you know the length and width of a rectangle, how can you find its area? _____

_____

Glossary

add to find the total when combining two or more numbers together

area the amount of space occupied by the face or surface of an object

array an arrangement of things (for example, objects, symbols, or numbers) in rows and columns

base-10 materials materials used to represent ones (ones squares or cubes), tens (tens strips or rods), hundreds (hundreds squares or flats), and thousands (thousands cubes)

centimetre (cm) a unit of measurement used to describe length, height, or thickness

cent notation a way to express an amount of money (for example, 40¢)

column things (for example, objects, symbols, numbers) that run up and down

decimal a short form for tenths (for example, 0.2) or hundredths (for example, 0.02), and so on

decimetre (dm) a unit of measurement used to describe length, height, or thickness; equal to 10 cm

decreasing sequence a sequence where each number is less than the one before it

denominator the number on the bottom portion of a fraction; tells you how many parts are in a whole

difference the "gap" between two numbers; the remainder left after subtraction

divide to find how many times one number contains another number

divisible by containing a number a specific number of times without having a remainder (for example, 15 is divisible by 5 and 3)

dollar notation a way to express an amount of money (for example, $4.50)

equivalent fractions fractions that represent the same amount, but have different denominators (for example, $\frac{2}{3} = \frac{4}{6}$)

estimate a guess or calculation of an approximate number

even number the numbers you say when counting by 2s (starting at 0)

expanded form a way to write a number that shows the place value of each digit (for example, 27 in expanded form can be written as 2 tens + 7 ones, or 20 + 7)

fraction a number used to name a part of a set or a region

greater than a term used to describe a number that is higher in value than another number

growing pattern a pattern in which each term is greater than the previous term

improper fraction a fraction that has a numerator that is larger than the denominator; this represents more than a whole

increasing sequence a sequence where each number is greater than the one before it

kilometre (km) a unit of measurement for length; equal to 1000 cm

less than a term used to describe a number that is lower in value than another number

litre (L) a unit of measurement used to describe capacity; equal to 1000 mL

metre (m) a unit of measurement used to describe length, height, or thickness; equal to 100 cm

millilitre (mL) a unit of measurement used to describe capacity

millimetre (mm) a unit of measurement used to describe length, height, or thickness; equal to 0.1 cm

mixed fraction a mixture of a whole number and a fraction

model a physical representation (for example, using base-10 materials to represent a number)

more than a term used to describe a number that is higher in value than another number

multiple of a number that is the result of multiplying one number by another specific number (for example, the multiples of 5 are 0, 5, 10, 15, and so on)

multiple of 2 a number that is the result of multiplying a number by 2

multiple of 3 a number that is the result of multiplying a number by 3

multiply to find the total of a number times another number

number line a line with numbers marked at intervals, used to help with skip counting

numerator the number on the top portion of a fraction; tells you how many parts are counted

odd number the numbers you say when counting by 2s (starting at 1); numbers that are not even

ordinal number a word that describes the position of an object (for example, first, second, third, fourth, fifth, sixth, seventh, eighth, ninth)

pattern (repeating pattern) the same repeating group of objects, numbers, or attributes

perimeter the distance around the outside of a shape

product the result from multiplying two or more numbers together

quotient the result from dividing one number by another number

rectangle a quadrilateral with four right angles

rectangular having a face that is a rectangle (for example, a prism with a four-sided base)

regroup to exchange one place value for another place value (for example, 10 ones squares for 1 tens strip)

remainder the number left over after dividing or subtracting (for example, $10 \div 3 = 3\ R1$)

row things (for example, objects, symbols, or numbers) that run left to right

set a group of like objects

skip counting counting by a number (for example, 2s, 3s, 4s) by "skipping" over the numbers in between

square centimetre (cm^2) a unit of measurement used to describe area

subtract to take away one or more numbers from another number

sum the result from adding two or more numbers together

T-table a chart used to compare two sequences of numbers

About the Authors

JOHN MIGHTON is a mathematician, author, and playwright. He completed a Ph.D. in mathematics at the University of Toronto and is currently a fellow of the Fields Institute for Mathematical Research. The founder of JUMP Math (www.jumpmath.org), Mighton also gives lectures to student teachers at York University and the Ontario Institute for Studies in Education, and invited talks and training sessions for parents and educators. He is the author of the *JUMP at Home* workbooks and the national bestsellers *The Myth of Ability* and *The End of Ignorance*. He has won the Governor General's Literary Award and the Siminovitch Prize for his plays.

DR. ANNA KLEBANOV received her B.Sc., M.Sc., Ph.D., and teaching certificate from the Technion – Israel Institute of Technology. She is the recipient of three teaching awards for excellence. She began her career at JUMP Math as a curriculum writer in 2007, working with Dr. John Mighton and Dr. Sindi Sabourin on JUMP Math's broad range of publications.

DR. SINDI SABOURIN received her Ph.D. in mathematics from Queen's University, specializing in commutative algebra. She is the recipient of the Governor General's Gold Medal Award from Queen's University and a National Sciences and Research Council Postdoctoral Fellowship. Her career with JUMP Math began in 2003 as a volunteer doing in-class tutoring, one-on-one tutoring, as well as working on answer keys. In 2006, she became a curriculum writer working on JUMP Math's broad range of publications.